Cowboys With Chrome Horses

A Historical Explanation Of
America's Most Popular And Unique Phenomenon

by

William G. (Lad) Carrington

Cowboys With Chrome Horses

*A Historical Explanation Of
America's Most Popular And Unique Phenomenon*

by

William G. (Lad) Carrington

Jarrett Press & Publications
Publishers Of Fine Books Since 1994

BUCKAROO

buck-a-roo also **buckeroo** (buk′a-roo′) *n., pl.*-**roos** also -**oos**.
A cowboy. [Sp. *vaquero* < *vaca, cow* < Lat. *vacca*] *American
Heritage Dictionary, Second College Edition*

The dictionary shows us that the word is actually an American-
ization of the Spanish word for cowboy vaquero, with the V
pronounced as B.
Thus Va-quer-o becomes Ba-kere-o or to an American
"Buckaroo"
We Americans do things our own way
Even in pronounciation.

This book is dedicated to all of those buckaroos who had so
effective an impact on me every Saturday growing up, and in
particular Lash LaRue, The Lone Ranger & Tonto, Roy Rogers,
Gene Autry, and the one who set all the popularity records and
exemplified the ideology of America, Hopalong Cassidy.

Also to my friends Dick Smith, Michael "Irish Red" Kelly, Dean
Lenihan, cowboys on chrome horses who had a profound influence on me and implanted the burr under my saddle urging me
to see America on my own iron steed, to my friend David K.
"Sheep" Winstead who knew I'd love motorcycling , and last but
not least my riding partners Gary Long, Fritz Voight, and Tim
Clark, brothers with whom I have shared many miles of
camaderie, in the wind.

ABOUT THE AUTHOR

William Graham Carrington is currently a freelance journalist who has successfully written, published, and nationally marketed a book of poetry, titled *Tomorrow's Promise*, with a completed second book to be published, titled *One Heart Beyond Tomorrow*. A popular and accomplished public speaker and lecturer, he performs his collective works for audiences of a variety of ages and lifestyles all across America.

Since 1992, Carrington has written articles on travel, history, business, personality profiles, and events, most of these featured in national or regional magazines.

Carrington began writing motorcycle touring articles in 1993 and in 1995 traveled across the US under contract to the Harley-Davidson Motor Company writing a series of five event articles for the Harley Owners Group membership magazine. During the period from November 1995 to February 1996, he had six pieces published in five national magazines. His poetry on motorcycling in America has been featured in several issues of the *Sturgis Rally News* magazine and other publications and performed live in two national video productions filmed at Sturgis in 1997. The poems, <u>Name On A Wall</u>, and <u>Rolling Thunder</u>® are featured on two Rolling Thunder commemorative posters. Articles and poems on a variety of aspects of motorcycling have appeared in issues of such magazines as *American Iron*, *Thunder Alley*, *Biker*, *Easyriders*, *VQ*, *Motorcycle Events*, *Bikes & Spikes*, and *Sturgis Rally News*.

Carrington, who has been riding motorcycles since 1964, has toured most of the 48 contiguous states since 1990, gathering material for books and articles and winning an award for the Longest North American Ride in 1996. In spite of being partially disabled, he has accumulated over 115,000 miles on his present motorcycle, a 1988 plain Harley-Davidson FXR. An unusual choice because this is a no frills machine without all of the comforts, bells, and whistles.

Prior to 1992, Carrington's writing credits include publishing two single-issue, target market magazines, serving as editor of three newsletters, two regional and one at UNC-CH and twenty-nine years of writing ad copy for both broadcast and print media.

Born in 1945 in Durham, North Carolina, the son of a newspaper man, he spent much of his childhood in and around the newspaper business.

At age seventeen, he began a career in radio which lasted until the spring of 1973. During that time, he acquired his first formal education which was in Radio and TV production and announcing at The Don Martin School of Radio and Television Arts and Sciences, in Hollywood, California. He received his diploma in the Spring of 1967. This is the same school that produced such famous personalities as Tom Kennedy and Bob Eubanks.

In 1973, Carrington evolved out of Radio and into commercial photography for the production of printed advertising pieces and brochures.

Carrington returned to school in 1988 to study computer publishing and history at the University of North Carolina at Chapel Hill. Under the urging of an academic advisor and several professors he changed his direction to writing, graduating in May of 1993 with a Bachelor of Arts Degree in Journalism and Mass Communication. In addition to the major, he earned a minor in History. He remained at UNC-CH for the 93-94 school year and studied corporate video production and script writing and additional coursework in history.

Additional background includes flying since 1962, five years of racing sports cars, working as an extra in several movies, and coordinating concerts and major events. One of the events resulted in the Vistascope audio visual program for the Cyclorama in Atlanta.

ACKNOWLEDGEMENTS

First I must express my undying gratitude for Thomas S. Clark M.D., M. S.,whose love of motorcycling, understanding the importance of history, and his belief in the writing of this book, made it possible for it to finally come to completion.

Since its origin, there have been many times it had to be shelved as business and survival became more imperative.

This book started life, October 1990, as the beginnings of a term paper for Professor Melissa Bullard's HIST 94-A Advanced Studies (capstone)course in myths and history. Professor Bullard instigated the subject while the collective influences of Dottie Bernholz, and Professors Charles Warren, Connie Eble, Dan Patterson, Donald Shaw, Gary Freeze, and my mentor Chuck Stone. All saw something beyond my vision and somewhat gently pushed me toward writing.

From the first idea to do this book in 1994 I have had the encouragement from friends in and out of motorcycling. My gratitude goes out to Bob Albright, Peggy Stovall, Gary Long, Nora Church, Tim Clark, and more others than I can remember.

I owe thanks to Marty Rosenblum for accepting my first motorcycling poem in the H-D Archives, and for Buzz Kanter and Linda Peavy for giving me my first opportunities to be published nationally. I owe thanks to Mike Corbin for believing in my writing and providing a good seat for me see America. To Robin Bagley who is a writer's editor, and has been a dream to work with on several writings, which have been part of the research for this book.

My sincere thanks is due to those who made completion possible. First among those is Mitchell Forest Lyman who made it possible for me to take the time to complete the book. To Kim Graham, Maggie Graham (no relation), and my sister Dot Starks. To Debbie Fisher, and Kate Trochum who worked with me the final two weeks almost around the clock editing, proofing and working hard to help keep me awake, and on schedule, arranging information and rewrites, while still working their regular jobs.

To Butch Knott of K Engines, and Jimmy Davis of J&D Custom Cycle who have helped keep my bike running sweet, and of course, those sponsors who have contributed parts, equipment, or assistance: Corbin Saddles, Barnett Tool & Engineering, Carl's Speed Shop, Crane Cams, JIMS, SPYKE Starters, Aerostch, Mikuni Carburetors, Wiseco Pistons, James Gaskets, Progressive Suspension, Atlantic Coast Plating, Chrome Specialties, Continental Tires, Leather Gallery, T-Bags, and Custom Cycle Engineering.

Thank you one and all, I couldn't have done it with out your assistance and support.

FOREWORD

William Graham Carrington understands that America needs folk heroes and finds them throughout history (and recruits them, sometimes against their own better judgement). He brings together in this book many different cultural identities but centrally locates a new breed of cowboy folk hero — — and this motorcycle riding individualist is a person that Carrington obviously knows well. William Carrington's official involvement in major motorcycling events such as Rolling Thunder®, a rally that is in celebration of the essence of American folk heroism, and his many years on a motorcycle himself, give his words that gas-and-oil truthfulness. If anybody can discover a new breed of cowboy, then it is, indeed, going to be William Graham Carrington

Dr. Martin Jack Rosenblum

Dr. Martin Jack Rosenblum is the Historian at Harley-Davidson Motor Company, and the Author of <u>The Holy Ranger: Harley-Davidson Poems</u> book and <u>The Holy Ranger's Free Hand: Music Taking Poetry Too Far</u> on compact disc.

11

PREFACE

Cowboys With Chrome Horses is perhaps the first book to look into the world of the biker from the inside out, and doing so from a broad and somewhat academic approach. It explores the phenomenon as a direct historical perspective, looking back in time to the earliest roots of each segment, then bringing the reader forward in a time line, to the biker of today.

Thousands of riders across the United States wear tee-shirts that sport the all too familiar eagle wings logo and the words, "If I have to explain you wouldn't understand." *Cowboys With Chrome Horses* presents that explanation. Making a correlation to America's history and cowboy image of itself, this book takes the reader from the origin of the word cowboy to today's multibillion dollar market, brought about by that image.

Each chapter takes an aspect of this uniquely American phenomenon and trace its evolution and development historically and sociologically. This information will be presented in a narrative form, understandable and interesting to the average reader, regardless of whether he or she has ever ridden a motorcycle, or wanted to.

The ever growing popularity of this American image has helped catapult the Harley-Davidson Motor Company into being the motor world's Cinderella story of success, earning it a second place world market share by 1995. This position is second only to Honda, in the world wide motorcycle market. No small feat, in as much as Harley-Davidson does not make cars or musical instruments, as does the main competition. The success of Harley-Davidson has paved the way, as we leave this millennium, for a number of new motorcycle companies to emerge and a few old names to reappear.

Cowboys With Chrome Horses gives the reader a visual

image of the people and issues discussed. To give more life to the reading, there are real stories about some of the players in the motorcycling world of today.

While it would be wonderful to cover all aspects and parts of this industry and tell the story of every fascinating individual involved, it is beyond the scope of this or any other single book to do so. The subject is broad enough to spawn and span many future books.

I have endeavored to take specific parts and people in the industry as representative, and tell their stories. Most specifically I have tried to present fairly, from the information made available to me, all of the present motorcycle companies in the United States with no prejudice, pro or con, toward any particular marque. Some have more history and have made a larger impact on America's history than others.

Many sources have been queried for detailed or historical information, and well meaning persons have promised to provide the requested materials but to date, have not provided promised material in time for this writing. If anyone feels left out who should be on these pages, or can show documentation as to mistaken information presented here, or provide subject topics and matter not represented, your positive input is welcome. Future and or revised editions will include additional and corrected subject matter.

While lists of books in print on motorcycling show many works dealing with technical issues, do-it-yourself manuals, and histories of manufacturers, there appears to be no broad scholarly work on the subject overall, or its connection specifically to Americana. The intent therefore, of this narrative, is to chronicle from its origins, the indominatable American spirit as epitomized in the American Biker and motorcycling in general. This I have tried to do by presenting the evolution of the persona, thus showing why this figure and this pastime has become the single largest signature representing America in the 20th century.

I have taken every effort possible to avoid libel or infringement. Most of this book has been written from my own collective experience and observations as part of the phenomenon and lifestyle, and as a rider and journalist for many years. A good bit of the material in this book is from articles written by me and the research for those articles, as well as dedicated historical research specifically for this writing.

It has been my policy since the beginning of this book to let each person or event presented, provide their own story wherever possible, and I as the storyteller, tell it in an interesting manner. I have attempted faithfully, to do so with the information at hand. This is especially so with the research on people who are no longer here to speak for themselves. I am a historian and a motorcyclist. These are things that I love and I choose to present them in a positive manner. This is my writing style and my preference. I will, therefore, continue to present my information in a fair light, without hype, as I find no need in gilding something I already see as beautiful, and always in keeping with accuracy in historical reporting.

I hope the reader is able to learn something about Americana, and its history, and motorcycling. If only one person who rides takes the time to read this book and at some point stops to say to him or herself, "Damn! I didn't know that." or a person who doesn't ride, after reading this book, shows a different attitude toward one of us at next meeting along life's road, or better yet, wants to join our unique fraternity in the wind, then that is enough in itself to have made the book worth the effort of its writing.

This book is written on a positive note about a part of Americana that I live, and believe in, and believe embodies the spirit of independence of the individual that prevails uniquely in the United States. It is a part of my life and I offer no apologies.

William G. Carrington

CONTENTS

Preface   12

Steel Horse Cowboys - The New Breed   16

Chapter One
Your Typical Biker   20
Chapter Two
America's Image - Cowboy Myth And Reality   26
Chapter Three
Before There Was America   42
Chapter Four
The Spirit Of The American Motorcyclist   52
Chapter Five
Ladies of The Road   93
Chapter Six
The Machines   115
Chapter Seven
The Long Riders - A Love Affair With The Road   140
Chapter Eight
Clubs, Organizations, And Angels With Wings   155
Chapter Nine
The Great Events   168
Chapter Ten
The Power Brokers   181
Chapter Eleven
Motorclothes And The Aftermarket   197
Chapter Twelve
The European Invasion   212

Conclusion   214

Bibliography   217

STEEL HORSE COWBOYS - THE NEW BREED
By Buck Montgomery

Do ya have a moment?
Do ya have some time to spare?
Well, this here cowboy has a story,'
A story that I'd like to share,
With all you folks out there.

It's about a cowboy, an outlaw through and through
A rip-roar'n, hell bent for leather, real buckaroo
Now truth be known,
This cowboy could very well be me
But it might just be you,
Read on, and you will plainly see.

Some say us cowboys, we are a dying breed
And our end may soon be near.
With our wide open spaces, our homes on the range \Disappearing
much too fast I fear.

But what of the cowboys, the cowboys of the new breed
Who ride an iron horse for their trusty steed
It's easy to see
He's very much like this cowboy _me.
Rolling down life's asphalt trail, both far and near
No different than the cowboys of yesteryear.

He's a loner, a drifter, a man of many parts
Following which ever way the wind blows
A man who finishes every ride he starts
So no matter how far he rides from home,
Alone, or in a pack, following the call of the wild,
It just proves he's a cowboy, clean through to the bone.

Now the longer that you read
The more you'll clearly see
That this modern day V-2 evolution buckaroo
Ain't all that different than me.

You see, us cowboys out west, we take care of our rides
We feed'm, we clean'm, even name them besides.
Like thunder, or silver'
Even old paint has been used a time or two.
Now don't you be laughin', you steel horse buckaroo
And don't think its odd, we give our horse a name
Cause I've seen it myself,
With your hogs, you've been known to do the same.

Like Knuckle-head _. Softail _ Road King
Why heck, once I even heard of one called, the fat Boy
Well, I'm here to clue ya,
They ain't like nothin' ever riden'
By Silver screen cowboys, Hoppy, Gene or _ Roy.

So, Just who are these cowboys who ride
Those thundering chrome horses with names like
Electra Glide!
I've heard tell some are doctors,
Even lawyers I've been told,
They might be single, or have a family,
And could be real young _ or very, very old.

I seen one once, way out on the prairie
I was ridin' and ropin' for the H-Bar-D
Twas my foreman, a Mr. Harley Davidson, if you please
Who pointed out this cowboy
To a bunch of the boys _ and me.

He was tool'n down the highway
Just as fast as fast can be
On his full dress Harley Hog
And sure as shootin', he was smilin' right at me.
He was proud of his ride,
The one that he did own
Had a passenger right behind him
This cowboy wern't ridin' alone
Cause there sat the biggest, ugliest,
Stink to high heaven ridin' partner
I ever saw upon a hog.
Sure enough, it was his best friend, his trail compadre
It was _ his dog.

Have ya figured out, just who exactly
These new cowboys just might be
Well, jus take a look around ya
Go ahead, and I'll tell ya what you'll see
Those are the cowgirls and cowboys
Of the new breed.

Ridin' for the Harley brand _ The H-Bar-D
And folks, there ain't no doubt about it
When all is said and done, you'll see

You are todays new cowboy
And not really any different
Than an old cowboy like me.

So when I'm too old to saddle up my horse
And hit the trail for a long hard ride.
Why, I think I'll go out and buy myself a Harley,
Heck, I'll get myself an Electra Glide!

You can bet, I won't be ashamed
And I won't have to hide
Because then I'll know, just like you,
What it's like to ride the very best
And ride, with good ol' American pride.

D. R. Buck Montgomery

A cowboy poet who over the years has worn many hats, some of which have included, stuntman, western artist, animator and radio personality. Buck now hangs his hat at the Ponderosa Ranch, in Lake Tahoe, Nevada, Home of TVs most popular western, Bonanza, where he is the resident stunt coordinator and entertainment director. Buck has also appeared in several commercials, both TV and radio and has performed his live action stunts across the country in concert with such recording artists as Vince Gill, Tim McGraw, Joe Diffee and Riders in the Sky to name just a few. Whether he's re-creating the west in art or poetry, or acting out the role of the badman of the old west during a stunt performance, you can bet that DR Buck Montgomery is keeping the west alive and wild!

Your Typical Biker

"Now listen, you don't go any one special place.
That's cornball style. You just go."
-Marlon Brando-
The Wild One - 1953

It's Friday evening and still light. Dinner's over and at least one after dinner beer is about finished. A few more spots touched up with the rag and he'll step back and admire his handiwork. The family car may be falling apart but this motorcycle will have the tenderest of loving care. The polishing rag gets stashed as he swings one leg over the seat to straddle the, as of now, inanimate machine. In no deliberate hurry he turns on the ignition and twists the throttle a couple of times, then touches the starter button. The machine that was so quietly sleeping a few minutes ago has now been startled awake and roars into life like a dragon that has been angrily awakened by twisting its tail. A twist or two on the throttle and the machine settles into the familiar pa-ta-put pa-ta-put of the Harley Davidson at idle.

One last swig on the beer and the can gets tossed the same as his cigarette had been a few minutes earlier. A couple of additional twists on the throttle and the bike gets backed out of its parking place and shifted into first gear. Then easing out on the clutch lever and he's rolling. In a short time he's on the highway and enjoying an emotional rush equaled only by the rush of wind in his face. In all too short a time our guy has reached his destination, or at least the first stop of the evening.

Even before he dismounts he can hear the strains of country music drifting out of the bar room door. There are already some other motorcycles parked outside along with a small group of people, wearing the distinctive markings belonging to that seg-

20

ment of our society affectionately and often very unflatteringly known as "Bikers." Most will be off to themselves talking and will keep apart from others not of this brotherhood, and just as the grade B movies depict, there may be an occasional physical conflict during the course of the evening.

The scenario just described is not out of the ordinary and will be acted out over and over again on any given weekend all across America in thousands of towns and cities. This is one phenomenon that knows no regional boundaries and will be repeated fifty two weekends each year in the United States. There is something distinctly American about this paradigm. It goes back to the mystique of the American Cowboy. The mythical character personified by such legends of the cinema as Tom Mix, Gene Autry, Roy Rogers, and of course the "Duke" himself, John Wayne. This image is one that immediately comes to mind whenever an average citizen hears the term biker.

The original cowboys were anything but the image we've come to believe in, and the rest of the world sees as American. In fact the real cowboy era only lasted about ten or fifteen years and if the Hollywood movies had been true to life, Roy would not look anything like the person we picture on Trigger riding along with Dale Evans and Pat Brady. The image of the cowboy has been distorted and broadened to include many others who happened to live in the late nineteenth century and have in the time that has passed become larger than life. However even such unsavory characters as William H. Bonney (Billy the Kid) did a stint punching cattle before earning his fame during the Lincoln County Wars. Our concept of the cowboy has become attached to an image that includes Wild Bill Hickok, Wyatt Earp, and Kit Carson, with a little Butch Cassidy and The Sundance Kid thrown in. Add the Hollywood Cowboy to this mixture and stir well to complete the impression. This mythical person lived a loner life but valued friendship. He was true to his own code and had an undying affection and attachment to his horse. To take this concept forward one hundred years you only have to take out the six gun and replace the wool trousers and linen suspenders with a pair of Levis and a leather belt. Trigger and the six gun have been combined and are now a new mechanical steed whose hooves are rubber and is many times more powerful and faster than even the greatest effort Man-

21

O-War could put forth.

The love affair between man and steed has remained unchanged and is quite possibly stronger than ever even though old dobbin is no longer flesh and blood.

The history of the cowboy, both real and myth, will be discussed in depth in the next chapter.

This typical "Devil-May-Care" biker is only part of the American motorcycle scene Let us take for example, that same Saturday night in another part of town, and we have a little different scenario.

Supper has been finished and mom is putting the dishes in the washer and straightening up the kitchen. Bob is out in the garage waxing and polishing a motorcycle with so many bells and whistles that you wonder how a two cylinder engine can pull the weight. This bike even has a built in CB Radio and a stereo that automatically increases the volume as the road and exhaust noise rises. Hard fiberglass cases on either side and in back hold everything from emergency tools to matching wet weather driving suits. Mom joins him in the garage to help put the final spiffs on the bike and they are ready to go.

With a grin he says, "Ready Doris," and they put on matching helmets. In addition to matching in style, these helmets are painted to compliment the motorcycle and have microphones which plug into an intercom so that they can ride and still carry on a conversation.

He pulls out the choke and twists the throttle a couple of times and the engine purrs into life. A few seconds of warm-up and the choke is pushed in and the motor settles down once again to the familiar rhythm of a Harley at idle. Doris climbs into the seat behind him and they pull out of the garage and up the drive way to spend yet another pleasant evening enjoying motorcycling rather than watching TV.

This particular evening could find them just out for a putt or joining friends for an evening group ride. The ride could be a random outing or have a specific destination and purpose.

Perhaps it would be appropriate to mention here that our couple is retired and in their sixties and this motorcycle is also their vacation vehicle. Their rides have spanned a variety of durations that range from similar Saturday nights to cross country excursions lasting weeks. They are not a rare example by any means. There are literally thousands of couples who spend their leisure time motorcycling. The only common denominator is a preference for being out on two wheels, and they share a kinship with our previously discussed fellow that can only be understood by those who prefer to be in the wind with the road rolling by underneath.

There are many other couples out and about on our typical Saturday night. They number in the millions and span virtually every walk of life and social strata.

Some will be riding together on a single machine and some will be on individual bikes. Some of them will be riding matching motorcycles. There are almost as many types of motorcyclists as there are types of motorcycles. The participants in this particular pastime ride a wide variety of makes of motorcycles from dirt bikes and big Hondas, to the super sport bikes called crotch rockets. For the purpose of this book, however, we will deal primarily with the iron horses made in Milwaukee, Wisconsin, and the phenomenon of the attachment that modern American cowboys have for their trusty steeds of steel and paint and chrome.

On the other side of the coin, or the view from the public perspective, picture this scenario:

It is not quite dark, and Cindy Citizen is driving home with the children after a day's visit with her parents. The day was pleasant and she is making a twenty mile drive she has taken literally hundreds of times before. Her husband John is probably at home by now and watching the evening news waiting for their return. She expects the drive home to be as uneventful as it has always been.

Something in the rearview mirror has caused her to take her eyes from the road ahead, and stare at the blacktop behind them. It takes a minute for her eyes to focus on the section of road far in their rear. There it is again: just a flicker of light, which turns into a single headlight rounding the curve a quarter of a mile behind them.

Paying more attention to the road behind than the road ahead, she watches as the lone headlight is joined by another and another, as more than twenty of the vehicles sweep around the curve, slowly closing the distance between them and the solitary automobile.

Involuntarily, Cindy's heart jumps into her throat and images from numerous movies and news stories flash through her mind.

The images are almost all the same. Mental pictures of Brando in the *Wild Ones,* or the bikers in *Stone Cold* as Cindy tries to hug the shoulder of the road unable to shrug off the momentary fright.

The column passes by her and she tries not to look as they ride by, but curiosity is stronger than the fear. Strangely enough there seems to be little or no attention to her as they file past and near the back a woman with a small child in a side car actually smiles and raises her hand in a friendly wave. Surprised and relieved Cindy continues home.

Fiction? Perhaps in this particular narrative, but this scenario is played out an uncountable number of times whenever groups of bikers take to the road and some people recoil in fear, the way they would at encountering a snake, whenever approached by a person in biker leather.

People in general are fascinated by things they don't understand and particularly by things they fear. This fascination is proven by the large numbers of people who regularly visit reptile farms across America or attend large aquariums such as Sea World and by the hundreds of thousands of spectators who drive by to gawk wherever a large bike rally is being held. Just the chance that a Hells Angel might be seen is enough to make the long wait in an endless procession of cars passing by worth the trouble. A woman coaxed to cross the street and enter the largest party along the main drag at the 1995 Bike Week at Myrtle Beach, South Carolina remarked, "Everyone at this beach wants to know what's going on over here and wishes they were in here."

In the past, Ward Bond, Keenan Wynn, Robert Taylor, and of course Cowboy Star Randolph Scott were bikers. The most prominent one of all, Clark Gable, was a biker and once confessed that he practiced his lines while taking long leisurly weekend rides in the country on his motorcycle. Buddy Holly rode a motorcycle which was given to Waylon Jennings as a birthday present by Buddy's band The Crickets. Malcom Forbes was a biker and so was Elvis Presley.

Wynonna Judd, Mickey Roarke, Liz Taylor, Larry Hagman,

Lyle Lovett, Sam Elliott, Jay Leno, Joe Piscopo, Dennis Rodman, and many championship wrestlers are bikers.

I know a prominent psychiatrist who rides his Harley-Davidson to work and my former business partner rides his to work every day. I ride mine an average of 15-20,000 miles per year and for the first two years after I bought it; I rode it as my only transportation. To date I have ridden that bike over 115,000 miles.

America's Image - Cowboy Myth and Reality

"Yippee Ki Yea Muther %#@&*!!!"
- Bruce Willis
Die Hard - 1988

In the 1988 film <u>Die Hard</u>, the antagonist is portrayed in a generic European appearing character while our protagonist is the stereotypical All-American Joe just trying to get by in his world. He inadvertently finds himself in the uncomfortable position of having to be involved in a high society and finance social function when all he wanted to do was try to resolve a domestic issue. He is resigned to make the best of it when he comes across the bad guy who has a gang.

Willis without thinking just goes into action and acting alone uses his wits, takes the hand he is dealt, and plays it out. In the end he, of course, is triumphant.

In the course of this action packed thriller there are interludes where the action stops while our two main characters have dialog and match wits in this now deadly chess game played with lives. In a classic case, the presumably foreign bad guy feeling intellectually superior, looks upon his advisory with disgust and deliberately insults him with a snide comment about cowboys. Willis who is now macho enough to be Tom Mix, Hop A Long Cassidy, and the Lone Ranger rolled into one, adopts the name Roy (for guess who) and defeats the 'owl hoot', emerging the victor with his symbolic ten gallon white hat (imaginary) still in place.

America has always presented a macho image to itself and the rest of the world that is epitomized in an historical figure that we identify as the American Cowboy. Although the cowboy era was a short lived period in our history, lasting only a few years in the late 1800's, this theme dominates our culture and seems to invade all segments and classes of our society. It is a central figure, or character, that is type-cast in all forms of our entertainment, and in many of our leaders; and an identity that we proudly display to the rest of the world. How did this mythical figure, whose time in history was so short lived, and whose life was so unglamorous, become our predominant image? How did it become so symbolic, that we actually backtrack and assign this image to heroes and figures that pre-date the cowboy more than a hundred years? If we explore this nondescript character, that now looms so much larger than life, and trace his evolution in American history, perhaps we can answer these questions and more about this uniquely American phenomenon. By examining the evidence at hand we can see how this figure evolved and how it came to dominate so much of how we see our history, both before his time and even through the present. Finally, maybe we can answer the question of why we identify so much with the cowboy that today we have a multibillion dollar industry based on this image. One that has led to millions of sales of large products such as pickup trucks and Harley Davidson motorcycles, the biggest part of the movie industry and even the electing of a president.

The Oxford English Dictionary defines cowboy as "a boy who tends cows." It further traces its earliest reference to 1725 but goes on to tell us that the term cowboy was first used in the United States during the Revolutionary War by a group of guerrilla fighters who would move about in the brush with a cowbell to imitate a lost cow. This would lure Patriots and continental soldiers into the brush foraging for food only to be ambushed. "A contemptuous appellation applied to some of the Tory Partisans of Westchester County, New York, during the Revolutionary War, who were exceedingly barbarous in the treatment of their opponents who favored the American cause" (OED, 1084). The word has gone through an amelioration since then. Robert Howard tells us that the term first appeared in Ireland in minstrel songs by 1000 AD. "The word cow is Old Norse; boy is Middle English and East Frisian." (265) Ireland had large herds of cattle and a beef industry but were destroyed during the conquest by the English under William of Orange. Howard goes on to tell us that the word cowboy was already in use at the time of the American Revolution as a "derogatory nickname for the illiterate roughnecks herding cattle in the back country from Maine to Georgia." With the added Revolutionary War usage the term acquired such an unpleasant intimation that cattle herdsmen in the East adopted the English term Drover. "Cowboy reappeared in Texas between 1830 - 1840 and was initially used to identify cattle rustlers and gunmen. Despite its popularity with Wild West authors and movie script writers, cowboy still holds derogatory implications among professional cattlemen east and west." (265)

In the late 1860's we have the beginnings of a real cattle industry in the United States with large herds and cowtowns popping up. Joseph G. McCoy is credited with being one of the first cattle ranchers. He actually opened the cattle market at Abilene, Kansas, in 1867. (Savage, 17) Joe McCoy is credited with being the name first used in the expression, "The Real McCoy". McCoy's own words show us that even at this point in time the term cowboy is used with a derogatory meaning. While a respectable person in the cattle business is still referred to as drover. McCoy wrote in 1874:

> In 1868 a party of young men, mostly residents of Abilene, numbering six or seven, were returning from a walk, at a late hour, when all of a sudden they heard the footsteps of a running pony, each moment coming nearer. Before they could scarce divine the meaning thereof, a mounted, crazy, drunk cow-boy was upon them. Yelling in demoniacal voice to halt; adding horrible oaths, abuse and insult. Before the young men fully comprehended the situation, the cow-boy was rushing around them at a furious rate of speed, firing both his revolvers over their heads in the darkness, demanding an immediate contribution from each one of a ten dollar note, swearing instant death to every one who refused to comply at once with his request. The party of young men were entirely unarmed, and in imminent danger of being shot. But no time was to be lost. As a subterfuge, one of the young men, a drover, began talking in the kindest tone of voice, saying to the cow-boy: "Now hold on; we are all cowboys just off the trail, and have been out to see a little fun. We have no money with us, but if you will just go with me to the Cottage, you shall have all the

ten dollar notes you want. Certainly, certainly, sir! Anything you want you can have, if you will only go with me to the hotel. Certainly, certainly, sir!" (Savage, 27-28).

The amelioration of the word cowboy came about because of the media as will be discussed later.

There were many who went west for various reasons including some European royalty. Walter Baron Von Richtofen immigrated from Germany sometime in the 1870's to Denver, Colorado and one of his business interests was cattle. Unlike most, however, his was a luxurious existence. He was the Uncle of the now infamous World War I German air ace, The Red Baron. (Savage, 41) The glamorous life portrayed in films and books was not the lot of the typical cowboy. He was none of the extreme images usually portrayed, but rather possessed the character traits germane to the business he was in. The typical cowboy was an average person living in the American West. The Roy Rogers outfits were not to be seen but would instead be clothing both comfortable and practical. Life was hard and always provided exposure to all weather conditions and months with no bed, no roof over his head, and no reading materials for entertainment (Savage, 99). We do have, however, evidence that cowboys sang both for their own entertainment and to soothe the restless cattle. Other pastimes included alcohol and all forms of tobacco use. The cowboy job was a twenty-four-hour one with the men working in shifts overnight watching the herd on a drive.

Many people moved west after the Civil War due to the shattered economy and lifestyle in the east and many of these became cowboys. According to Savage, "The roughest of the west's immigrants drifted into the business because of its excitement and good wages, and this class by its excesses gave the world its standard for all. But hundreds of cowboys were sons of Christian parents, and when they had made a start in life settled down at last as good citizens of the great West they had helped to develop (99).

The word cowboy usually invokes an image of a white man in the form personified by an actor, depending on your favorite, ranging from Ben Johnson, veteran of many horse operas to the outlandishly dressed Roy Rogers. Ben Johnson's characters would come closest to being authentic. The real cowboys were not, however, always white. If those pictures had been accurate, Roy might have been the only white man at some of those campfires if, in fact, even he had been white. There are no accurate records or numbers of cowboys nor their proportionate racial mix.

According to Durham and Jones, "a typical trail crew had among its eight cowboys two or three Negroes. Its boss was almost certain to be white, although a few Negroes led crews up the trail, its Wrangler might be a Negro....Its cook was likely to be a Negro - usually an ex-cowboy." (45)

Many cowboys were Mexican and Indian. The best cowboys were said to be Indians, probably due to adaptability to living out in the weather. Some Tribes said to produce the best cattle herders are Coddo, Kickapoo, Osage, and Pawnee, according to pictorial records and comments by contemporary cattlemen.

Durham and Jones estimate the total number of cowboys at 35,000, but there is no accurate data to support this figure. No one counted cowboys but records were kept of cattle because cattle translated into profits.

We know that average trail crews were composed of 8 to 10 cowboys. According to Savage in "The Cowboy Hero", modern estimates of total cattle number between four and six million with the average herd size at 2 to 2 1/2 thousand. This allows for a total number of cowboys of only 12 to 30 thousand figuring from the smallest possible cowboy to cow ratio, to the largest possible. One early cowboy historian, George W. Saunders, estimated about one third of the cowboys made more than one trip. If this is accurate then the total figures would be less. In any case, nowhere near 35,000.

This historical description would be terribly incomplete if I did not mention the women cowboys or cowgirls as it were. The majority of women in the West were wives who spent their time raising families or ladies of somewhat dubious repute. In some cases, however, photographic evidence shows that some women were present on cattle drives. How many were just accompanying their men, as opposed to those who were independent, is not known. Of the latter some notable exceptions are Calamity Jane, Annie Oakley, and the famous female outlaw Belle Starr. To be sure just as some women donned men's clothes and served in the military surely the same occurred among the cowboys. The women of the American West, just as their men, were cut from a different

30

bolt of cloth. William Forrest Sprague quotes two descriptions of western women; one by Lino Carr in 1855 and one from a European traveler named Boyesen in 1869:

> The western young lady is a cross between the southern and eastern - the intelligence of the one, and the grace in showing it of the other, with a spice of half a dozen European nations thrown in, and fearlessness and dash which belong only to a rearing west of the lakes and Alleghenies. The first woman whose acquaintance I made in the United States (in 1869) was a pretty western girl.... She was slangy in her speech, careless in her pronunciation, and bent upon "having a good time" without reference to the prohibitions which are famed for the special purpose of annoying women .... Patriotic she was - bristling with combativeness if a criticism was made which implied disrespect of American manners or institutions. She was good-natured, generous to a fault, and brimming with energy.
>
> This young girl is the type of American womanhood which has become domesticated in European fiction. She is to the French, English, and German authors, the American type par excellence" (Sprague, 230, 231).

The common denominators that shaped settlement of the West were the same ones that had characterized the settlement of the rest of the United States. Hard times have paved the way and existed throughout our history forcing people to be tougher than other cultures. They were predominantly beset by hard times until the twentieth Century and then there were no real periods of luxury for many until the decades beginning after World War II. Social scientists have determined that there is a subculture of violence in the United States that seems to be non existent in most other parts of the world. This subculture is most prevalent in the Southern United States. Perhaps, then, it is no small coincidence that the majority of the cattle industry was in the southwest. To this day the most dangerous city in America to live in is Dallas, Texas. This statistic is from the FBI Uniform Crime Report based on number of crimes per 100,000 population. This is not a hard statistic to believe. The road traveled throughout the settlement of the United States was paved with violence. Many of the people, both immigrating to America and migrating from the East westward were escaping from something, either a life style or pursuit as criminals. Being rough, roguish, restless, volatile and fast moving are all character traits which help in living that sort of lifestyle. Many of the ancestors of those migrating westward fled England and other countries to escape harsh sentences or even the hangman's dock. During the time Defoe was writing *Moll Flanders* and *Robinson Crusoe* there were twenty one capital offenses in English law. Many were pardoned if the offenders were willing to migrate to the colonies. With such a heritage, their personalities should be no surprise. My own first ancestor to come to America, arrived as an indentured servant.

Two tools that were essential to the conquest of America and the job of cowboy were also the stock items necessary for violence and crime. Of course these are the horse and the gun. America has always had a love affair with guns that persists even today. In the seventeenth, eighteenth, and nineteenth centuries they were a necessary way of life for protection.

Many of the wilder western figures found the gun a useful tool to earn a living in a few different ways. These men, and a few women, became the gunfighters, outlaws, lawmen, and bounty hunters. All of them held life much cheaper in value than did those of a more respectable nature. These are the ones most remembered. The gunfighters were not very different from the outlaws. Even though a person didn't have to be one to be the other, in most cases, they crossed over and were synonymous. Gunfighters generally were drifters, or gamblers, or hired guards (guns) when they weren't outlaws. Outlaws were out and out criminals and a good many would drift back and forth between the two categories as it suited them. All but a very few exceptions were cold blooded killers.

The lawmen in most cases were separated from the outlaw side by only the thinnest of barriers. Some had already been on the other side, while others eventually crossed to the other side of the law also. It took a ruthless person to control ruthless people. With little respect for the law prevalent, a lawman had to be as tough or tougher than the lawbreakers. Those who hunted the outlaws for the rewards had to be tougher still. For the most part those on both sides had worked for a time as cowboys.

These men and women are the ones who became legends.

32

The names of the average cowboys have been lost to antiquity but those whose exploits earned them a footnote in history have become larger than life; each one's exploits becoming greater with the retelling.

The device most used by all of these characters of course is the pistol. The pistols were revolvers of six shot capacity and were more portable than rifles or shotguns. Earlier pistols were cap and ball and were unreliable. They took a long time to reload, therefore those who used them would carry two or more. This created the image of the two- gun gunslinger. As technology and reliability coupled with metal cartridges which were easy to reload came into use the necessity of carrying more than one gun passed and gave way to a single six shooter, usually 44 or 45 calibre. Although there were better made pistols, those of Samuel Colt became the most famous and used.

Joseph Rosa wrote in 1969:

The instrument of a gunfighter's appeal is his pistol. Without it he is meaningless, for the gun signifies his strength and purpose. In his hands it is the tool of justice or destruction, each shot finding its mark, for "Judge Colt and his jury of six" is unerring in its verdict of death to wrong doers. No other make of revolver has enjoyed the fame of the Colt,....the gunfighter's particular favorite was the 1873 army model, the Peacemaker - without doubt the most famous firearm ever made (5).

Interesting that this instrument should be called the peacemaker.

Somehow we tend to straighten crooked pictures and we do this with our past. As time progresses it tends to retouch the photographs of our past figuratively just as we have family heirloom pictures retouched to make them look better. We've combined these characters: cowboy, gunfighter, lawman, and bounty hunter, under the generic term cowboy.

Looking back in time this image has softened. We have turned this cold, rough, hardened character into a myth. With the transformation into myth we have attached this good badman status even to our heroes that preceded the cowboy, (gunfighter). Rosa also argues that the gunfighter cowboy image traces its evolution from the men with the long rifles who gave a good accounting of themselves in the American Revolution and the early wars against Indians. The long gun has evolved into a pistol, specifically the revolver, invented in the 1830's. This six shooter became the instrument of the lawman and the lawless and its importance in legend as well as fact, "cannot be over emphasized." "The long rifle was to earlier days what the six shooter was to the West. It is an easy matter to trace the evolution from frontier figures such as Boone and Crockett through the Texas Rangers to the gunfighters in the figures of Earp and Hickock." (28-31)

We like this figure. In him is something we as Americans admire. We see this person through dark glasses that hide flaws we would rather not notice. Modern processes of law, order and retribution are cumbersome and usually an extended process and terribly frustrating. We are not always satisfied with the outcome either. In our mythical figure of the cowboy gunfighter we have an American Robin Hood. A person who can be at once judge, jury, and executioner, and in him we see ourselves as that person (Rosa, 4).

Thanks to Nineteenth Century media, the cowboy was already becoming a mythical hero before his time had completely passed by. The first cowboy hero was William Levi (Buck) Taylor who was promoted in PR materials and Buffalo Bill's Wild West Show in the 1880's. He was titled "King of the Cowboys" and later a dime novel hero (Savage, 66). Wild West shows and dime novels were printed in abundance and literally gobbled up by a waiting audience in the east and in Europe. Of all the folk characters used by feature writers none have enjoyed more space on the printed page than have cowboys.

In 1887 a British traveler wrote:
The cowboy has at the present time become a personage; nay, more he is rapidly becoming a mythical one. Distance is doing for him what lapse of time did for the heroes of antiquity (Frantz and Choate, 69).

The invention of moving pictures before the turn of the century provided yet another medium to promote the cowboy myth. The popularity of this figure was money in the bank for movies and more than any other genre put Hollywood on the map. The earlier cowboy stars such as Tom Mix and William S. Hart actually were cowboys before becoming stars. Many others were

34

also, or at least were rodeo cowboys.

Hollywood far outdistanced all other media in promoting the myth and reshaping the image. The Tom Mixes were replaced by a generic cowboy character personified by men such as John Wayne. With Wayne we have an example of an American hero image that can span time and fit many roles without changing characters but slightly, if at all. You can place John Wayne in a part not identifiable by date or location within the dialogue and by changing his clothes and background scenery he can be any American hero from a Revolutionary War soldier through all of our periods in time and locations to end up a green beret in Viet Nam. With the magic of Hollywood we see the cowboy image transported to other times and places or even eons into the future on other worlds through the characters portrayed for instance by Harrison Ford in the *Indiana Jones* series or the now infamous Han Solo of the *Star Wars* Trilogy. These are actually only feature length serials like the Lash LaRue Saturday morning shorts of long ago.

A really good example of the ability of Hollywood to reassign the cowboy and gun image is easily evidenced in the 1938 version of Robin Hood, starring Errol Flynn.

There are no records of Robin Hood, as the character we know, ever existing and certainly no recorded quotes. In spite of this, in the movie when Robin is asked why he didn't use his signature weapon, a black arrow, he says, " that's my court of last resort Sir Guy. Its verdict is always final." Remember the previous quote from Joseph Rosa? Curious that he would use this terminology, literally decades before the Magna Carta and our modern court system were in existence.

American visitors to Sherwood Forest, by the way, are frequently shocked when encountering the monument to Robin Hood and discovering that the figure is in traditional twelfth century attire instead of lincoln green tights.

With the stereotyped Hollywood, and now television, figure we have our western good badman. Suddenly this person who in life was probably a psychopathic killer now is a 'Robin Hood' of the old west. The term has actually been used as the introduction to TV western series. We have literally put the white hot image of the good guy over the bad guy, even to such homicidal maniacs of history as William Bonney (Billy the Kid). K.L.

Stechmesser, in his book, *Western Outlaws, The "Good Badmen" In Fact, Film, and Folklore,* devotes chapter fourteen to a complete profile breakdown of this good badman Robin Hood of the American West.

In the twentieth Century the cowboy image completed metamorphoses to become the symbol by which Americans as a whole identify themselves. We no longer can separate the reality from the myth although more and more the media strives for authenticity. The myth is a vital part of our lives.

Early in the twentieth century we elected Teddy Roosevelt president because he was immensely popular due to his cowboy lifestyle and fame. If Ronald Reagan had been more of a comedian, or a Fred McMurray type, or had been more identified with *Bedtime for Bonzo* instead of *Death Valley Days,* I will wager he would never have achieved the presidency.

The cowboy image coupled with modern media magic has made sponsorship of westerns a huge profitable venture. Many fortunes have been made from this image, both in movies and on television. Most adult Americans are familiar with the success of the spaghetti westerns which catapulted Clint Eastwood to stardom and made his one-liner dialogue household expressions. The first color television show was Bonanza in the 1960's and Bonanza and Gunsmoke have become two of the longest running series in media history and are still in syndication.

But for this rugged American image there might not be the enormous sales success of the Harley Davidson Motorcycle. So successful that almost all of the Japanese manufacturers have revised both the body styles and the engine configuration over the last several years to resemble the Harley Davidsons.

On any given day, as an average motorist take note of the enormous number of old pickup trucks, nicknamed Cowboy Cadillacs, to be seen in use as everyday transportation by men and women on their way to and from white collar jobs. A quick scan across any radio dial will uncover stations playing Merle Haggard, Willie Nelson, and Waylon Jennings songs with cowboy themes.

On any Saturday night you will find hundreds of thousands of Urban cowboys and cowgirls, all across America, riding their Harleys or in their cowboy Cadillacs, on the way to local clubs with names like The Longbranch or the Silver Dollar Saloon or even The Cowboy Barn. On the way there they will listen to amplified CD players belting out Willie, Waylon, and Merle songs. Once at their destination, they'll Texas Two-step to the same music performed by live bands using names like Pamela Jean and The Texas Rangers. Come Monday they'll be back in coats and ties at work trying to survive until next weekend. It was the film <u>Urban Cowboy</u> about just such Saturday night outings to a cowboy club in Houston Texas that helped boost John Travolta's star status in motion pictures.

Speaking of pictures making stars, Sam Elliott, who bears an uncanny resemblance to Buck Taylor the first cowboy hero, ascended to stardom portraying characters from Louis L'Amour western novels brought to the screen.

In the last few years we see this good-badman image assigned to Michael Douglas, son of famed actor Kirk Douglas, and responsible for much of his success. Michael, who soared to fame as a tough detective co-starring with Karl Mauldin in the hit TV series <u>Streets Of San Francisco.</u>

Since his Streets days, Douglas has portrayed this good badman character that we seem to love so much in a series of successful movies. A list of examples, none of which are actually westerns, includes <u>Romancing The Stone</u>, <u>Jewel Of The Nile</u>, <u>Black Rain</u>, and even <u>Falling Down</u>, <u>Fatal Attraction</u>, and <u>Disclosure</u>. In all of these he portrays a character who is clearly involved in something we as a public would ordinarily consider unacceptable. Things which range from being a con man to cheating on his wife, and even murder. Yet through it all we are able to identify with, and even like his character.

Need a clearer example, then take Sam Elliott. It is hard to imagine an American movie goer who doesn't like Sam Elliott. It matters not whether the film is <u>Road House</u> or <u>Sackett</u> or any of the many others. The only change Elliott needs is to change from a four legged horse to one with rubber tires.

Like Sam there have been through out the 20th Century real two wheeled cowboys, in and out of the movies,who embody this image. Elliott really rides a motorcycle as did Roy Rogers.

The 1990 blockbuster spectacular is the immensely successful three hour super western <u>Dances With Wolves</u>, filmed where else but in the Sturgis and Deadwood, South Dakota area. The director and star of the movie, Kevin Costner, had some significant cowboy or cowboy type characters as roles prior to Dances. He played a maverick in the military stationed in Washington, DC, in No Way Out and a devil-may-care gunfighter in the popular western Silverado.

Since Dances he has successfully potrayed similar characters in movies such as Waterworld and The Postman.

While Waterworld and Postman are futuristic they are by no means unique. Going back to the future, if I may use a play-on-words from another movie title, has been as immensely successful with more actors than just John Wayne.

Aside from Rocky how would Sylvester Stallione (sounds like stallion to me) made out in his career without the Cobra and Rambo characters. Where would Mel Gibson be without the Mad Max movies. The characters he has portrayed in Lethal Weapon, Braveheart and even Ransom have been this type of character as well and all of whom were "Good Badmen."

It is hard to take this image much farther afield than with the Robo Cop and Terminator movies. Here we have gunfighters who are not only the heros but robots rather than human. Arnold Schwarzenegger has certainly proven that he can do well in other characters and genres including comedy, he always seems to be somewhat a tough guy ready to go to the mat over an issue. His best known rolls are in the Predator and Terminator movies. While clearly the robotic 'gun-totin' villain in Terminator, he comes back as the same character but is now the hero, in Terminator II, and riding a Harley.

Even the modern cowboy comedies are a sure hit. A good example is City Slickers which as of summer 94 had a sequel which was equally successful.

The Cannonball Run movies with Burt Reynolds are based on a rally type race named for Erwin G. "Cannonball" Baker, (see chapter 8) who not only was a motorcyclist, but set many of the time and distance records in the first half of the 20th Century. Baker also won the first race ever held at the Indianapolis Motor Speedway and it was a motorcycle race.

Few magazine or TV commercials in America can be examined without revealing the inevitable cowboy, or motorcycle, or both, oriented ads. One of the longest running ad themes of all time is the stereotyped cowboy images used for Marlboro Cigarettes, followed closely by Winn Dixie Beef. Who could have missed the influence the western has had on industry and advertising including all brands of denim jeans. The western image has been particularly used to advertise Levis and Wrangler brands. Just the word wrangler conjures up a western image. One note of interest is the dyeing process for the indigo blue which I am given to understand is done in Hong Kong. It really doesn't matter because the jeans worn by the original cowboys were made of a coarse weave wool and not denim at all.

A short list of additional ads and commercials include but are certainly not limited to the following:

Joe Camel for Camel Cigarettes. (A Harley-Riding Biker Camel)

Ford Country. (Features the cowboy look with pick-up trucks and Harleys)

Ford Explorer. (Going to Rodeos)

Pontiac Montana. (Cowboys all piling into a Montana in Montana carpooling to go to work but like a chase scene from an old Gene Autry movie)

Chevrolet Silvarado Trucks. (Herding horses and cattle)

Lincoln Navigator.(Luxury sport utility vehicle advertisement uses play-off on the theme of *Home On The Range* both in design and as background music)

Dodge Caravan. (Minivan ad uses *Home On The Range* as background music)

Honda Passport. (Biker ype character in a sleazy Bar & Grill)

Amoco Gasoline. (Stampede of cars and trucks to gas pumps to get special deal on prize headphones from Wild Wild West)

McDonalds Breakfast. (Everyone on the ranch piles in the truck when the breakfast bell rings to ride to the nearest McDonalds restaurant)

Orkin Exterminators. (Robo Cop character killing termites)

Orkin Exterminators. (Toy Story type wooden cowboy character getting rid of bugs)

Wal Mart. (Price rollback features a smiley face in a cowboy hat with the theme from Rawhide playing in the background)

Wendys. (One ad has Dave Thomas trading his nerd coat for leather and a motorcycle and the other has him as a cowboy sitting around the campfire)

Domino's Pizza (Ad has a motorcycle)

Burger King. (Sunglasses ad has western shootout)

Resolve Carper Cleaner. (Little boy with cowboy outfit)

Post Cereal. (Little boy from the 50s with a cowboy outfit)

Fruitopia.

Stetson Cologne.

Zantac 75 Antacid.

Just For Men Gel. (A cowboy in the ad)

Maxwell House. (Businessman sitting on a motorcycle)

Big John Homestyle Red Grape Wine. (Bottled in Petersburg, VA, it features a John Wayne type caricature on the label)

Author's Note: From experience, if you open the cap and down a couple of swigs, then screw the cap back on tight and store the rest of the bottle in a dark camp box for about a year, it will turn really good and sweet and becomes a campfire favorite.

Successful TV shows and music videos for TV are good examples of vehicles which use western and or motorcycle themes, but modern, are Walker Texas Ranger and the videos of Bare Naked Ladies, Celine Dion, Meatloaf, Shania Twain, and Toni Braxton. Even the scenes behind the opening credits on David Letterman's show have motorcycles.

During the 1999 TNN Music City News Country Awards Preview fans were asked to explain the reason why George Strait and Tim McGraw were able to maintain such loyal popularity. Their explanation was the cowboy and rodeo appearance and actions on stage.

One final point dealing with movies is the connection of the American type cowboy to the horsemen in Australia for American moviegoers. Themes which have been tremendously successful. Some of these include The Man From Snowy River Parts one and two and the release featuring Tom Selleck, who has starred with Sam Elliott on occasion, called Quigley Down Under.

David Dary tells us that "by the 1880's being a cowboy was already romantic." He then quotes Frantz with the comment, "The feel for the cowboy is everywhere; the symbol of the cowboy is just as pervasive" (332, 337).

Frantz says, "...the American cowboy is the composite, the blood and sinew prototype of all the frontiersmen....In him are all the qualities and characteristics of every frontier folk hero from the Indian fighter of Daniel Boone's day forward (8). Those images arising whenever the word "cowboy" is mentioned - the man on horseback, armed with his six-shooter, trailing a thousand longhorns across virgin prairie, keeping a spirited eye out for Comanche, Apache, or Sioux (69).

We as Americans are identified with the cowboy. Not because people in other lands call us that, often in jest, but because we have adopted the image for ourselves. "From the outset, the range rider has embodied all of the virtues and vices of the Anglo-American in one folk type (Frantz,71). We aren't stuck with this identity, we embrace it. It is the basis of our pride and our confidence. It's the emotional backbone that makes it possible for us as a country and as individuals to face adversity with a bravado that is amazing to and unmatched in most other societies. On the down side it is our deliberate identification with this dubious and mythical figure that has helped get us branded in other parts of the world as "The Ugly American". As Americans we are immersed in this identity from birth. Think back to your cowboy or cowgirl outfit that sooner or later almost all children in the United States have. Dating back to the 40's, America's oldest, continuing, popular singing group, the Sons of the Pioneers, still evoke images with their sad harmony in Tumbling Tumbleweeds. Relax in your most comfortable chair at home in front of your stereo and feel the slight chill caused by the haunting lyrics of Ghost Riders in The Sky. For good or bad the mythical cowboy is our image. An inseparable identity that will be with us and be uniquely American for a long time to come.

Joseph C. Rosa on pages 12 and 13 of The Gun Fighter says: To the American, the story of the west is the story of his country's youth - A brief yet long to be remembered stage in the growth to maturity - one time when the frontier was an identifiable place without distinct boundaries, a place apart. The gunfighter is now a firmly established character in American folklore —

41

Before There Was America

"How is it that you didn't use a black arrow today"
-Sir Guy with Prince John-
"that's my court of last resort...
Its verdict is always final."
-Errol Flynn-
Robin Hood, 1938

There is a lust for life among Americans, that only a feeling of freedom as an individual can produce. This is an inborn attitude or overpowering ilk indiginous in Americans, and something that all of us native-born, to some extent, are here possessed. Even the most timid seem to have a spark of it in his or her makeup.

From where did it come? Being human is the start of it and the nature of being human as opposed to other animal life on the planet. According to the great Anthropologist, Dr. Richard E. Leakey, in The Making Of Mankind:

What is particularly interesting about our species? For a start, we walk upright on our hind legs at all times, which is an extremely unusual way of getting around for a mammal. There are also several unusual features about our head, not least of which is the very large brain it contains...Other forelimbs, being freed from helping us to get about, possess a very high degree of manipulative skill. Part of this skill lies in the anatomical structure of the hands, but the crucial element is, of course, the power of the brain....The most obvious product of our hands and brains is technology. No other animal manipulates the world in the extensive and arbitrary way that humans do. The termites are capable of constructing intricately structured mounds which create their own "air conditioned" environment inside. But the termites cannot choose to build a cathedral instead. Humans are unique because they have the capac-

42

ity to choose what they do. (Lerner, Meacham, & Burns, 3)

Being human just isn't enough of an explanation, however, for there is something which is different, which is unique and special. It can't be explained by the extra chromosome theory either because it lives as strong in women as in men, as will be demonstrated in the 5th chapter.

To find the American character's earliest beginnings we must go back before the settlement of this country, which began at the end of the Later Middle Ages. Development of Western Civilization from the foundation of Christianity was based on of conformism to mass popular acceptance and deference to higher authority. Everyone was governed by a variety of authorities in the form of levels of government and church which at that time were intertwined. Average citizens did not read nor vote and were at the mercy of any information or rulings handed to them by these institutions of authority. Many of these governing bodies held the power of life and death over the common person anyway.

Notable exceptions over the ages have been those figures of legend, song, and cinema, such as Spartacus or William Wallace. The masses for the most part over time, have followed where they were led.

Glen Turner, the man who originally developed the pyramiding concept into a money making scheme, used to tell a motivating story to his audiences. His intent was to instill into each person the idea that people are limited only by what they think they can do. The story was a lesson to make people think about human nature and where he or she was in life. I was in one of those audiences and I have never forgotten the story. A mesmerizing speaker, he would tell about a jar of fleas. The fleas once in the jar would jump up and down and hit the jar lid on every leap. Eventually they would hit the lid enough time that they would began to jump with less force until the leaps would stop short of the lid. Some would give up and stop jumping at all. Once they reached this state, you could remove the lid and the fleas would still remain in the jar. I do not know if the flea experiment will really work on fleas, but it works really well on humans. Hundreds of thousands of listeners followed like sheep and invested in his products expecting to walk into an easy fortune.

The flea principle has worked through the ages to surpress

43

the masses and keep populace in check. The many must be controlled by a few. It has always worked better everywhere else in the world than in the USA.

Historians, this one included, must go back and study many aspects of history to determine not only what has happened over the ages, but how and why.

We know from Leakey's observation of the distinguishing differences between humans and animals, besides appearance. That tells us why, but what tells us what and how? It may be traceable to a particular incident or person.

Although some may choose to argue the point that it could actually be related to historical figures much farther back we will not go into that much depth. I am sure that some historian could nit-pick all the way back to a Mesopotamian Bedouin bandit on a camel, but for the sake of argument and the size of this book we will direct our attention to a later time and an identifiable person of some notoriety.

The Middle Ages were a miserable and dark time for most people. The whole western world seemed to be under a gloomy oppressed state and poverty and plague prevailed. It is imaginable that to the average person life was a hopeless struggle and one could not escape his position in life. If a person was not born into affluence it was not likely that he would stumble into it. The Christian Church (Roman Catholic) in Europe was all powerful and ruled until one man became unable to digest any longer, the doctrine of the church as it affected human individuality. After all, going to Heaven is not a group effort. No matter how much you do things in a group or conform to the mass order of things, leaving this life and going to another seems to be a matter of individuality of the highest degree. If a bus came along offering rides direct to Heaven and stopped to pick up your group, some would elect to take their chances and wait for a later bus. This is not a hard fast rule, however, for in some cases comets come by and take a bus load all at once. Even then a few didn't make the trip.

In 1521 Martin Luther decided after much anguish, and rereading of Scripture, that the doctrine and theology as presented by the Church was contrary to the Scriptures themselves. He wrote out his theories and presented them to the Church. He subsequently was called to stand before the Church Authorities and stood his ground instead of backing down defending his position even though he knew this would place him in peril. (Do you see a connection forming here?) His answer to those confronting him was:

Since then your serene majesty and your lordships seek a simple answer, I will give it in this manner, neither horned nor toothed: unless I am convinced by the testimony of Scripture or by clear reason ... I am bound by the Scripture I have quoted, and my conscience is captive to the Word of God. I cannot and I will not retract anything, since it is neither safe nor right to violate one's conscience. I cannot do otherwise, here I stand, may God help me. Amen.

-Martin Luther, addressing the Diet of Worms, 1521. (465)

Luther was excommunicated for his stand against church doctrine.

This comment by Luther at his trial seems to be similar to the position of Walter Brennan's character in the TV western series The Guns Of Will Sonnett. Sonnett would state his position on some issue or make some threat and close it with the following, "No Brag just fact."

The English had made significant progress 306 years earlier in a confrontation with King John (If you are an old classics or movie buff, this is the same character who earlier was the Prince John of Robin Hood fame.) and an agreement was signed which would alter the order of things forever and bring out the first ray of light in the dawning of independence and civil liberties. In a meadow at Runymede in 1215 King John was forced to sign the Magna Carta. This document some historians say was modeled after a similar instrument, signed almost a hundred years before, by Henry I in 1124. There is even some speculative thought that this was in reality a political statement and designed to undermine John from the inside of his administration.

It doesn't matter what the motives or the subversive reasons, it did set a precedent which has carried over through to the present. Individuals do have rights, and collectively have the power to enforce those rights, and may claim them against an oppressive authoritarian figure. (king, ruler, etc, in short, government entities) This opened the door for individuals of a free thinking mind to see that they might have a chance at personal liberty.

The Magna Carta was no where near perfect and certainly provided no real freedom for the common person but it was a start.

This was the start of a spark which would not be extinguished. However, St. Thomas More, an equally famous figure in history, stood his ground for what he believed, and this time on the side of church doctrine. He was executed just 14 years after Martin Luther made his famous stand. Go figure.

World trade had been increasing as more spices were sought to enhance food, which was somewhat rancid a lot of the time. Remember refrigeration was a thing of the future and in warm weather meat would not be so delectable except when fresh. I would guess that meat went from good to jerky in no time with lousy in between. The search for spices led to the discovery of the New World around 1500 and just about the time Martin Luther and Thomas More were asserting their independence.

Colonies were established with the intent to produce an expansion of holdings and create revenue for the mother countries back in Europe. These colonies were to be the incubators for the American Spirit to have a birthing place.

Almost every historian writing about colonial America and beyond has mentioned this particular trait in Americans, or have skirted around it not quite hitting on it but coming close to the mark.

Most of those earlier authors writing about Americans from the very first stages of settlement of the new world, have noticed a fierce independence not native to, or at least not so apparent in the rank and file of other parts of the world. It is an attitude of defiance, and do it standing alone, that seems to permeate those of us native to this soil.

Maybe it is something in the soil itself or maybe the water or maybe for the first time in civilization as Europeans knew it there was a place to go, which would allow by its very remoteness and expanse, an incubation chamber for that spark of a desire for life unfettered.

There is a place on one of the few remaining sections of pavement along old Route 66, between Clinton, Oklahoma and Shamrock, Texas. This place is Texola, and on the side of a building there which used to be an old Route 66 icon, I remember from my youth, there is a sign still visible. It reads, "There's no place like this place anywhere near this place, so this must be the place." That sums it up and that is America or at least that part of the northern half of it staked out as the United States.

Although Australia may run a close second, according to reports I hear, there is no place anywhere quite like this place here in America. From the continuity among the people all the way across to our unique Constitution, nowhere else in the world can you ride as far on good roads across different cultures, dialects, regions, and tastes and get along and communicate without real difficulty.

We are a different breed of cat and that difference has been the attraction since day one. That difference has been obvious and there is plenty of historical data to support it's being there and being recognizable.

My theory is that the spark was brought with the colonists and the land was to be the incubator for it to grow. An examination of historical data and observation will demonstrate why this theory is valid.

Many, if not most of the early colonists came here as less desirables or for less desirable reasons. Jails in Merry Olde England were overcrowded and I am given to believe that there were some 21 offenses which were capital crimes in England during the colonial era. Now comes the ticket out. If you will go to the New World you can get out of the Hoosegow, cheat the hangman and have a new start. I know I would have been on the next boat. My own earliest ancestor over here came as an indentured servant. In addition there was terrible poverty and over population and a variety of diseases making this period, in spite of some bright spots, accepted by most historians as pretty bleak.

On the other side of the coin there is religion which should have been the bright side. By this time Europe is full of religions, and some are involved in violent altercations either perpetrated by them or on them. Chiefly targeted are those who are non Christian or are those Protestants who have spawned from Martin Luther's successful departure from the Mother Church. Both sides will be responsible for horrendous numbers of needless deaths.

To begin with, many Jews have been persecuted and massacred periodically, all over Europe for centuries. (I'll bet you thought Hitler originated the concept.) Basically the start of this butchery was the concept of Christian Soldiery by those noble Knights in the first Crusade which was ordered by Pope Urban II.

Even though Early Christianity is basically pacifistic and St. Martin, in the 4th century set the precept that Soldiers of Christ do not fight, the religious leaders were able to get around that one itty bitty hindrance. St. Augustine and St. Gregory worked out theories which would allow them to bypass this block, which sort of allowed the bypassing of several of the Ten Commandments as well. Pope Gregory VII managed to affix the Papal seal of approval on Christian conquests against the Normans, Muslims, Greeks, and Slavs under the terminology of "Gaining the right order in the world." With this precedent set, Urban ordered the first Crusade.

Only eldest sons were entitled to inheritance in Europe at this time. The idea of going to foreign lands and perhaps acquiring some fortune and lands for themselves, rather than sitting around feeling miserable and sorry for themselves, looked good to a lot of younger sons who stood little chance of enjoying an inheritance at home. They among others of various reasons, flocked to join in the great Crusade forming. Even though the overall reason was religion, it was to present a great opportunity for mob rule to get out of hand and be sanctioned at the same time. Preachers went a step beyond the Pope's special dispensations for the Crusaders, and promised them forgiveness of all and any worldly sins with a ticket straight to heaven if they were to be killed while crusading.

Now they have a sanction by the church and are 007 licensed and marching for God. This added perk really swelled the ranks with volunteers. The results of this situation were disastrous. As they flocked together they were further whipped up by the preachers into a religious frenzy that approached mass hysteria. They were convinced that they had been chosen to cleanse the world of unbelievers. One terrible consequence was that even before they fully set out for the East they started slaughtering European Jews in the first really virulent outbreak of Western anti-Semitism. (344)

The mayhem didn't stop there, and there was wholesale slaughter in the Holy Land as well with some of the devoted sending letters home that they had ridden on Solomon's Porch and in the temple with their horses knee deep in Saracens' blood.

We see this pattern repeated in France under sanction by Queen Catherine in 1572. In an all night slaughter of Protestant

48

leaders, which expanded to include all enemies of those doing the butchery, the streets of Paris were found to be littered with bodies at daylight. This event is known to this day as the Massacre of St. Bartholomew's Day. Somehow a lot of these massacres happen for religious reasons. Perhaps religion is a convenient excuse for people to do terrible deeds they already want to do anyway. Then a Saint gets his name tagged onto the deed because his day is a convenient time to do it. Reminds me of St. Valentine's Day in Chicago.

The Anabaptists, who were forerunners of modern day Mennonites, Quakers, some Baptists, and Pentecostals, had a run of terror in 1534, by taking over Muenster and ruled for a year. Their leaders were captured, tried and executed in 1535 and their corpses suspended in iron cages in front of the church. The cages are still there to this day.

Calvinists had a period of religious terror marked with many executions for violations of church law. Calvinists were very prolific and helped pioneer missionaries and evolved into the religious orders of Presbyterian, Dutch Reform Church, Huguenots, and Puritans.

In 1649 England's actual monarchy was over thrown by Puritans under Oliver Cromwell and King Charles I was beheaded. During Cromwell's rule Ireland was dealt a horrible fate as well. The Puritans ruled for eleven years before the monarchy was restored and they fell under the heavy hand of religious persecution.

This theme of religious ideology which advocates the raining of God's judgment on the infidels would be repeated over and over in history, even here in America, proving that mob rule led by a "religious right" knows no geographical boundaries or place in time. One such incident in the United States was led by Col. John Chivington, "The Fighting Parson," who led the cavalry assault on Black Kettle's sleeping village at Big Sandy Creek, in Colorado on November 29, 1864. This event is to this day laced its width and breadth with controversies and unknowns, as well as unprovable, elements. Some of the officers attempted to deter Chivington with the argument that it would be murder to attack the sleeping village which was under the guarantee of a treaty. Chivington is quoted as saying:

The Cheyenne Nation has been waging bloody war against

the whites all spring, summer and fall, and Black Kettle is their principal chief. They have been guilty of arson, murder, rape and fiendish torture, not even sparing women and little children. I believe it is right and honorable to use any means under God's heaven to kill Indians who kill and torture women and children. Damn any man who is in sympathy with them.

In a clash of cultures, Cheyenne Chief Black Kettle was trying hard to keep his warriors in check and establish a lasting peace with the whites. At the time he was living under a treaty with his band, near Fort Lyon, and had no reason to expect hostilities. There is evidence that Black Kettle's encampment was chosen only because it was the closest and that the troops under Chivington were thirsty to earn a reputation. They were already the victims of a teasing and unflattering nickname, "Bloodless Third," which they wanted to shake before their soon to be up term of service ended. Chivington attacked before dawn, with the intended victims still asleep in their bedding, just as Queen Catherine's henchmen had done in 1572. After a miserable forced march in bad weather, he assaulted the village with 750 troops, accompanied by four 12 pound howitzers, and the now "Bloody Third" returned home victorious.

Between the tyranny of laws and governments and the domination of Papal Christianity there was a third menace during the middle ages which would over a 320 year period wipe out over one third of the population. This pestilence was the Bubonic Plague or Black Death. Spread by the fleas from black rats, this killer knew no social class or geographical limitations.

Lasting from 1320 to 1640 approximately, this plague was able to spread all over the known world and eventually to be transported over here where it still crops up in the Rockies and points West. Many people believed the plague was the wrath of God and turned to the church. This brought the black death into the church cloisters where it decimated the ranks of the clergy.

Fanatical religious groups sprang up in various parts of Europe and some of their directed attacks were once again against Jews who were blamed and murdered. Many were burned to death in group executions. In 1349 nearly 200 were burned to death in one day by an angry mob. Nothing but suspicion was necessary for these terrible acts and eleven were burned over the populace thinking that the town well had been poisoned with the plague. The Jews in order to be kosher had preferred to drink from country-side springs. Church rulings against this sort of activity and even the efforts of Pope Clement VI, who pointed out that the plague was killing Jews at the same rate as everyone else, were to no avail.

History points out to us that with the decimation of the clergy from the plague there followed a decline in the accepted societal moral standards of the time and at the same time a revival of an interest in individual spiritualism. (note the operative word here is individual)

The problems caused by all of the wars, religious upheaval, and the constricted economy of Europe were compounded and exacerbated by the Black Death and all that was left for many was to get as far out of town as possible.

During all of this turmoil in Europe an amazing thing had happened which changed the world as mankind knew it. A fellow from Genoa named Christopher Columbus discovered the New World. This happened around 1500 while all of the rest of Europe was having its calamities.

It must be pointed out here that the Discovery of the New World and the religious upheaval and the plague had no more in common than having happened around the same time and as pure coincidence. The discovery of America was simply due to the need of finding a more direct and less costly way to get to the source of spices to improve the taste of food. Not for religious reasons or even gold. So here we are, all over a search for nutmeg, cinnamon, ginger, cloves, and pepper.

Once the New World was discovered the gate was open. The "civilized" world, aching for something different, something better, poured in and the tide hasn't been stemmed yet.

The Spirit Of The American Motorcyclist

Now the worry is the Americans
We meet the right sort, this will work
We get some buckaroo...
-Sean Connery-
The Hunt For Red October, 1990

The explanation of this chapter, and in fact this entire book, can be summed up with simply the word "American." Fortunately that is not enough. That spark which lives in those who, for four hundred years or so, have called this part of the North American Continent home, is not well understood. Were it so, then this book would have no purpose.

In this chapter the American motorcyclist is explored from the first pioneers on this continent to the "yuppies" and RUBS (rich urban bikers) seen in ever growing numbers today.

Lets explore the rider of today through the evolutionary stages before motorcycling and trace the spirit or driving force behind the love of riding. If we accept the theme or idea that such an inner spirit is the fuel which drives the phenomenon of motorcycling, then we can explore the concept that, what makes the phenomenon unique, is the independence of the American heritage of its spirit. We can achieve this by understanding the history leading up to this travel medium's popularity. This can be done via the personalities themselves and their times.

This pastime has today grown to symbolize the last means of total personal freedom left in America, and representative of the concept of individuality maintained in a melting pot society in danger of losing its identity.

It's a simple story in itself. A typical youngster sees and hears motorcycles all through his years of growing up. In my experience there seem to be two types of kids around motorcycles.

One doesn't like them and is frightened by the noise, while the other one is fascinated by them and loves the sound. (I am using little boys here for example purposes only and no sexism is intended or implied.)

Odds are that the probable outcome is the first kid will never develop the love of the machine and what it represents deep in his heart of hearts. The other one, however, is a different story. He'll pick up on the sound of a bike of any sort a mile away and smile at the knowing. He'll tug on mommy or daddy's sleeve until the parent(s) acknowledge that he's heard it or looked to see where he has seen it. We've all heard it, "mo'cycle daddy, mo'cycle."

This is the kid who can't wait to get on his first bicycle, and you can't keep him off of it once he has tasted the new found freedom it provides. He is the kid who puts the playing cards with clothes pins in the spokes. This is the kid who's heroes are cowboys and who's heart and mind can't be contained in a narrow sphere of confinement. This is the first metamorphic stage of the person who will be found at a later date with his boots on the highway pegs, his hands loosely caressing the handlebar grips, and with his hair blowing back has his face in the wind. Now he's tasting the freedom he could only experience earlier in the wanderings of his mind.

What is this lust for life, the high only this feeling of freedom can produce, that the guy just mentioned is possessed with? From where did it come? There is something else and special which makes our guy different? There is no sheep in wolves clothing here, just a lone wolf.

With the settlement of North America came something besides people. A new order was starting even if it was unknown by those who brought it in. There was a concept of freedom hammered out by centuries of living in a world developing all of the checks and balances to prevent it. This concept was the idea that mankind was not here for the system but that rather the system exists to be for mankind, and if it doesn't then the system is what needs changing.

From the very first moment things were different. Most of those who came over after the initial explorers had paved the way were out of the norm anyway. Some of the English colonization was specifically used to rid the country of undesirables and overpopulation.

Sir Humphrey Gilbert, Sir Walter Raleigh's half brother, was one of the first to attempt a colony. He devised of a plan to dispose of the excess numbers of people in England and according to information published on the World Wide Web from the English department of tourism:

Sir Humphrey Gilbert devised a plan to dispose of the "surplus" population of Britain by founding colonies in America (the "New World") and intended to eliminate the native peoples first. He annexed part of Newfoundland and left a settlement there but he was drowned in a storm on his way back and the colony was soon lost.(www.devon-cc.gov.uk/tourism/pages/woodbury/raleigh.html)

Raleigh provided a ship named for himself (modestly) which led an expedition to America and took posession of the central portion of the eastern shore of America. This area he named for Queen Elizabeth and called it Virginia after her nickname "The Virgin Queen." There is a good chance that she wasn't, and that Raleigh had a first hand knowledge she wasn't. His actions earned him his knighthood in 1585 and gave him the title of Lord and Governor of Virginia. Virginia at that time included much more territory than the state would later occupy.

Raleigh wasn't as extreme as his brother and he planned a colony also, but composed of families, many from his home area of Devon, rather than just men.

His early exploration teams returned to England with such rare commodities as Tobacco and the first Potato which was planted on Raleigh's estate in Ireland.

In 1587 his colony was settled on what is now Roanoke Island, North Carolina, and England had its first colony in America. The first British colonial child, a girl, was born into this colony and named Virginia Dare. This colony was not to receive support from the mother country for three years due to problems back home and the hostilities with Spain. When English ships returned with supplies there was no one there and no trace as to their whereabouts. Although there are theories, their fate remains a mystery to this day.

In 1607 a new colony was established with 104 men and boys. More ships would follow containing additional settlers which included twenty Africans as indentured servants and finally a ship with ninety young women in 1620. Brides resulting from this cargo were bought from the Virginia Company with the husband's tobacco crop.

Many of those settling the new colonies were an odd sort and were there because of conditions back home as has been previously discussed. Lets look back and summarize what our settlers have in common. First they are all or almost all of common stock. They are almost all from circumstances which are miserable even at best. Almost all of them are from segments of society that the gentry would rather be rid of anyway.

From squalid living conditions, religious persecution or prosecution, prison or execution, they all were willing to flee their circumstances and take a chance on the unknown wilderness of America. All believed that whatever was to lie ahead had to be better than what they were leaving behind.

The one sure thing they could almost count on was that they would have more of a say in their circumstances even if that wasn't a conscious and universal thought. Some if not many were in their individual circumstances because they had done things to upset the order of things, such as steal rather than starve in a society where the farm animals had a better lot than the poor of humanity. Many of them possessed a fierce and defiant attitude and a willingness to fight down to the wire for survival rather than go as sheep to the slaughter. This attitude, which is easily translatable into a stubborn love of liberty and a sense of individuality, would immediately take root and grow in this new land so vast as to be boundless.

We find that this trait shows up immediately in the American character and leaders develop whose names will become legendary even while they are alive and people step forward to stand and fight or stand and die but stand their ground regardless.

The first sign that functions as an alert to this shared independent spirit between men and women is the very act of settlers building their homesteads in this new wilderness and having to work in unison in the production of shelter, provisions, and defense. To take a fitting passage, perhaps out of context but fitting never the less, from Seward & Williamson:

An exception to the pervasive deterioration of women's status appeared in the American colonies where the frontier served as a leveling influence that gradually altered the patriarchal tradition of the continent and raised the status of wife and child in the evolving democratic family.(115)

The authors continue with this train of thought and tell us that an attitude of individualism, "was in the air." This attitude would be a driving motivating force but would create a stress and conflict as well, in a society which would attempt to combine standards of community and family inherited from the Old World culture and ideology.

Here we have a society developing from a group of people who were unable to just march along with the accepted norm of the prevailing culture. For one reason or another, they have migrated to a land where the world as they knew it doesn't exist, but has the opportunity and space to develop a life as they wish. Cities grow and societal boundaries develop to keep social order, and rules become more and more pronounced. America was no different during that first one hundred and eighty years or so as the New World developed an identity which would lead to stresses within and directed without.

As our society began to place more emphasis on the family and community it did not manage to suppress whatever gene was inherent in those who first paved the way which demanded the right of individualism. Seward & Williamson state:

In addition to the emphasis upon the family, Western culture has another tenet, one potentially in conflict with a family-focused orientation. This tenet stresses the rights of the individual; the dignity of the individual should be inviolate and the pursuit of happiness is an inalienable right. These concepts have been concretized in the political and social philosophy. (72,73)

We believe this so strongly that our forefathers made it part of the language of the Declaration Of Independence, adopted July 4, 1776. Our authors continue with the thought:

Our social structure-based upon the family yet guided by the philosophy of the sacredness of the individual, requires the individual to function well within the family unit and, simultaneously, to sustain a sense of self-uniqueness. These elements, have the potential to be either incompatible or compatible... (73)

This potential has from time to time created the predict-

56

able and inevitable problems and still does and as our society grows the individualism seems to be winning out as evidenced by the unusually high and growing divorce rates.

On the other hand this same strong willed spirit of individualism is what creates those who will not stand for the infringement on personal rights and showed strong in the development of this Nation. It produced many of our leaders and heroes during the transition and revolution to procure independence.

Prior to the war itself we have men who would publicly demonstrate this attitude and who would spark or shame if necessary others to take action rather than be imposed upon by any authority. Many of these are our most cherished figures among our ancestry.

These people were not limited to the American Revolution and they are not in small numbers as worldly standards go. It is beyond the scope of this book to name and tell about them all, but a few over the passage of time are in order for they have taken their place in our collective memory of our land's development and are today larger than life. Sometimes it is hard to realize that they were ordinary people who just stopped and said, at least figuratively, "Wait a minute here, I'm not taking that crap."

Their deeds are the fuel of legends and their very words can be quoted by almost any person on the street, even if he or she can't recall who said them.

Thomas Paine, who is considered to be one of the spark plugs of the Revolution, fired the imagination with words like, "These are the times that try men's souls." His commentary about summer soldiers and sunshine patriots and liking the King to a, "common murderer, a highwayman, or a house-breaker," was effective enough for George Washington to use it as recruitment propaganda. Paine went on after the American Revolution to be one of the instigators of the French Revolution against Louis XIV. He was ruined when he attempted and failed to effect a similar circumstance in England.

A favorite and collateral ancestral relative of this author is Patrick Henry. Henry, a lawyer and land owner as well as politician, virtually ad-libbed the most famous speech in American history when in St. John's Church, March 23, 1775, he spoke with the concluding remarks:

There is no retreat but in submission and slavery! Our chains are forged! Their clanking may be heard on the plains of Boston! The war is inevitable—and let it come! I repeat it, sir, let it come.

It is in vain, sir, to extenuate the matter. Gentlemen may cry, Peace, Peace—but there is no peace. The war is actually begun! The next gale that sweeps from the north will bring to our ears the clash of resounding arms! Our brethren are already in the field! Why stand we here idle? What is it that gentlemen would wish? What would they have? Is life so dear, or peace so sweet, as to be purchased at the price of chains and slavery? Forbid it, Almighty God! I know not what course others may take; but as for me, give me liberty or give me death!

It is worthy to note here, that in speech and song both in the American colonies and in Ireland the recurring theme is to refer to being under the rule of Mother England as being in the chains of slavery. A curious objection in its terminology, over here in a land which was in the practice of allowing indentured servants of all races and the forced slavery of Africans. This would be a point of hot contention in the drafting the soon to be U. S. Constitution.

Slavery would exist until 1865, ninety years later. Many popular songs, from this era in Ireland, would be adopted and sung in the field in the 1860s during the American Civil War. Their popularity and lively tunes providing much entertainment for the troops in the field and the civilians back home as well, even though the spirited lyrics against slavery were actually referring to British oppression. One of the most popular of these songs, even today, is The Minstral Boy which has found its way into a Master Card commercial and on to the distant future, to be sung by Commander Picard in a Star Trek episode.

What then is meant by the term "Liberty" when used by those who would forge a new form of society which preached this state of being above all else, even life itself, while allowing the enslavement of other human beings. The American Heritage Dictionary give us this definition:

lib·er·ty (l¹b"...r-t¶) n., pl. lib·er·ties. 1.a. The condition of being free from restriction or control. b. The right and power to act, believe, or express oneself in a manner of one's own choosing.

58

John Stuart Mill in the 19th century would define this in his essay on Liberty with these words:

The struggle between Liberty and Authority is the most conspicuous feature in the portions of history with which we are earliest familiar, particularly in that of Greece, Rome, and England. But in old times this contest was between subjects, or some classes of subjects, and the Government. By liberty, was meant protection against the tyranny of the political rulers. (5)

The dictionary further defines the concept of liberty as, "Freedom from unjust or undue governmental control, a right and power to engage in certain actions without control or interference, a breach or overstepping of propriety or social convention, and a statement, an attitude, or an action not warranted by conditions or actualities."

What we have here is the concept of individual rights and freedoms all wrapped up in the term liberty. It was a start and enough of one to be a driving force even though it was in reality not yet fair nor did it yet provide "liberty and justice for all." You might say the fledgling American Eagle had broken from its shell but was still in the nest where the egg had been incubated, not yet able to fly.

This concept was to burn so strong in the hearts of many of those in the field of conflict that it produced valiant defenders who's words like those of Henry and Paine would remain, like their deeds, with us as long as there is an America to provide inspiration.

Among those from the American revolution are Nathan Hale and John Paul Jones.

Nathan Hale was a brilliant student and had graduated from Yale by the time he was eighteen. Although he probably intended to become a minister like his older brother, he became a teacher in the public school in New London, CT. Hale believed in the higher education of women as well as men and by special arrangement with the school he taught a class of twenty young ladies from 5 to 7 a.m. the same studies taught to the boys later in the day.

As soon as word of the conflict at Concord and Lexington reached New London a town meeting was called. Nathan Hale though only twenty and still under age, was one of the speakers. He made the statement, "Let us march immediately and never lay down our arms until we obtain our independence." This is the first recorded public use of the word "independence." Hale was commissioned a First Lieutenant and was involved in recruiting new troops and the fighting which drove the British forces from Boston.

General Washington turned his attention to New York and Hale's regiment went with his army. A special service corps was formed as Knowlton's Rangers. The officers and men were officially listed as "detached on command." Nathan Hale was part of this unit.

Washington was desperate to know the British plans in New York City and it became necessary to have a spy infiltrate and bring back information. The first person asked, refused, fearful of the potential consequences. Nathan, the youngest Captain in the command, spoke up and said, "I will undertake it." He had been late to the meeting having been ill but willingly volunteered to serve. Major General Hull spoke with him letting him know that this mission was not in the line of duty and the fate would be a disgraceful death if he failed. Hale's reply was, "I wish to be useful, and every kind of service necessary to the public good becomes honorable by being necessary. If the exigencies of my country demand a peculiar service, its claim to perform that service are imperious." These would be the last words ever cited from him until the moment of his death when he uttered the statement that would forever seal his name as synonymous with the word patriot. He was captured as a spy trying to make his way back across the river. General Howe ordered him hanged and turned him over to the most notoriously brutal man in the British army. This man, Prevost-Major William Cunningham, was hanged himself back in England after the war for causing disgrace to the British army with his actions during the war.

Hale was refused a request for a Bible and letters of goodby written to his mother and a fellow officer were destroyed by Cunningham, who reasoned that the rebels should not know that they had a man in their army who could be so firm even in his death. We know of the details from one of the British officers who was in attendance to guard Hale in his last hours.

He was taken to an apple tree near the present day inter-section of East Broadway and Market. Gripping tightly the com-forting hand of the American Spirit, Nathan Hale stepped up to the hangman's rope, and looking his executioners in the eye stated, "I only regret that I have but one life to lose for my country."

American naval hero John Paul Jones, began the war in command of the Providence and under his command this vessel became the most victorious American Ship of the war. He would say later, "she was the first and she was the best." Jones was com-manding the *U. S. S. Bonhomme Richard* (named for Benjamin Franklin) when he encountered the British Ship *Serapis*. Lashing the *Richard* to the *Serapis* he fought the battle at point blank range. With the damage from the encounter and the result of two of her cannon bursting the *Richard* was sinking. The British captain of-fered to accept Jones' surrender and Jones replied with the now immortal words, "Sir, I have not yet begun to fight." The battle continued until the British captain was forced to strike his colors and the crew of the *Richard* boarded the *Serapis* victorious, only to watch the *Richard* sink. The words of John Paul Jones have remained to this day as an icon representing the American Spirit.

That spirit prevailed over all adversity. The Continental Army suffering tremendous losses and seemingly insurmountable setbacks held on with the tenacity of a bulldog. (maybe over here a terrapin would be a better comparison) The British at one point in the war had taken every major city in the colonies. The situa-tion to an observer would seem hopeless. George Washington has even been credited with saying that if he were to wish the worst curse this side of the grave on an enemy, he would wish him to be in his place and with his thoughts. The British were close to win-ning the war at every turn but close would not be close enough. The American spirit held indomitable and carried the day.

During the Revolutionary War era another man would loom larger than life but not so much for his wartime exploits although he is credited with fighting in the last battle of the Revolution. He was Daniel Boone, and would be a legend in his own time for expanding the frontier and establishing settlements in Kentucky and beyond. Fighting with bears and Shawnee alike this man's legend grew in story until he became <u>The American Folk Hero</u>. Boone was a man, according to his later and more accurate biographers, who wanted to have his love of exploration and settlement of the wilderness, and his life as a family man, to coexist in harmony. He didn't mind being a hero as long as the other aspects of his life could be there too. Boone seemed to come along at a time when real life heroes were plentiful. The American public, however, had a need that could only be satisfied by the image of a larger than life and almost super human figure. A necessary icon representing the embodiment of the spirit of this new country, experimenting for the first time in history, with a government for the people and by the people.

Daniel Boone's autobiography was written in a land speculation pamphlet, published in 1784 in Wilmington, NC, and written by John Filson. Filson was a schoolmaster from Pennsylvania, and his pamphlet was titled <u>Kentucke</u>. This work enjoyed a popularity over here and later printings would be very popular in Europe. The first real adventure story as a biography of Boone, and a forerunner to what would be considered pulp fiction in the 20th century, came along in a work by a distant cousin, Daniel Bryan. Titled <u>The Mountain Muse</u>, this book was written in 1813, seven years before Boone's death and about the time the exploits of another well known frontier figure were earning him fame and glory in the Creek Indian War. This figure was Davy Crockett.

Over the last two hundred years there have been many stories and biographies written about Boone, including one by Teddy Roosevelt in 1889. Boone has become the quintessential early American folk hero. This is a curious thing because, unlike his contemporaries, his adventures were not as public and with a lot of flash. He died a normal death in his home as an old man rather than going out in a blaze of glory. He did not have brilliant or fiery quotations attributed to him as did his contemporaries, but he did have something better. Boone had great PR rather than great deeds to build his legend.

According to Dr. Thomas Clark, former professor of history, at the University of Kentucky, and University of Indiana, Boone had good public relations. He said, "The Filson book was the springboard to Daniel Boon's fame." His research indicates that Boone's exploits were mediocre compared to some others. The much touted last battle of the Revolution was in August 19, 1782, almost ten months to the day after Cornwallis had surrendered at

Yorktown to end the war. This fight was primarily a frontier skirmish between Boone and the other defenders, against some out-of-touch British traveling with marauding Indians.

We know that Filson's book was an attempt to make a fortune, quite literally, from promoting settlement in Kentucky. He had a large investment in Kentucky land and Boone had been the front man, paving the way into the area for the Transylvania Company. (The title has nothing to do with vampires by the way, but rather the name means across the forest.)

This is a forerunner to modern sponsorship and hype. Boone was already in there preparing the way for settlement. Making him a natural candidate to be the national icon representing virtue, bravery, and the spearhead of the efforts of a country expanding into its future, and fulfilling its manifest destiny. This was just good advertising. It worked well and Boone is still that icon to this day, even though in all probability, he was trying to escape or stay as far ahead as possible of society with its rules, refined ways, and taxes.

Bring that advertising concept forward a hundred and fifty or so years and you have another great example. Kellogg of Battle Creek, selling cereal with the adventures of Wild Bill Hickock. Hickock was resurrected, dusted off and a halo, that the real character never possessed, polished and applied. The real character historically was just another one of those good badmen Americans love so much. I can still remember faithfully watching Guy Madison each week as Hickock with his trusty sidekick Jingles P. Jones, played by Andy Devine of Buster Brown show fame. I also remember the thrill of meeting Devine as the sheriff of Knott's Berry Farm and getting an autographed picture. There was even a movie produced later on with Guy Madison as a cowboy fighting a dinosaur. Now that gets both popular genres in one movie.

There is perhaps a valid argument that the country needed a hero figure such as Boone. W. H. Bogart argues this point in his 1857 work titled <u>Daniel Boone and the Hunters of Kentucky</u>. Bogart believed strongly in the manifest destiny of the nation, and saw Boone as an unwitting even if willing instrument of that destiny, thus having really no choice.

The country was moving west and the spirit of the concept of America was traveling right in step with the explorers who continually pushed the frontier ever farther. It needed a westward hero of bigger-than-life proportions. Hale and Henry were eastern society and of civilization. Seafarers like Jones were even farther removed. Someone had to be the representative of the American spirit across the dividing line into the frontier and Boone won the luck of the draw.

It is strange that Boone came to be in his position in American lore. Others who were not the fiery ones have taken a back seat to others who were even when more qualified for the fame that history awards. Commodore John Barry, for instance, and the real father of the American Navy, took a back seat to John Paul Jones. In the case of our Kentucky hero the reverse is true. There were others who could have been the symbol and maybe were even more qualified than he, but Daniel Boone was the man who came to symbolize America's destiny, its image, and he still is.

As discussed in the previous chapter, like John Wayne, you can put him in any time period and change the clothes to fit the era and the image still fits whether he is on the Mayflower or the Millennium Falcon. All the while, the American spirit just sits on his rail fence rolling a cigarette and chuckles as he watches and waits.

A brief look into the life of Davy Crockett is appropriate here and a good example of the type of character Americans think of as exemplifying the American spirit. Like Boone, Crockett was a frontiersman. Unlike Boone he was flamboyant and outspoken and maintained a very high profile during his life, and he did go out in a blaze of glory.

Born in 1786, just a few years after the Revolution, David Crockett would have probably been the role model that Boone became had they perhaps been doing their respective deeds simultaneously.

Crockett was full of fire and vinegar and was going to be his own man no matter what anyone else said. He had a motto which became a household saying during the run of the Davy Crockett series on TV by Disney. Every one could quote Fess Parker saying, "Be sure you're right, then go ahead." The actual saying attributed to Crockett is, "First make sure you are right, then go ahead." The former rolled off the tongue a little easier for TV I'd guess. The series and slogan made a star out of Fess Parker, who would later return, to TV as Daniel Boone.

The real Davy Crockett was as big as the legend and as independent as a hog on ice and ultimately that was his political undoing. He earned his reputation in the military under Andrew Jackson in the Creek Indian War. He was a good soldier and achieved the rank of sergeant but became dissatisfied with both military life and the unfairness of the conflict with the Indians. He commented that if he had remained in the military it would have used him up.

An avid woodsman and hunter, he once killed 105 bears in a single season. In addition he was a family man who was absent a lot from the family. Remember the conflict between family and individuality mentioned earlier. Crockett was married twice and as a widower with three children remarried to a widow with two of her own. Family seemed to be important to him.

He was a very gregarious person, and an immensely popular storyteller which led him into politics. Beginning at a local level he was elected to the rank of Colonel in the local militia and in three years was being sent to the State Legislature. Election to the U. S. Congress followed, where Crockett was a direct contrast to the standards of social class in the East. He was much ridiculed in the press and labeled with such nicknames as the "Canebrake Congressman."

Davy Crockett would not be intimidated and quickly made it clear that he was his own man and would vote his own conscience at all costs, rather than along party lines. This stand won over many critics and made him beloved all over America.

He was a fierce defender of the squatters rights for those who had pioneered western lands and a defender of Indians' rights to their own lands. He was very outspoken against the cruelty of the removal policies directed by the administration against the Eastern bands of Indians. This removal and the huge death toll of Indians in the process would later come to be called the Trail Of Tears.

He made many enemies in the Jackson camp and they worked hard to undermine him politically. He was defeated in 1831 but came back reelected in 1833. The work of his enemies along with mistakes on his own part led to his failure to be elected again in 1835. It was this event which led to his second famous quotation. He announced to the voters of Tennessee and the Congress that since they had seen fit not to elect him again, "you can go to hell — I'm going to Texas."

Crockett stated to friends that he was going to Texas and had every intention to, "have Santa Anna's head, and wear it for a watch seal."

Davy trekked to Texas and an old mission at San Antonio where his destiny awaited him at the Alamo.

Texas was gearing up to fight for independence from Mexico under the leadership of another Tennesseean and acquaintance of Crockett's, Sam Houston. Davy and his companions, now calling themselves the Tennessee Mounted Volunteers, found a small group of defenders at the Alamo who had been ordered by Houston to destroy the Alamo and remove the garrison and armaments further East. This group was under the joint and incompatible leadership of Colonel James Bowie (of Bowie Knife fame) and Colonel William Barret Travis. Bowie was to command the Volunteers and Travis the regulars. Now there are Col. Bowie, Col. Travis, and Col. Crockett. Davy volunteered to be just a high private and fight with them in the cause of liberty. He was, however, still referred to as Colonel Crockett.

Travis had been one of the main spearheads of the rebellion to free Texas from Mexico and was determined to command this outpost. Bowie was the more serious fighter and took command, as well as the Mexican army threat, more seriously. Leadership was decided when Bowie took ill with a fever and was bedridden, apparently with pneumonia. He would die there in his bed when the Mexican soldiers overran the mission.

The Alamo was a three acre mission with a perimeter of walls ranging from nine to twenty two feet high. The only exception was a fifty yard open stretch with no wall and makeshift earth and log fortifications. This is the position Crockett and his volunteers were assigned to defend.

During the siege, when there were lulls in the fighting, Crockett would become Davy the entertainer, playing his fiddle, and telling jokes and stories.

Although this was Crockett's assigned position, Travis proved to be somewhat inept in command and Davy unofficially took over. In a dispatch Travis noted, "The Hon. David Crockett was seen at all points animating the men to do their duty." Another witness made the same observation and noted that Travis willingly deferred to Crockett's judgment. He said that Davy was at every point to direct the fighting.

A Mexican soldier's diary, discovered in recent years, describing the events there stated that a tall man in buckskins would stand up from behind the low earthworks as if he were impervious to bullets, take careful aim, and each time he did a Mexican soldier would fall. He had written that the soldiers assaulting that section of the fortifications soon learned to duck when this man stood up to aim.

All combatants defending the Alamo were slaughtered save seven worn out and bloody men. General Manuel Fernandez Castrillion halted his advance and offered clemency for their surrender. Crockett was among this seven. He presented his captives to Santa Anna who was angry that his troops had taken the fortress at a cost of fully one third of their number. In his rage, Santa Anna ordered the execution of the captives. When the regular soldiers refused to move he was embarrassed and ordered his personal staff to do it. The seven were hacked to death with sabers.

An officer's wife, Susannah Dickinson, and some other civilians were discovered hiding in the church. As she was being escorted from the Alamo she saw Crockett's body complete with his signature coonskin cap along side. Santa Anna had all the bodies of the defenders cremated but not before our American spirit dusted himself off and once again headed into the future.

Now we know that people like Crockett andbefore him by not too many years Nathan Hale , and others who had a specialness about them, and an intrinsic quality which was observable but seemingly not identifiable. We know that it developed from people of a different sort who were the first to be sent here to colonize and different than those who would be content to have a city existence relatively the same or similar to society in England.

H. G. Wells (Time Machine & War Of The Worlds) spoke of those first immigrants in his extensive work, The Outline Of History, published in 1920. He describes the make up by religion, ethnically, and sort of sociologically. He also inadvertently presents the potential for conflict.

Moreover, the absolutist efforts of James I and Charles I,

67

and the restoration of Charles II, had the effect of driving out from England a great number of sturdy-minded, republican-spirited Protestants, men of substance and character, who set up in America, and particularly in New England, out of reach, as they supposed, of the king and his taxes. (Wells, 844)

Thorpe from England, who had taken pity on the miserable people imprisoned for debt in England, and rescued a number of them from prison to become the founders of a new colony ... So by the middle of the eighteenth century we have these settlements along the American coastline; the New England group of Puritans and free Protestants ... then came Catholic Maryland; Cavalier Virginia; Carolina (which was presently divided into North and South) and Oglethorpe's Georgia. Later on, a number of Tyrolese Protestants took refuge in Georgia, and there was a considerable immigration of a good class of German cultivators into Pennsylvania.

Cromwell sent Irish prisoners of war to Virginia ... convicts were sent out, and there was a considerable trade in kidnapped children, who were "spirited away" to America to become apprentices or bond slaves.

Such were the miscellaneous origins of the citizens of the Thirteen Colonies. The possibility of their ever becoming closely united would have struck an impartial observer in 1760 as being very slight. But they rapidly became equal under colonial conditions. The English class system disappeared. Under colonial conditions there arose equality "in the faculties both of body and mind, and an individual independence of judgment impatient of interference from England.

But if the inhabitants of the Thirteen Colonies were miscellaneous in their origins and various in their habits and sympathies, they had ... very strong antagonisms in common. (871, 872)

It is important to remind ourselves of these antagonisms in common and some of the things we have to this point observed. We have a homogenous mix of settlers over here who range in scope from colonist to convict, and all either running from or to something believing that life will be better over here. As soon as they settle and set up communities we have our conflict between the conventions adopted for our society and the independence we seem to so want. The conflict between being an individual and not standing out of the norm is ever present.

In the first part of the 19th Century two observers from overseas visited here and published their observations. They weren't the only ones but were significant and astute in their observations. They saw the same things and about the same time but they are as different in their writings and opinions as they are from each other's nationality. They are Charles Dickens, and Alexis de Tocqueville. Dickens in <u>American Notes</u> presents his as a criticism or perplexion while Tocqueville's two volumes on <u>Democracy In America</u> are presenting his observations as a warning. American society has missed the point on both author's observations and warnings.

Dickens notes fit in 1842 when he toured America and oddly enough they still do. He observed that we are, "by nature, frank, brave, cordial, hospitable, and affectionate." (Dickens, 286) He also said we as a people are warm hearted and enthusiastic which is enhanced by cultivation and refinement. He noticed, however that there are influences at work which endanger our very societal make up.

One great blemish in the popular mind of America, and the prolific parent of an innumerable brood of evils, is Universal Distrust. Yet the American citizen plumes himself upon this spirit, even when he is sufficiently dispassionate to perceive the ruin it works; and will often adduce it, in spite of his own reason, as an instance of the great sagacity and acuteness of the people, and their superior shrewdness and independence. (287)

According to Dickens, we carry this distrust into every part of our public life and run away good people from our governmental offices and have, "bred up a class of candidates for suffrage, who in their every act, disgrace your Institutions and your people's choice." He said we are as a public, so fickle, that we, "no sooner set up an idol firmly than you are sure to pull it down and dash it to pieces." We reward our benefactors and public servants and our idols and no sooner do so before we start looking for a chink in their armor to attack them. Dickens observed that anyone whom we put in a high place from the president down can number his days, because anyone can say anything about him and the public will believe it and attack.

Dickens presents a lot of examples and speaks of the excuses we use to forgive scoundrels who succeed by the degree of intelligence they possess. He noticed the unwarranted attacks in the press without any other reason than to destroy or achieve personal gain. He said we have many publications which are good but they are powerless to counteract the poison of the ones which are bad. We reason that all these conventions are right and natural and when polled by Dickens answered unilaterally and invariably, "There's freedom of opinion here, you know. Every man thinks for himself, and we are not to be easily overreached. That's how our people come to be suspicious." (288)

Dickens wrote these observances in 1842 and in an after dinner speech in 1868 allowed that he was not so rigid in his thoughts or opinions that he could not be wrong on an observed point, or that things might just have changed over here. I, however, think not. Along with that spirit we so admire marching along in our psyche is a built in distrust which leads us to attack it whenever it shows its face, except when we need it for a boost to our own identity. This negative side of our society has been the nest of iniquity that hatched the likes of the Salem witch trials, Joe McCarthy, and recently the independent council. Davy Crockett's political career fell victim to this all too American syndrome.

I picture our American spirit during these times in the image of the late Iron Eyes Cody, standing amid a pile of garbage with a tear running down his cheek. We never seem to remember the quote, **"He that is without sin among you, let him cast the first stone."**

Tocqueville wrote upon his return from America in 1832, a warning to contemporary Europe, which was filled with curiosity about the "noble experiment" going on in America. The warning was also meant for America itself.

Tocqueville was not a romantic nor a poet but he was caught up in the excitement of being alive as well as young during these changing times. What he was however was a keen observer with an understanding and perception of society and politics. He was able to assemble his observations, which were written around the same era as those of some of the greatest literary giants of the day, yet Tocqueville's alone stand today as the classic source of early American observance. We find the general synopsis of this warning in the introduction by Daniel J. Boorstin:

Tocqueville's twin purposes were to awaken his contemporaries to the "providential" currents of equality, which they could only vainly try to obstruct, and at the same time to awaken the beneficiaries of the new currents to impending dangers. His book was to be as much about the threat of the Tyranny of the Majority as about the Promise of Equality. Nowhere are his prophecies more poignant. In the worlds of thought and feeling, he announced, democracy itself had created a new tyrant—Public Opinion (Tocquerville, ix)

This was a potential monster observed Tocqueville, which could easily get out of control if we weren't careful. He was acutely aware that the possibility was there that as our new country grew with its attempted experiment in democracy, and the first since ancient times. The majority rule, warned Tocqueville, could suppress the rights and will of the individual. The definition of this system of government includes the following: 1. Government by the people, exercised either directly or through elected representatives. 2. A political or social unit that has such a government. 3. The common people, considered as the primary source of political power. 4. Majority rule. 5. The principles of social equality and respect for the individual within a community. (AHED, 3.0A)

The last one, definition number five, is the key here. Here is the danger and the one easiest to forget, overlook, or simply violate by number four. It is the danger to five from four which is the base of Tocqueville's warning and what we face in the U. S. today, and have since wartime. Had he not gone out in the manner which he did or perhaps even if he had but Texas never achieving statehood, Davy Crockett might be known only to historians today. After all he was a loose cannon. He upset the apple cart and refused to go along with the majority. He dressed funny, he talked funny, and he went against public opinion. Daniel Boone did exactly what he was supposed to do and even though he wanted to be as far as possible from civilization he did so quietly. His most radical quotation was in passing Cincinnati on his way to settle in Missouri. Someone called out to his boat to ask why he was going west and leaving Kentucky, his simple answer was "Too Crowded." He didn't go against anybody's grain, he didn't defend Indian rights, and he didn't tell anybody to go to hell. Making no waves, save those of his canoe paddle on the river, he quietly slipped into

71

legend and died a peaceful death, in a fine home, as an old man. Wartimes came and went leaving us with daring figures of legend to read about such as John Singleton Mosby, the Gray Ghost, and we would make heroes of more Croquet like figures who would later be determined to be really bad.

I am of course speaking of one George Armstrong Custer. Custer was an egomaniac with great political ambitions who had made his name being willing to spare no lives to achieve his goals. This pattern was his hallmark during the civil war and the Indian wars and would ultimately cost him his own life along with a couple of hundred of his troops. Many needless deaths red and white had preceded the final day at the Little Big Horn. H. G. Wells would later comment in 1920, no Red Indian Jengis (Wells' spelling) Khan ever arose among these nomads of the New World. (872)

The vast Western Territory was opened and our American spirit enjoyed about thirty five years of breathing free air while a still relatively young nation, thirsty for another hero, discovered that it had a tremendous thirst for stories which epitomized this American icon. The good badmen were doing the dastardly deeds and some marginal ones which would later be the subjects of a whole century of entertainment.

During that time America was involved in another war, and this time with Spain, which made a hero of a wild western type of adventurer from New York. This fellow was brash and bold and seemed to be the very image of the American spirit. His popular image would pave the way for Teddy Roosevelt to move to Pennsylvania Avenue in Washington, DC.

America was gobbling up stories made up about cowboy stars and watching Buffalo Bill's Wild West Show. Dime novels were selling like hot chocolate in the Arctic and someone somewhere hooked an engine on to a bicycle. The new century dawned and less than two decades of progress saw us going every where on machines that rolled and flew and we were to find ourselves back at war.

Once again America had a hero pop up from, where else, Tennessee. Alvin Cullium York was born December 13, 1887 to parents each descended from Civil War Veterans who fought for the Union. Both had died from conflicts which arose due to their Union allegiance.

On his father's side the grandfather, Uriah York, was trying to escape pursuers after receiving word that they were coming after him. He was very ill and escaped through bad weather only to become so sick he died from the additional complications from the exposure to the weather.

His mother's grandfather, William Brooks, was a deserter from the army who left to pursue Alvin's grandmother. After the war a feud with another man led to him killing the other and fleeing to Northern Michigan with his wife and daughter joining him later. At a later date Alvin's grandmother wrote a letter to her family which was intercepted by the dead man's friends and relatives and Brooks was brought back to stand trial for murder. The next night he was taken from the jail by a band of men who tied his feet to a rope attached to an unbridled horse's tail and fired shots to frighten the horse into running. They then rode down the road behind Brooks who was struggling as he was being dragged by the runaway horse. The vigilantes fired bullets into Brooks until they were sure he was dead. Recent occurrences remind us that history often repeats itself.

Alvin's father was a simple man who believed in honest work and fair play. He was such a fair person in his dealings, his nickname was "Judge York." York was an avid woodsman who understood the forest and the animals. He was a master tracker and loved the hunt. It was how he put most of the food for the family on the table. He imparted these skills to his sons, and not the least of these to learn well the lessons was Alvin.

Eventually Alvin would go through a phase where he was a hard drinking rounder but his mother was able to convert him to religion and from this he never strayed. Alvin was planning to marry Gracie Williams when he was drafted into the army and had to go serve in World War I.

At first York had a problem reconciling killing with his religion, but just as the crusaders had done centuries earlier, he was able to find a way. Alvin felt a close kin to Boone and Crockett and wanted to serve his country. He was fiercely patriotic but needed to know it was all right to kill the enemy. In the book of Ezekiel in the Bible, Alvin C. York found the approval he needed.

He has been labeled a conscientious objector by history and listed as such in the War Dept. records. By his own words this isn't true. He just needed to be able to reconcile shooting people.

He didn't see much action right away but on September 28, 1918 his unit went into the battle of the Argonne Forest. By October 8th York was in a group of 17 assigned to circle around a hill and attack machine gun nests from the rear. They came under fire from the machine guns and the small unit was reduced to 8. Our hillbilly sergeant went into action, with his remaining comrades mostly pinned down by machine gun fire, armed with a rifle and a .45 automatic. By the end of the encounter, and almost single handed, Alvin C. York killed at least 25 of the enemy and captured 132 and took out 35 machine guns. These are confirmed numbers. For his exploits he received the Distinguished Service Cross, the French Croix de Guerre, and the Congressional Medal of Honor. America had a real honest to goodness hero returning home from the war as America's most decorated W.W.I soldier.

York spent the rest of his life dedicated to improving education and roads in his home area and helped in the national recruiting drives when war was again looming over America. At one point he even volunteered to lead a unit in W.W.II but couldn't pass the physical.

Alvin C. York came to be the symbol of the American spirit to Americans. When a movie of his life was made, Gary Cooper was chosen to portray Alvin. Cooper has probably portrayed more characters representing the American Spirit than anyone else in Hollywood. That includes the movies High Noon and The Virginian which have become signature films of the American western genre. High Noon was actually a political statement by Hollywood representing the American spirit of resistance, in response to the McCarthy communist witch-hunts.

A grateful government repaid Alvin York for his wonderful contribution to America. The IRS ruined him financially by denying him the tax deductions for contributions to the educational facility he helped to start. He was charged $85,000.00 which, with fines he was unable to pay, escalated to $172,000.00. After his third stroke, leaving him a complete invalid, the IRS agreed to settle for $25,000.00. Fans from all over America sent in the donations to pay the fines for this American Hero. He died at the VA Hospital, in Nashville, TN in 1964, aged 76.

While Alvin York was learning to shoot like Davy Crockett

in the woods of Tennessee, other things were going on in the United States as the century turned over from one to another. Automobiles and motorcycles were making their way across the country. Dime novels, and moving pictures were showing Eastern America and Western Europe that there was fully half of this country which was vast and not crowded. People had discovered the freedom provided by motorcycling. Races, Gypsy Tours, and transcontinental records were happening and the motorcycle went to war just like Alvin York.

The American had made the transition from foot to horseback, and now to motorcycle. Events and gatherings began to spring up around the country, usually in conjunction with races. People like Cannonball Baker were setting records of endurance and speed, and the sport or avocation as it were had its own publications such as the Motorcycle and Bicycle Illustrated.

Some Americans did extremely well for about a decade or more and the unthinkable happened to take the American spirit on a crash dive. The 1929 depression hit and the nation's economy was devastated. A little over a decade later we were coming out of the depression by gearing up once again for war. Men, machines and of course motorcycles were once again heading into battle in foreign lands and The American spirit would emerge in America's last giant war hero.

Giant is in this case a figurative term because Audie Leon Murphy, unlike Boone, Crockett, and York, was a little guy. In spite of his size he would become the most decorated war hero in the history of this country, receiving 33 citations.

Murphy enlisted in the army at age 18, two years younger even than Nathan Hale, and served for three years. Audie became a legend while in the service and is credited with an all time record for valor. He was awarded every honor for such that the United States has to offer. Some citations he received twice. Both France and Belgium honored him with awards, and he holds a record of over 240 enemy killed with many others wounded or taken prisoner.

After being discharged he was enticed to come to Hollywood where he eventually would be featured in 44 films over a twenty five year career. Murphy starred as himself (something most celebrities are not allowed to do) in a 1955 biographical film titled

<u>To Hell And Back</u> and based on his 1949 book of the same title. This movie would hold the record as the largest grossing movie ever filmed by Universal until <u>Jaws</u> surpassed it in that category in 1975.

Audie Murphy had charisma. He had good looks and a boyish appearance. He looked like the boy next door, was tough, and all patriotic American rolled into one package. Murphy with his grin and soft spoken, and polite voice, was the epitome of the kind of boy parents wanted their daughters to date. And above all he had the American spirit through and through.

I vaguely recall an incident where he was taken to court by someone who claimed Murphy had taken a shot at him. If my memory doesn't fail me too terribly, I believe his defense was to inform the judge that the charge was preposterous. If he had been shooting at the other person then someone else would have had to call the police and testify. You gotta love that statement.

Audie was an outspoken person and was instrumental in bringing the government's attention to Post Traumatic Stress Syndrome. A sufferer himself, he helped in the fight for medical benefits for the treatment of this disorder for Korean and Viet Nam war veterans. When Murphy came back from W.W.II this condition was known as "Battle Fatigue."

In addition to his other accomplishments (as if they weren't enough) Murphy was a poet and a successful songwriter, composing several hits in the country music field.

Murphy was an example of everything we call great in the word American, and he takes a rightful place in the roll book of heroes. In spite of his height, he stands tall along side the likes of Boone, Crockett, and York, and we who are living in this time are lucky to have been able to know of the exploits and heroism of Murphy and York while they lived and while it was still possible for persons of their character to exhibit those traits. Besides his excellent marksmanship and determination of character, his ancestry stems from the same areas of North Carolina as did York, Crockett, and Boone. An area which produced the fiercest defenders during both the American Revolution and the Civil War. As a historian, I find it a little more than curious that all four seem to have this North Carolina / Tennessee connection while Crockett and Murphy both have Texas in common as well.

Audie Leon Murphy would be taken from us in a 1971 plane crash. He was buried with all due military honors in the National Cemetery at Arlington, where his grave is second only to John F. Kennedy's in annual visitations. The State of Texas honored him by designating an official Audie Murphy Day for June 20th, Audie's birthday.

Between 1900 and 1975 the popularity of motorcycles would provide a way for the American spirit to continue to feel the freedom it found necessary, and the not so silent majority looked on with a disdaining eye. As Tocqueville had warned, the mass of the majority had settled into an image of itself as a standard of what is to be right, and the American Way. The majority rule Government had achieved a measure of power which would have frightened the founding fathers.

Motorcyclists still crossed and recrossed the country and were only mildly noticed by the rank and file of society. Motorcycles and riders went to war in both World Wars and the Korean Conflict. In W.W.I, Corporal Roy Holtz was the first yank into Germany, and he was riding a Harley-Davidson.

Although in the States free spaces were shrinking, for a while there were still plenty of areas to go to and feel free. They, as well, would gradually dwindle. Rallies (gatherings) where motorcyclists could congregate, feel a camaraderie, and watch races, would develop in predominately remote areas. Some of these places, like New Hampshire and South Dakota, and Eastern beach areas would become perennial events.

Homo Sapiens has always loved speed and the piloting of this two-wheeled vehicle was no different. Racing competition is one thing we did inherit from the old world and we have done our part to make it the largest type of sporting event for spectators in the whole world.

As the general order of society began to march in step locked into a pattern, the American spirit looked over a set of handlebars and said to itself, "somehow that ain't quite right." It turned away and rode in a different direction. This spirit of individualism isn't just marching to a different drummer, it's listening to a whole different band.

One of the things governments and oppressive societies do to maintain control is to promote forced sameness. This isn't a

77

new thing, nor is it unique to our country. It comes with civilization's perceived need to control. A very real necessity in some instances and a violation of individuality in others. It is easy to see where it is a necessary thing in organizations such as the military. In the prison system we have the uniform dress which used to be distinct stripes, or the lock-step developed at New York's Sing Sing, for moving prisoners in a controllable manner from one area to another. Take an identity and reduce it to a number and you remove any individuality. Remove individuality and you have control. This method was effectively used at Alcatraz where no names at all were used, just numbers. In the private sector it can work well also, and profitably. No one can dispute the success of IBM with its army of blue blazers and white shirts.

Motorcyclists had been more or less in the background in the early years. Like the actual cowboys of the second half of the 19th Century they were just a class of different folks, possessed by an independent spirit, who preferred wide open space, blue sky, and the thrill of the road. They had no desire to submit to a mundane existence. That is still to this day why hard-core bikers ride.

They had always had the Gypsy Tours, races, and various gatherings since the earliest days and polite society feared or at least disapproved. At the least, they were just different. They didn't look and dress properly. As early as 1919 we find articles mentioning the disdain of society over the bikers at events wearing the same clothes for two or three days straight and especially women in men's style pants appearing in public places. (Motorcycle and Bicycle Illustrated, June 19, 1919) Wonder what they would say of today's events where many women wear nearly nothing at all in public.

The end of W.W.II would throw things in a different light as motorcyclists and their inherited independent spirit would assert the right to freedom and any attempts at suppression would cause much conflict.

Barely two years after the war's end a Gypsy Tour and motorcycle race weekend in a little California town would make history. July 4th weekend in Hollister, California, would forever stigmatize the bikers in the minds of the American mass consciousness. A confrontation which took place between motorcyclists and local authorities, blown out of proportion by the press, gave precedent or at least proved two significant things. One, that bikers made good fodder for headlines and that the public was easily frightened into enough curiosity to devour the accompanying media hype, with the same feeding frenzy that had previously made dime novels about cowboys a hit. Second this would also prove to be a major area for political manipulation and an excuse for designating funds and manpower to control these loose Cannons on two wheels.

The Hollister incident, which by all eyewitness accounts was blown way out of proportion, became the plot for the first of three movies which would enjoy immense popularity.

Post W.W.II America was an affluent era which saw much prosperity and relegation of citizenry into a loss of identity. Tract houses and Beaver Cleaver were the order of the day. Father knew best and those who didn't conform to society were looked down upon as bad, or outcasts of society. Not since the banishments from the Puritan colonies was nonconformity so despised in this country.

Even the TV shows such as Father Knows Best and Andy Of Mayberry were pumping the message to the American public that there was one right way to be in society and the authoritarian leadership was there to guide you. Albeit subliminal, the message was there and these shows worked well. There were other benefits for some as well. Just because Andy Grifith chose a Ford for the Mayberry police car, Ford sales increased.

As long as a person did, "what was right," the institutions of authority would be there to take care of everything. They were also there to punish those who got out of step. America discovered just how horrible things could get, in the maligned paranoia which would rampage, under Senator Joe McCarthy.

Moving pictures which are about, or star personalities that represent the take-no-guff attitude enjoy an almost cult following in America. This is an indication that the spirit of independence and freedom of the individual is still strong, even if it is lurking beneath the surface. They represent that rebellious spark in us all, and the very public which fears them the most, is simultaneously fascinated. This trend or trait in a public, which is uncomfortable when encountering square pegs which do not fit neatly in round holes, is somewhat of an oxymoron. Perhaps in the depths of his heart, even the most reticent of Americans has within his or her makeup, some of the spirit which makes a motorcyclist driven to this lifestyle. Some celebrities owe the crux of their total and enduring popularity to this phenomenon. Somehow they almost always have a love for motorcycles. James Dean is a very prominent example. His was a short career, and he starred in but very few movies. He lived and died a rebel and was gone in a short time. His popularity continues to endure almost forty five years after his death. Dean became an image which represented the post war generation of Americans. Those who would chart their own course, regardless of the norm, or social pressure. He did live fast, and he did die young, but his legend lives on and his movies (there were only three) are popular still today. His death even caused some fans to commit suicide. Many visit his grave site to place kisses on the tombstone or leave notes and Marlboro packs. Fan mail still pours in and on several occasions his tombstone has been stolen. (Sheesh! give him a break) On display, as of my last visit to the Hard Rock Cafe at Universal City in Orlando, is a motorcycle custom made for a Dean movie. None of the scenes, however, made it into the final cut. This is an unusual looking machine and the plaque says that it was a joint effort of the Harley-Davidson and Indian motorcycle companies just for the film.

About the time James Dean was building his reputation, a movie was to come along and set the stage for the public image of bikers in America. Filmed six years after the actual event, this motion picture was to make stars of Marlon Brando and Lee Marvin and was based on the Hollister incident. The title was The Wild One and is still popular. The immortal image of Johnny is and will remain an icon in American motorcycling. The film was, of course no more accurate than the press.

The pop singer Donovan recorded a hit song in the mid 60s titled, Rikki-Tikki-Tavi after the mongoose in the Kipling story. This song was not one of the greater hits of the 60s nor even the biggest by Donovan. The song was, however, a prophetic political piece, telling of the disillusionment of a public who had come to realize that the ideology behind the things their generation had been told were not true. Since W.W.II we had been led to believe that everything would work out as it should and that the authoritarian institutions, like the mongoose in the Kipling story, would

80

have solutions, and answers. They would be there to kill all of the snakes for us. Donovan's song says it ain't so and Rikki-Tikki-Tavi is dead.

The 60s also brought a lot of public attention to motorcyclists. 1964 seems to be a significant year with adverse publicity and headlines about California's Hells Angels Motorcycle Club. The 1966 movie, The Wild Angels, with Peter Fonda, Nancy Sinatra, Bruce Dern, and Diane Ladd, fired up the public excitement in addition to the news media reports. Although some viewers were just entertained, many identified.

The Viet Nam war era brought the realization that perhaps the enemy of individualization was from within. Just maybe the entities which were frustrating the freedom of the individual and suffocating the spirit of America was society itself, as were the very institutions pledged to safeguard the concept. Maybe just maybe Tocqueville's warning was coming home to roost.

In 1969 and in 1971 the other two aforementioned movies of significant impact were to become signature films of a generation. Even though they were relatively low budget productions, compared to today's megabuck films, these two movies have enjoyed an unparalleled cult following, producing clichés, and Viet Nam era musical hits. They represented an emergence of disillusioned young Americans who had become disgusted with the status quo and no longer believed in the Father Knows Best image of America. These two films were Easy Rider and Billy Jack and the generation representative characters in both were motorcyclists who had become fed up with society and dropped out.

Called "one of the ten most important pictures of the decade," Easy Rider, stars Peter Fonda and Dennis Hopper, as two bikers, who hook up with Jack Nicholson, an alcohol saturated lawyer, and try to go look for America. The cover of the video reads, "A man went looking for America and couldn't find it anywhere." Specifically the film deals with three guys, possessed with the American spirit who take to the road only to come face-to-face with the violent nature of a society which will not tolerate anyone out of step with its accepted social norms.

In this writer's opinion some of the commentary from Easy Rider is classicaly socially significant. An enormous point is made in a conversation between Nicholson and Hopper as they sit by a campfire after being treated unfriendly in a small town with an open and obvious prejudice toward them.

Nicholson says to Hopper that America used to be a good place but no more and he doesn't understand why it has to be that way. Hopper tells him about being turned away from hotels because of the fears of people and he guesses it's the long hair. Nicholson says it isn't the hair it's the fact that they represent freedom. Confused, Hopper asks what is wrong with being free. That is what it's all about. Nicholson says, "Oh yeah, they're going to talk to you, and talk to you, and talk to you, about individual freedom, but when they see a free individual it's going to scare 'em." Dennis says, "Well that don't make 'em running scared." To which Nicholson replied, "Naw, that makes 'em dangerous."

The point of this film is the point of Tocqueville's warning. The have nots will always attempt to destroy the haves. The ruling majority will see those not bound by the shackles of the status quo as a threat. Once perceived that way, all stops will be pulled out in an effort to prevent such a menace to the norm from existing. Even if violating its own rules becomes necessary to do so.

Suppression comes from many things.Small items which slowly erode away minuscule bits of individual freedom of choice. Items in the form of legislation targeted at minorities, or social groups, which then have nowhere to escape or hide from the oppressiveness. In the late 1860s it was in the form of Grandfather Clauses. In the 1900s it can take the form of something like insurance company instigated legislation, or the Racketeer Influenced And Corrupt Organizations Act (RICO). While initially prima facie, this law seemed a good thing as presented on paper and in intent. In reality it opened the lid of a Pandora's Box of abuses and violations of individual's rights by authorities. It allows arrests for guilt by association, and although it wasn't intended to target bikers, it has been used against motorcyclists with club affiliations. This type of attack brings us to the significance of the last of the movies mentioned which had a tremendous social impact.

<u>Billy Jack</u> is about a man, by the same name, who is a half White and half Native American biker. He returns to a Southwestern Reservation from the Viet Nam war, trying to find a place where he can live in peace, without interference from regular society. The regular society is represented by the population of a nearby small

town. Again the town's prejudiced populace can't leave well enough alone making for a situation whereby Billy and his friends at a school for Native American and other children with problems run afoul of the status quo. The situation, of course, leads to a direct and violent confrontation.

This movie like <u>Easy Rider</u> appeals to a segment of America thirsting for truth and the freedom of living in harmony and peace without a hassle from the not so silent majority. Some of the commentary in <u>Billy Jack</u> also serves to explain what is wrong with our society. Situations seem to prevail where the majority is guilty of outrageous actions and activities which they would find intolerable if they are practiced in reverse. Billy argues pertinent points in several scenes and his words highlight some of the ills of a society in violation of its own rules which have their origin in the very declaration of the rights of its citizens.

Early in the story Billy makes a fundamental statement of significant importance. "When policemen break the law, then there isn't any law. Just a fight for survival." Throughout the film Billy and his friends are constantly having trouble with those in the oppressive majority who fear the lifestyle of personal freedom practiced by the school's passive minority. Billy, the protagonist, who is the unofficial champion of the passive minority, is pitted against the antagonist, Posner, who is the unofficial dictatorial head of the aggressors.

Near the end Billy makes a challenge to Jean, the female lead in the film, to tell him where in the entire world is there a place men really do live in peace and harmony. Jean is unable to name such a place and is forced to remain silent. Billy says, "That's what I thought," and rides away on his Triumph. Did I mention, Billy Jack is also a biker. He makes some other good points and presents logic, wisdom and other lessons at many points through the course of the movie. He also points out that, "being an Indian is not a matter of blood. It is a way of life." (The same thing which ties bikers together in brotherhood.)

That concept alone could be the subject of another whole book. There is no better example in the history of this country, of a majority forcing the destruction of a freedom-to-be-different minority, than the treatment of Native Americans.

In the case of both films we have the exact situation red

flagged in Tocqueville's warning. Both movies have left us with comments from the dialog which were not only pertinent then, but relevant today as we close the millennium and freedoms are being eroded under the cloak of being for the public good or forced safety.

Since Viet Nam many Americans have been on a quest for the freedom of the American spirit. A great many of those seeking the Spirit have chosen to do so on two wheeled transportation as they ride back into their heritage. This is evidenced by the sound of a growing voice resonating from the pipes of the motorcycle ridden by our character described at the beginning of this chapter.

The American spirit lives in the freedom concept of an individual being allowed to be free. That simply means freedom to choose.

Today as we ride out of one millennium and into another, we are faced with a challenge to the American Spirit as an entity all its own. This spirit will fight for its rights and the right of individual freedom. A fight that must be won, for if any one rightful freedom falls, all are then in jeopardy. If one is lost, any can be lost. It should be equally important to every freedom loving American to resist and fight, regardless of whether he or she rides a motorcycle.

Historical precedent tells us that once a government or a majority gets a foot in the door then it is a matter of time before the door is wide open. Today it is helmet laws for our own safety. Tomorrow it will be body armor so that we look and feel like Robo Cop or an Imperial Storm Trooper from Star Wars. Bikers would rather feel the wind, regardless of the risk. Eventually it could be no motorcycles and finally no freedom. These are the things today's motorcyclists fear and are fighting to prevent.

In his book, The Holy Ranger, Martin Jack Rosenblum says, "your hands can hang on to graceful courage all the time with graceful force & a power rises from history that will not be toppled by fashionable modern laws." (47)

Today there are many hands hanging on to powerful throttles on the end of handlebars. Some have collective monikers and acronymous designations such as "yuppies" and RUBS. They are as different in backgrounds as they are in Paint schemes but they all go by the term Biker. Many belong to clubs such as HOG or the AMA. Some, like Paines Summer Soldiers and Sunshine Patriots, will only be found on bright, dry, weekends out for a putt. All seem to belong to an elite fraternity. All are proudly willing to proclaim their claim to be bikers.

There is something which ties all of these folks together. Something more than the smell of leather and gasoline. It isn't a desire to get dirty and have grease under their fingernails. It's that spirit, and it walks hand-in-hand with each and every one of us and it only cares that we want to enjoy breathing free air.

Those of us who have been riding a very long time and go the long rides are linked by this common bond of paint and chrome and leather, However those new riders among us, who are in the higher dollar brackets and buy the really expensive machines, are making a real statement as well. They work for places where they are in the uniform of corporate America. A world of offices and fluorescent lights. Many are in sales and marketing and spend their days in cubicles. Days are spent in meetings and phone calls, and churning out lots of paper. They have now discovered that the only free life left is the one on two wheels. They have slipped the shackles and even if it is only for a few days, or even hours at a time, are enjoying the exhilaration of the heady wine of having the wind on your face, the rank and file world at your back, and the sweet taste of freedom on your tongue.

The American spirit welcomes all into the family. Just as the ones in the past who inadvertently brought the spirit to these shores, they have a pursuit factor involved. Their forefathers were running to or from something. Then and now they are in pursuit, or running from pursuit, and it is a freedom thing. It is the freedom to be one's self. Regardless of the degree of freedom sought, each is an independent person, driven by the spirit, who resents and rebels against being told what to do, or not to do, or how it has to be done.

Sometimes called "hardheaded," all possess strong wills and have a need to be free or not to be contained by the norm. Just as it is for the hard-core, the yuppies with motorcycling have the opportunity to be a rebel or feel free and like an individual within the guidelines of the law.

We still have to fight for our rights and counteract those who would do us in for no more than the sake of control or preventing us to continue enjoying our freedom which is as precious as life to us.

In the words of Rosenblum, once again from The Holy Ranger:

> The present fear of conflict is producing reactions that weaken those who would prefer freedom. If we choose to ride our motorcycles without helmets, drive our autos without seatbelts, then we have an insurance controlled legislature to reckon with, which creates laws that favor our own best interests whether we like it or not. This is not a proper function of my government & especially since it operates out of scare. We learn that we cannot take care of ourselves unless it is written that we are doing so well. The point is not to go without a helmet, nor without a seatbelt but to decide without assistance. (67)

It is appropriate here to tell of another fighter for freedom who is waging his war against a system which would take his freedom to ride away. So for a present day example of the American spirit in conflict let's consider the strange case of Jeremiah Gerbracht whom I consider to be like Dr. Dolittle under siege.

Jeremiah Gerbracht has a way with animals. Actually 'way' is a masterpiece of understatement. Describing him as a man who loves animals is tantamount to describing a motorcycle as a thing with wheels. He will tell you readily that he has had a variety of pets and at one time had as many as 21 dogs and a couple of monkeys.

Talk to his parents and you'll find out that he was an animal phenomenon much like a latter day pied piper growing up.

Marvin and Sophie, his eighty-one year old parents, seem to beam with pride when they tell of the continuous stream of dogs which regularly followed him home. Somehow the animals always received a treat regardless of any objections from Mom as Sophie prefers to be called. Mom tells of the milk horse which Jeremiah was fascinated with, and which he decided to take off with when he was five years old. Marvin Gerbracht laughs as he recalls the numerous other pets in Jeremiah's Marvelous Menagerie. Included in the unusual assemblage was a snake that lived in the hall, several cats and one fine feathered friend, not your usual parakeet, but an owl. It was for this owl that he first modified a vehicle. The owl rode with him in his convertible on a special perch attached to the rearview mirror. His Dad said the owl would fly off from time to time but would always return to the perch.

In the Dr. Dolittle movies with Rex Harrison and more recently Eddie Murphy, the animals are able to talk to the doctor and in the latest version they spread the word that here is a guy who understands us and will take care of us. There seems to have been a spreading of the word about Jeremiah also.

Unlike Dolittle the animals do not outright speak to Jeremiah and in all probability he might not be able to hear them if they did. Jeremiah Gerbracht is hearing impaired.

This is where the story takes a bizarre twist. Jeremiah is being hounded by the LAPD both for his love of his current partner and companion, Lady Harley, and his need to have her with him at all times.

Even if animals don't talk to him, he talks to them and they listen. His unusual attachment to his non human friends and the extraordinary feats they are able to do for him did not end with the car-riding owl. His previous dog, Jenny, learned to climb trees like a cat and was even awarded a license to do so by the city of San Francisco. This was the world's first dog ever licensed to climb trees, according to the Guinnes Book of world Records.

An avid motorcyclist, Jeremiah has modified his motorcycle to make it possible for his companion to ride with him on the bike. His present partner, Lady Harley, who followed the beloved Jenny, is no less loved and is also extraordinary.

She rides everywhere Gerbracht goes on her special saddle, (I wonder if Corbin has seen that), allowing her to straddle the tank safely and ride nestled between the tall handlebars. She is a licensed signal dog and is trained to alert him to warning sounds such as sirens and horns which are beyond his hearing range.

Therein lies the tale, The LAPD, it seems, is determined to put a stop to Gerbracht's freedom of the road. He has been repeatedly stopped and ticketed for having Lady Harley on the bike.

Until now, he has beaten all charges and tickets. With the dismissal of the latest ticket the charge has arbitrarily been bumped up to misdemeanor level based on an obscure city ordinance from 1935 making it an offense to ride an animal on the running board or tonneau of a vehicle. When was the last time you saw a tonneau

87

on a bike or one with a running board large enough for even a gerbil to ride on?

There is an undertone here of a vendetta.

Gerbracht's longtime friend David Phillips, AKA Deacon, says this whole fiasco goes back to 1991. Deacon, who was the founder of ABATE in California, sheds a good bit of light on the reason for this controversy. It seems that in 1991 when the helmet law was passed, the problem began. (See chapter 7)

Jeremiah, who was a member of ABATE, started wearing a helmet cover which looked like a top hat. He would be stopped for a helmet violation only to have the last laugh. After finding out he was legal, they stopped pulling him over for the helmet and began ticketing him for the dog. Gerbracht wears the helmet cover to make two statements. The first is to protest the helmet law. The second reason for the top hat motif is class. He reminds that even the earliest films of motorcyclists have shown men in top hats riding.

According to Jeremiah, the unusual style of protest chosen is a way of speaking out. He said, "I wear it to emphasize the exercise of freedom of speech, and to make the statement that says bikers worldwide, male or female, are a class act, and a top hat is a symbol of class."

Gerbracht wears a leather outfit off the bike as well which includes a real leather top hat identical to the helmet cover.

At one point, Lady Harley disappeared for two months and Gerbracht advertised widely for her return, even offering his motorcycle as a reward. This even earned a moral support letter from Willie G. Davidson offering his well wishes in Jeremiah's search.

A Rabbi in LA found the missing Siberian Husky and being a dog lover himself, returned Jeremiah's partner without accepting any reward. The man, the motorcycle, and the four legged friend, were all once again united and back on the road, and back into trouble with LA's finest.

At least five attempts have been made to stop this dynamic duo from being in the wind together.

The latest attempt has elevated what started as a moving violation to a misdemeanor criminal charge stemming from the aforementioned 1935 city ordinance dealing with animals on running boards. They are also bringing in the 1997 vehicle code in

California which prohibits dogs from being transported in the backs of pickup trucks unless caged to 46" or cross tethered to prevent the animal from being discharged, being thrown, or falling from the vehicle.

Numerous allies have taken up Jeremiah's cause and joined in the fray. His team of attorneys looks like the O.J. Simpson dream team. They are being called "Lady Harley's Paws For The Cause Doggie Defense Dream Team."

Gerbracht is defended by Robert Sheahen, long-noted defender of motorcycle rights and issues, the team of Alison F. Bloom, and Alana G. Corman who practice on both coasts. In addition, the services of Christopher Lee and Associates are involved. Collectively, the four attorneys have filed a 36 page brief with the courts.

This brief requests in six places that the complaint be dismissed. Included within the brief are four arguments which address all of the relevant aspects of the state's charges against Gerbracht. In addition to pointing out that all previous charges have been dismissed, the brief addresses that overriding all other factors, city ordinances state laws, and federal, is the Americans With Disabilities Act of 1990's provision that Jeremiah, as a hearing impaired person, may take his dog wherever and whenever he wishes without fear of restrictions.

These laws render municipalities powerless in these matters. His rights in this matter are also covered by the California civil code and the California penal code which prohibits any person, establishment, association, or entity of any sort from interfering with a disabled person and guide dog. The penal code provides for stiff fines and the possibility of imprisonment to any offender.

Jeremiah's attorneys make a good point of showing that the LA courts and district attorney proudly boast in press releases the swift retribution visited upon those who interfere with a disabled person and dog then turn around a week later and try to thwart Jeremiah's freedom of access.

They argue that there is no precedent for the application of the charge to motorcycles and even if there were, Gerbracht is not in violation because of modifications to the bike to protect the dog. They further point out that the officer issuing the most recent cita-

89

tion never saw the animal being transported, but instead only observed Gerbracht and Lady parked in a private parking lot.

Lastly in the brief, the legal team cites the California penal Code's prohibition of charges being set then elevated to a higher offense.

Jeremiah heaps mountains of praise and appreciation upon his lawyers and witnesses and can't seem to say enough in their behalf.

The attorneys, all of whom are working pro bono, believe in the rights of this cause and the righteous indignation that an authority should dare attempt to undermine and deny any individual's just and due freedom of access. They feel that an agency of the people, charged with the protection of the rights of the populace, which misuses it's authority simply because it can, frustrates the life force of our society as a whole, and in this case, seemingly with no more provocation than winning and a purely get-even motive.

The defense attorneys support their brief with five exhibits. These range from official recognition by the city of LA of "Lady Harley" as a signal dog and motorcycle dog, to the press release demonstrating the determination of the courts to protect access for persons with disabilities and their service animals.

Other exhibits are testimonial letters from the SPCA in LA as to the safety of Gerbracht's transporting his dog on his motorcycle because of its modifications and medical testimony as to Gerbracht's hearing impairment.

The final exhibit consists of copies of the California civil and penal codes as well as court disposition of other violators convicted of access denial to a disabled person and service animal.

David 'Deacon' Phillips is a witness providing expert testimony in the case as well as Gerbracht's friend. Deacon is a motorcycle story writer and was an original member of the C.M.S.P. (California Motorcycle Safety Program). He is also an accident investigator and former member of the Philadelphia Police Department Motorcycle Squad.

Deacon says, "This is a vindictive attack by the authorities who are determined to get at him for embarrassing them in previous attempts." He further states, "He shook up the good-old-boy system and they are determined to get even."

The attorneys are equally outspoken on the matter.

Robert Sheahen, with noticeable agitation, commented, "He has been singled out, and it is senseless and barbaric. One week they are prosecuting a restaurant for not allowing a guide dog and the next week they turn around and prosecute a hearing impaired man for using a signal dog. It is outrageous."

Jeremiah has won the admiration and respect of all involved with him. Said Alison Bloom, "The more time I spend with him, the better I like him. He is a champion for what he believes."

Not unlike the figure of Billy Jack, Jeremiah Gerbracht does see himself championing a cause in this. He believes strongly in his dedication to being a freedom fighter and is totally committed to the point of putting it ahead of his social life.

All agree that there is a principle at stake here and even if Gerbracht were not hearing impaired they should let him alone because it is not illegal to ride a dog on a motorcycle.

This is the first time he has had to answer to the current charge and he has won on every previous case. The first time he won an officer said, "See you next time."

Echoing Deacon Phillips and Robert Sheahen, attorneys Alison Bloom and Alana Corman said, "His repeatedly having to answer the same charges is harassment and vindictive prosecution."

This is now much bigger than Jeremiah and his dog. This strikes at the right of all people with disabilities as well as motorcyclists who are being denied their basic freedoms, not the least of which is the right of an American with a disability for unlimited access of his service animal.

David "Deacon" Phillips

After years of fighting a system with an unfair power advantage and bent on a vendetta rather than an honest upholding of the law, Jeremiah and Lady Harley had their final day in court.
And They Won!

Dr. Dolittle maybe but perhaps Jeremiah Gerbracht is rather a modern day Billy Jack after all - even to having a distinguishing hat.

Today's popularity in motorcycling is an outcome that was was as inevitable as it was unpredictable. In retrospect, it doesn't matter whether Daniel Boone was the most qualified for his place in history or not. It is, after all, the spirit that counts and what it represents in our collective identity. It is a love of freedom, it is unique, it is American, and today it rides a motorcycle.

Just as fish grew legs and marched from the sea to end up as man, the American persona of today marched through time in a likewise manner as well. The spirit of our iron horsed American cowboy of today came ashore with that first wave of colonials to hit the beach. He stepped from the boat with wonder in his eyes, a smile on his face, and determination in his expression. He stood there a minute then hitched up his jeans, straightened his ten gallon hat, and with spurs jingling marched off the beach into the future, headed for his first motorcycle.

Ladies Of The Road

I am woman hear me roar
My pipes are too loud to ignore
And the open road I've come to claim as mine...
-William G. (Lad) Carrington-
(To the tune of I am woman by Helen Reddy)

In 1722 Daniel Defoe, the author of <u>Robinson Crusoe</u>, wrote what many believe to be his greatest work. The story is about a woman of dubious repute who begins life in the slums of England and ends up in America as a member of the gentry. The book is titled <u>The Fortunes and Misfortunes of The Famous Moll Flanders</u>, and although it was written in the eighteenth century was about a seventeenth century person who might well typify some of the key players in the settlement of the North American Continent. Moll Flanders is a girl born in Newgate Prison and raised to be a prostitute and thief who is caught and sent to prison herself. In the time the story is set there were no less than 21 offenses in English law which were punishable by death and she was guilty of enough to swing for them. As many prisoners were offered the option of having their necks stretched or being on the next boat for the American Colonies, she decided on the latter. In Virginia she starts her new life and makes the transition from felon to a rich colonial lady of respectability.

Although this is a fictional story the character isn't atypical. Both men and women were a major part of the early development of what was to become the United States. (see chapter 4)

Just as the previous chapter told the story of the individuals who pioneered the sport, this chapter tells the story of the ladies who have come into a prominent position in their own right. This chapter also speaks about individuals who have made a place in our history as pioneers who helped pave the way for women and some who still continue to make up a vital part of the continu-

93

ation of this history, and who now have taken a place alongside the men as equals in sharing this lifestyle.

The Cowgirls with their Chrome Horses are women who range from very literally taking a back seat to the men (as well as figuratively), to those whose individuality rivals their male counterparts. These women cover a full range of personas as citizens of this eclectic community who span the gamut from those who only ride behind boyfriends and husbands to piloting their own custom machines across the American landscape independent of the men altogether.

Ladies Of The Road of today are women basking in a different light than the stereotype "Biker Chick" who is the property of her "Old Man" and second in value to his scooter. The ladies profiles collectively are a group of women who are as varied as the men in this sport, from corporate executives and screen idols to the mother and schoolteacher from Maine who packs the kids in the family wagon and tows her Harley to South Dakota to race at Sturgis.

This is not a new thing for women, although it may seem so to those who think of the American woman as Beaver Cleaver's mom, or are just not accustomed to the numbers of women seen today at events and riding the highways.

Women have always had those individuals in their midst who stood out, and offtimes stood alone, but stand their ground they did.

From the very earliest of times in the American colonies there have been women who distinguished themselves even though the norm was a wife and mother who was the stay in the background type who cared for her home and raised a family.

If we take the case of Margaret Brent, for example, we see how a situation paved the way for her to set a precedent and a first for one of her gender.

Margaret Brent in 1647 was appointed by the terms of Lord Calvert's will as his executrix. In this capacity she served also as attorney for Calvert's brother, Lord Baltimore. In order to look after the Calvert estate to the best advantage, Mistress Brent went before the Maryland Assembly on January 21, 1647, and demanded a seat, "thereby unconsciously distinguishing herself as the first woman in America to claim the right to vote." (Price, 1)

Ms. Brent may have been considered unique for her time because the prevailing opinion was that women should play a diminished role in society. Society was by and large a patriarchal system and men had their own ideas about women's roles.

In her 1945 thesis, about Southern Women and their evolving leadership, Margaret Nell Price describes this prevalent attitude by quoting a passage from the biography of George Fitzhugh:

He believed that woman was sent into the world to be a helpmate to men and the highest practical wisdom on the conduct of human affairs resulted from the unison and interfusion of male and female minds....Woman should accept an 'inferior position', for whenever she becomes the equal of man, she loses his respect and fails to fulfill her God-ordained duties. In Asia, where she is secluded from public gaze she is almost an idol; and in China where she is crippled and kept in the background, she is protected and honored. So long as she is nervous, capricious, delicate, diffident, and dependent, man will worship and adore her. Her weakness is her strength, and her true art is to cultivate and improve that weakness. (13)

While Fitzhugh's statement may seem to some as an advantage to women, and it could be argued that women, for the most part, may have learned to manipulate the position and skillfully navigate the system to their advantage, they were still under a system which held immense power and restraint over them. After all, a bird in a gilded cage is still in a cage.

A good example is Teresa of Avila, who in the fifteen hundreds became one of the most important women in the history of the Catholic Church. This was at a time when Europe was in turmoil and Christianity was being split apart over Martin Luther and the Protestant Reformation.

The power of the Church bore more of a resemblance to the yet to be Nazi Third Reich than a benevolent institution leading its flock to heaven.

Teresa rose to be a mighty influence upon her contemporaries as well as those to follow and was eventually canonized and became Saint Teresa Of Avila. A study of her biography reveals a smart and savvy woman who, beyond practicing her beliefs, had to learn and manipulate the politics, successfully navigating a hostile system, and did it brilliantly. She did so, however, under the constant suspicion of her male superiors, who had for the most part the power of life and death over her.

In chapter two we saw how even pirates could be portrayed as the same as, or similar in character to, our mythical representative figure of the cowboy or the "good badman". This figure, in the form of a pirate and portrayed as fierce of demeanor and valiant of heart, was to be found in the women as well.

While Hollywood has always had its horse-opera-heroines, the real life figures were even more possessed of this spirit than those played in the motion pictures by such wide screen stars as the fiery haired Maureen Ohara and girl next door, Doris Day.

A few years ago the movie <u>Cut Throat Island</u> portrayed a woman pirate, played in the movie by Geena Davis. This figure had a counter part in real life in the form of lady pirate Anne Bonny. Actually there were two of them since our Swashbuckling femme-fatal had a cohort named Mary Read.

When these notorious ladies of the bounding main were eventually captured they were dueling it out on deck with the King's boarding party. The men in the crew were cowering below decks including the infamous Calico Jack Rackham. According to legend, Anne Bonny, who was carrying his child, is supposed to have been allowed a visit to Rackham's cell door just prior to his necktie party (notice the western pulp fiction terminology) at the Jamaican prison where they were being held. She is reputed to have admonished him saying, "I am sorry to see you hang, but if you'd fought like a man, you need not have been hanged like a dog."

This incident took place in October, 1720 in the very time period that the novel, <u>Moll Flanders</u> was written by Defoe.

Both women were pregnant and given stays of execution but Read died from disease while incarcerated. Bonny gave birth and was reprieved about two weeks after her baby was born.

Anne Bonny was reputed to be under 20 years of age and the daughter of an Irish plantation owner in Charleston. Possibly Bonny's family may have immigrated earlier from circumstances similar to those depicted in Defoe's novel. Rumor has it she returned to South Carolina with her child and there is no further record of her beyond that point.

Many women in this country have since stepped into history to carve their niche and establish a place in what was considered traditionally to be a man's world. They have not only done so in an inhospitable environment but with as much flair, gumption, and panache as any man.

Some of our favorite figures in history are women whose names live on today in legendary proportions. They include Sacajewea, without whose help as interpreter and guide, Lewis and Clark's monumental expedition might surely have failed.

Among others, equally notable, who stepped up to take their place in history are immortalized in the personages of Belle Starr, Calamity Jane, Poker Alice, Annie Oakley, Ma Barker, Bonnie Parker, and Amelia Earhart.

Along the way most women in the US , with the exception of war times, for the most part lived under the assumption that their skills were to be domestic in nature and each was to strive to be a good wife and mother. A young girl was expected to bring to marriage skills which included but were not limited to proper cooking and baking, stove tending, cleaning and sewing, gardener, teacher, and nurse. This concept prevailed into the 20th century and is described in great detail in <u>American Women Today</u> by Margaret Mead and Frances B. Kaplan.

Her home was largely self-sufficient, her outside activities chiefly in her church, its missionary society and its women's circle. Neighboring families, however, could rely on mutual aid at times of crisis—illness, accident, or death; fire; or crop failure. (81-82)

Every society that ever existed has classified people by their customary usage and each category was expected, and trained respectively, to behave and function in its specific role. This has been particularly true of the sexes, but it seems that in the far past the roles became more logically equivalent.

Historical research shows that even in ancient Minoan civilization women were roughly enjoying living on a par with their male counterparts and the same can be argued for the Renaissance.

Ancient Minoan women were able to, "hold their own with the most advanced of our times. We find them mingling freely, unveiled and bare-breasted, with men at the theatre, the bull dances, and other public events." (G. H. Seward & R. C. Williamson, 109) The women were also able to hold their own with the men in jobs which would seem to be traditionally men's places and still get the household duties done. It sounds like a combination of Bike week and then back to the office or construction job of today doesn't it?

This same sense of balance between the sexes seems to be the situation for men and women of the Renaissance era as well. The self-actualized "universal man," bold in boudoir and battlefield, knowledgeable in art, letters, and philosophy, found his female match. The energy, beauty, and courage of the Renaissance women have been immortalized by such heroines as Caterina Sforza, for her defense of Foprli, and Bianca Visconti, for governing Milan (Burkhardt, 1937; Durant, 1953).

On all fronts, the Renaissance showed life being lived intensely with both men and women eagerly making the most they could of themselves and of one another. (114, 115)

For some reason, and that would be the subject of another book, women had deteriorated in status by the settling of the American colonies. It seems that surviving in primitive frontier environments has somewhat of an equalizing effect. This is not to say that it brought equality but a number of factors began to cause a gelling effect which would began in colonial America and gradually grew through to today.

The individualism and independence of character discussed in chapter four was as much a part of the American woman as it was in the men. This was to grow from the woman homesteading beside her man to a spark of independent spirit among women in the towns, that would not be extinguished by any patriarchal dominance. It found a way to grow and break free and penetrate the Victorian era and the stage was set for its incubation by man's most foolish of all games, war.

The seed of this independence was sewn literally by women gathering together to make quilts. The reasons were more the gathering than quilting. Sandi Fox in For Purpose And Pleasure tells us about women using quilting as a reason to assemble:

In colonial America, the quilt was often already on the frame when family and friends arrived to stitch together its multiple layers. In this particular exchange of labor, a concept integral to preindustrial America, creativity was often secondary to companionship. By the middle of the nineteenth century, however, women had more fully involved themselves with the surfaces of those quilts they would complete together, particularly in the construction of album and friendship quilts, but even at that century's end, the simple circumstances of "quilting together" seem to have remained constant. (9)

Early quiltmakers' letters and diaries speak often of "circles," and of the comfort and continuity they provided.(127)

Companionship, safety in numbers, voices united for power, the results are the same. You get out of the day-to-day routine and away from someone telling you what to do and how to behave. Is it starting to sound familiar?

There were numerous, if isolated, instances of women proving their worth and making a bid for their rights during the American Revolution. Abigail Adams wrote a letter to her husband John while the very government was being formed and its blueprint being written. She requested women be included in the doctrines of liberty and made free from husbands' unlimited power over wives. She claimed men were, "Naturally Tyrannical." (Tindall, 253)

Some other women making history during this time were Margaret Corbin (no seat connection here), and Mary Ludwig Hays who took the places of their husbands when the men fell in battle. Deborah Samson actually enlisted, disguised as a man, and served for two years under the name Robert Shurtleff. Although there are stories that this feat would be repeated in the Navy during the War Of 1812 with a woman named Lucy who, disguised as a man, served for three years as a marine aboard Old Ironsides, they have been proven false.

Things were beginning to change for women and an individual identity came with it. Quilting circles may have been a leap ahead but the strides were to become even longer. By the second quarter of the 19th century academies of higher learning for women began to emerge.

As soon as the functions of women were no longer narrowly linked to physiological factors and ceased to be shaped exclusively by demographic and economic imperatives, a search for moral justification started. The role of women developed a 'sacred' character and any modification in it triggered off an ideological debate, so that at present all discussion of their position has moral and ideological overtones. (Stearns, 6)

Tocquerville, in what has become the greatest classic work of observations about Americans, wrote in his second volume, published in 1840, that anytime several Americans have an opinion they wish to promote they seek each other out and combine and from that point on are seen as a power and example to be listened to. He also observed that American girls are hardly out of childhood before they begin to think for themselves, and act on their own impulses to speak out with a freedom not seen in the young ladies of Europe.

Probably of greater importance to American women was the tendency toward association that made such a deep impression upon Tocquerville, and that continues to be so distinctive a feature of American life. In church auxiliaries and missionary societies, and then in philanthropic and charitable bodies, thousands of women found outlets for the altruism and wider fields of enterprise beyond the domestic circle. Barred from the society of men they discovered among themselves talents and resources enough to advance many good causes and perform many good works. By the 1830's there were literally thousands of separate women's groups holding meetings, collecting funds, discussing public issues, and variously improving themselves. In this manner a revolution of rising expectations was launched. (57)

In what even the least observant historian couldn't fail to notice, these two distinctly American traits would form catalysts for one another and lead to a demand for suffrage by a convention hosted in 1848 by Elizabeth Cady Stanton and Susan B. Anthony. Anthony is now honored by the newest silver dollar which oddly is a misfit in US currency standards. Check out your change carefully, and especially if you receive it from a stamp machine at a post office. You may accidentally give away dollars thinking them to be quarters. Could there be a hidden message in the size difference between a regular silver dollar and the Anthony one.

The Civil War Amendments to the US Constitution, 13,14, and 15, passed between 1865-1870, covered in their very language freedom, equality, and suffrage for all legitimate citizens of the United States. Obviously the men making the laws did not allow that women were citizens and apparently believed them to be something less than the former male slaves. For in spite of these amendments, and the equality demanded by the women of 1848, suffrage would not come until passage of the 19th Amendment, August 26, 1920, fully 72 years later.

Wars bring great changes along with the death and destruction and many of those changes were to bring out a much broader potential in American women than their male counterparts probably wished for.

Because of their relatively small sizes, the Revolutionary War and the War of 1812 may not have had as noticeable an impact on those back home as later wars but the seeds were there and significant never the less.

No war did more to change the face of America than the Civil War. Its great battlefields still dot our landscape and well over a hundred years later we are still discovering new aspects and finding recently uncovered material. This is true historically, archeologically, and sociologically.

This war decimated a large part of the male population of the US killing some six hundred thousand plus of our citizenry collectively. Four days alone accounted for seventy eight thousand overall casualties. That is some twenty five thousand or so in one day in September, 1862 near Sharpsburg, MD and about fifty three thousand in July, 1863.

While these figures are not all battlefield death tolls they bring into focus the huge waste of humanity because many who were not killed in battle were to die later from wounds or resulting infections. Many many more were maimed or at least partially disabled from the loss of limbs and eyesight. This devastation was not to affect only those in battle and the landscape where the battles

101

took place.

Four years and one month the War Between The States dominated all of the United States and its territories and associates. It wreaked havoc on economies, supplies, attitudes, and lifestyles. This had a profound effect not only on those who fought, but on those who waited back home as well.

The women and children were left to do all of the things they had traditionally done plus all of the things the men had previously done and the added burden of supporting the war effort. Even the wives of generals were doing their part making things, like socks, for the troops in the field.

Women were the employees who did much, if not most, of the work in munitions factories. These workers rolled cartridges by the millions on both sides of the conflict. Southern women in some areas were urged to save their chamber lye (the urine from chamber pots) to refine or filter out the nitre which is potassium nitrate (saltpeter), an essential element in the manufacture of gunpowder. A couple of postwar poems printed in national publications told of this practice. One made humorous spoof of it saying the fragrance of the nitre from the women back home was what accounted for the fierce fighting ability and marksmanship of the Confederate soldiers.

The women made much more than bullets, however. Uniforms and shoes are as essential for troops on the march as weapons and women formed a good part of the labor force used to produce these things. Many women organized to generate support for the war effort and raise funding. This was true for both sides.

Although women were not allowed to go into combat as soldiers there were some on both sides who actually would be in the battles. Wearing a uniform of sorts and sometimes carrying guns these women, known as Vivandiers, would provide all kinds of aid in the field. Running up and down the lines of battle assisting with everything from communications to water and ammunition delivery and help to the wounded.

One such woman of the war was Marie "French Mary" Tepe of the 114th Pennsylvania Regiment also known as *Collis' Zouaves*. Eye witnesses have recorded that this well known and decorated woman (the famous "Kearney Cross" awarded to III corps members for bravery) was cool under fire and continued to do her duty unshaken under conditions which left the most seasoned soldiers unnerved. French Mary was wounded in the ankle by a bullet at the battle of Fredricksburg which evidently, according to newspaper accounts, remained there, painfully, for the rest of her life.

The enormous casualty rate of the war provided the learning arena for many advances in the field of medicine and one specific aspect of this field was to be the beginnings of a new area of medicine, nursing. It was not a new thing for women to volunteer to tend the wounded and dying but this war produced some exceptional ones.

Daring and resourceful (like the Lone Ranger) Clara Barton was one shining example and throughout the war carried the nickname given her by a brigade surgeon, The Angel Of The Battlefield. Although women were technically not allowed on a battlefield under fire, she established the precedent of getting supplies to the front early in the war. She volunteered to be a battlefield nurse after being turned down in her attempt to be a soldier.

Barton remained in nursing and in 1881 founded the American Red Cross.

Another exceptional woman of the war was Dorothea Dix who was Superintendent of the Female Nurses and had more authority than any woman connected to the military prior to the war. One of the nurses who served under Dix was Louisa May Alcott who would go on to become one of America's most beloved authors, writing the classic <u>Little Women</u>.

Mary Ann Ball Bickerdyke was nicknamed by the soldiers, "Mother Bickerdyke" and was also known as the "Calico Colonel." Bickerdyke was honored in the grand reviews and through a special bill congress granted her a pension in 1886.

Others include Mary Edwards and Elizabeth Blackwell. Edwards, was known before the war for dressing like a man because she didn't like the frilly bloomer styles women were expected to be seen wearing in public. She became an assistant surgeon, was captured by Confederate soldiers and was awarded the Congressional Medal Of Honor. (rescinded in 1917)

Educated at Geneva Medical College in New York, the forerunner to Hobart College, Blackwell became the first woman doctor in America in 1851. (bet you thought it was Dr. Quinn Medicine Woman) She then studied in Europe and returned to the US to open an institution to assist other women in becoming doctors and established a place where women and children could buy medicine. Blackwell trained nurses for the army and after the war established a hospital for poor women and children. She later returned to Europe to study more medicine and devoted the balance of her life to writing, lecturing, and working for women's rights.

On the other side of the battlefield was Sally Louisa Tomkins. Philanthropist and humanitarian, Miss Tomkins was the only woman who was a comissioned officer in the Confederate Service. She established a hospital at her own expense in Richmond and her facility had the unusual honor of being well liked by her patients and contemporaries, which was rare in wartime medicine. Many of the nurses and doctors were not well liked because of conditions, temperment, and discipline. Her hospital had the most impressive record and the lowest death rate of any hospital in the war, North or South. Tomkins passed and was buried with full military honors in 1916.

Some women did make it into the ranks disguised as men and no doubt did so on both sides. Historians believe that most of these would likely have been wives or sisters, wishing to serve with husbands and brothers. The body of one woman in a man's uniform was discovered among the dead North Carolina troops after the illfated assault on the third day at Gettysburg.

Last and most notorious were the camp followers. These ladies were the most discussed by the press and ladies of polite society and most popular with the troops. Their numbers and the red light districts rose to enormous proportions as did venereal disease. There are no concise Confederate reports but an average reported by the Union Army Medical Department in 1861 gives a rate of 1 out of every twelve soldiers infected. (ouch) It is popularly believed that the lenient policies for recreation for the troops by General Hooker, established when he took command of the Army Of The Potomac, are where the slang term "Hooker" came from, meaning a lady of the evening or a drink of whiskey taken neat.

Kate Sperry, of Winchester, VA, was one of the women who stubbornly maintained her independent spirit during the recurring occupations of the city. Valiantly she was outspoken, kept a high profile, and recorded a detailed diary during the Civil War.

Thanks to a great extent to her efforts, we know what daily life was like during the occupation of the city which most often changed hands during the war. At one point she was even smuggling some things through the lines. After the war she broke some new ground for women's liberation. She married a surgeon from NC and moved to Mississippi, where she shocked polite society by going into business for herself.

After the war women were to find that huge numbers of the men who did return were crippled or in some way impaired. This made it necessary for women, and the children who were big enough, to work the farms and seek employment elsewhere as well.

The postwar era of the 1860s and 70s saw the rise of factories in areas of production which had not been in evidence much before the mid-century mark.

Textiles and tobacco factories sprung up in the south and needed a labor force. Factories were already a prominent feature of the more industrialized North and after the war multiplied in both regions with the spread of the Industrial Revolution. Factories produced everything from pencils to paper goods and from textiles to tin cans and until the next generation of men were of a workable age women filled in the ranks. This was not just a trend, but rather a necessity for the survival of their families.

The years after the war also accelerated the formation of women's clubs and societies. Most for cultural or preservation efforts and benevolent organizations. These types of philanthropic and professional groups gave the members a feeling of purpose and usefulness beyond the role of being a homemaker, even more so than had the quilting circles of the colonial era.

These organizations for women outside the home, with perhaps the exception of church activities, tapered off as the country began to revert to a more 'normal' state of being. "The philanthropic and professional services which southern women had given during the war and reconstruction period were no longer required and a void was created in the lives of women who had once tasted social usefulness." (Price, 36)

The exception to this picture seems to be those women of Victorian America who were from wealthy enough families to take advantage of the Gilded Age, that period from about 1880 to 1915.

The Spanish American War just before the turn of the century created some advancement but not terribly significant. World War I would began the acceleration of trends for women that would set the tone for attitude and achievement in the 20th century.

Mead and Kaplan tell us in <u>American Women Today</u>, that the war produced an increase in the kinds and variety of work for women to do. This left performance models for women in America of the 1920s thus producing a standard for the young ladies of the time to achieve if not best. By the Great Depression and the 30s, "... a considerable number of women attained standing in the professions." (86)

The turn of the century produced more than just a liberation platform for women. It gave them and their male counterparts new conveyances which promised to add to the concept of human mobility in ways superior to anything which had preceded them since fish grew legs and crawled from the ocean. They were airplanes, automobiles, and motorcycles.

Although these devices were primarily the tools and toys for men they would play a real role in the various stages that women would take over the rest of the 20th century to assert their independence and equality.

For the most part the new age of machines departed from the focus of being war machinery and began to make life easier for civilians. Life was better for many people and Americans enjoyed a period in the twenties of afluent living and a false sense of security since recession and depression were less than ten years away. More people than ever partied and enjoyed night life as the Gilded Age came to an end and gave way to the machine age. A growing number of Americans bettered themselves but women by and large were regulated after WWI back to the role of Susie Homemaker.

Once again Susie had been put back on the shelf after proving that she could hold her own and was left with no clear independent identity in a male dominated society. A late but token gesture was handed women after 72 years of fighting for it, in the form of the 15th Amendment. Suffrage did not, however, solve all of the problems even though it was a milestone. It did still some ruffled waters amid the confusion of identity. People like things to comfortably fit in familiar niches. Round pegs in round holes so to speak and when they don't we have loose cannons and folks get very uncomfortable with the situation.

Up until then men had seen American society gender roles as fitting the natural order of things, i.e. round pegs were fitting in round holes. Women rather had felt like square pegs in round holes. The machine age was providing the machinery for change and some did indeed change.

Men at one time undoubtedly felt secure in their identity because non-males brought out the contrast. When women found their identity undermined by changes introduced by the machine age, and found themselves with no identity they could admire, they sought a new identity. As a model, they accepted that which they had always admired; they would be the equal of men. (Seward & Williamson, 88)

The big fight for equality which might have risen from the final achievment of suffrage was to be put on hold as the house of cards came tumbling down with depression and war.

The great war was to come along and put an end to the great depression, and get women out of the house in numbers of enormous proportion. We find once again a war is the vehicle which provides a way for mom to take off the apron and leave the house. Now we have an army of women workers stoking the war machinery, and this time she is doing more than sewing uniforms and knitting socks. This time she is making airplanes and battleships.

The outbreak of World War II in 1939, and United States entry in 1941, brought another period of full employment, and with it new opportunities for women. In 1940, 48 per cent of the country's single women were working; by 1944, 59 per cent. The women's components of the armed services put 266,184 women into uniform. Tillie the Toiler and Rosie the Riveter became classic figures on the American industrial scene; under the Lanham Act, day-care centers took care of the youngsters of many working mothers while they boosted war production. (87)

This war, as do all of them, eventually came to an end and Rosie had to put down her rivet gun and surrender her coveralls so that GI Joe could trade his uniform and M-1 rifle for them. Rosie went home and assumed the role of June Cleaver, taking care of

Ward, Wally, and The Beaver.

From the Civil War to WWII there were women who would really stand out and carve their niche in the American historical landscape. Standing on both sides of the law we have the figures such as Belle Starr, Annie Oakley, Bonnie Parker, and Amelia Earhart so much intwined in American image and folklore.

Both before and after WWII there was one woman who would be influential to Americans of all genders and races in a tireless fight for equality and personal liberty, and that was Eleanor Rosevelt. Born near the begining of the Gilded Age (1884) and living until just before the Viet Nam War (1962), Eleanor was a tireless worker for just about every aspect of social reform in this country. She became the First Lady and as such was one of the most active in the history of the office. It is perhaps possible to speculate that Franklin D. Roosevelt might never have been President had he not been married to her. She has had a profound effect on paving the way for more equitable circumstances for the poor, blacks, the nation's youth, and of course women.

For another twenty years American women were once again back in the role of Susie Homemaker, for the most part, as the United States went through the most affluent period in its short history.

During that time the Korean Conflict came along and women were the support structure back home as the men expended record amounts of gunpowder and testosterone and then in the mid 1960s the one event to shake the entire American psyche came along and we found ourselves at war again and this time in a little place in Southeast Asia no one had ever heard of Viet Nam.

Once again Women answered the call but things were different this time. Many women were in harms way and gave their lives as the full measure of their service or at least gave their sanity as the price of the sights and experience. Many others participated in protests to the war and for the first time in history more than fifty thousand American mothers saw their children's remains delivered back to them in plastic bags.

Somewhere between 1800 and 1980 enough became enough and all of the injustices and setbacks stacked up until the last straw was piled upon the camel's back. June Cleaver got pissed-off and told Ward and The Beaver to go to hell. She threw down her apron, burned her bra, stormed out of the kitchen, leaving dinner burning on the stove, and made herself heard as never before. Some of that noise came from the pipes of a motorcycle.

Women have not always been bound to wartimes or war machinery to do great things or make a mark in history. The most popular dessert in America is ice cream. Invented in China and making its way west via Italy (Italians like to claim its origin), it made its way to North America via England and is recorded as being served in Philadelphia at a party honoring the new American independence. It was crudely made at best and was really iced cream. It was not easily available to the public until a woman in New Jersey invented the first portable ice cream freezer in 1846.

Not exactly a machine but an unusual means of transportation anyway was the padded barrel built by Annie Telson Taylor. Annie it seems was the first person to ever go over Niagra Falls in a barrel and live.

Women have, however been among the first to ride motorcycles. There is ample evidence to support this statement as fact even though it is sketchy. There seems to be little documentation or records kept about women two-wheelers. There are, however, references which indicate that there were indeed women among the pioneers of motorcycling. This disparing lack of records is noted in the <u>Mechanix Illustrated Motorcycle Book</u> of 1951 and also in the New book by Susie Hollern, <u>Women and Motorcycling - The Early Years</u>. The Mechanix Illustrated book does mention that in spite of a lack of records, "it is probably a sure bet that the first motorcyclist had a wife or sister who sneaked his bike out of the barn, figured out how it worked, and went for a spin when he thought she was doing the weekly wash or canning tomatoes." (79) The book mentioned that most of the participation by women was in the form of lady's auxillary groups attached to motorcycling organizations, but goes on to say that in addition by 1951 there were an estimated 1000 "girl cyclists."

Some of the evidence we have is found, in the records of the development of some of the earliest, motorcycles are that Coventry Motor Company, The Humber Company, and Shaw produced motor bicycles for women in 1897 just two years after the first motorcycles appeared in a public exhibit. (The Stanley Cycle Show) Susie Hollern's research for her excellent book, <u>Women and</u>

Motorcycling - The Early Years, discovered that there was a manual for women motorcyclists as early as 1828. This manual was titled, A Book For The Lady Driver, Sidecar Passenger, and Pillion Rider, by Betty and Nancy Debenham.

Famous for riding Harley-Davidsons and Indians were the Motor Maids of the 1930s. This group of two-wheeling women is still in existence as we close the millennium. The 30s also saw movie actress, Beverly Roberts, riding her 45 twin around Hollywood. She was actually featured in a few issues of the H-D magazine, The Enthusiast.

Women are still breaking new ground in the motorcycling industry. One prominent example of this new wave of women at the forefront is Jennie Hanlon, a CEO with the new Excelsior-Henderson motorcycle company.

Ms. Hanlon along with husband Dave and His brother Dan founded the company in 1993. The three were at the 1993 Sturgis Rally And Races. Hanlon who has been an active rider, along with her husband, was a participant from the very first discussion considering the possibility of creating a new marque in the world of two-wheeled travel. Since 1993 the trio have worked diligently to create an all new machine which would take to the road and take its rightful place in the field of motorcycles made in America. Jennie has been no behind the scenes stereotype of the corporate wife. Taking the high profile position, she has been a hands-on person from day one, working tirelessly with the two guys, as this project took form from merely an idea in the collective minds and hearts of the three.

Ms. Hanlon who is an attractive example of todays leadership in corporate America, is also a warm and outgoing individual. A true example of the American spirit mentioned throughout this book.

With her sharp sense of style, Hanlon has spearheaded the development of a line of Excelsior-Henderson clothing and attire which is attractive yet practical. Her goals are that wearing apparel should be functional without sacrificing comfort or femininity for the women riders.

As if that were not enough, Jennie Hanlon, not only rides, and maintains her own scoot, she is working on a custom Super-X bike and still finds time to be a full time mother. Hear her roar!

She is no doubt an example of what the business world of motorcycling can expect in the industry of the future.

The spirit demonstrated by women who love to ride is not necessarily exhibited by the size of the motorcycle or the distance ridden. The impression that the spirit of America has to be mounted on a fire breathing, ground shaking, stump puller goes wide the mark. Therefore I'd like to present here, a lady who has as much gumption as the hardiest of our pioneers and loves being on two wheels better than most bikers love chrome. I call her the Baddest Biker Babe East of the Badlands.

Nestled between two rolling hills in central South Dakota is the sleepy little prairie town of Murdo, so named by the railroad for Murdo Mackenzie, a cattle rancher. Its actual location is about equidistant between the Missouri River and the Badlands along I-90, putting it about 160 miles east of Sturgis.

Now during most of the year Murdo is primarily known for being the home of The Pioneer Auto Museum, which boasts having one of Elvis' motorcycles. Most notable when approaching the town is the large billboard which says "Murdo Exit Now," and then tells you that Murdo has 10 motels, eight restaurants, five service stations, two campgrounds and complete services. What the sign doesn't tell you is that Murdo also has Laura Grace Heyden.

Laura Heyden (pronounced Hi-Den)was born Laura Grace Hay, 85 years ago. With a twinkle in her eye and an impish smile she says, "Mother was a Moss and Moss married Hay." L i k e her namesake, Laura Ingalls Wilder, she was born in a little house on the prairie in 1913. She started life in Bijo Hills near Platte for about the first 10 years and would be the first of seven girls and no brothers. She had to help her dad with all the work on their farm. Around age ten the family moved to Mellette County between White River Wood and Mission, SD to homestead near the grandparents. Sharp as paint, she reminisces with a smile about the times she rode on the lead horse to help her father break the sod with a gang plow to get ready to plant each years crops.

Laura lived just over the state line in North Dakota for a year with a lumberjack's family named Brooks in order to finish high school. She was going to a nearby school in Morristown close to the border in South Dakota. So she rode an old gray mare (no play on words intended) across the line to Morristown daily to attend classes. In addition to school she tended the livestock and gathered cow chips for fuel to pay for her room and board.

She can keep a listener spellbound for hours with her tales of being a teacher in one room prairie schoolhouses and the life of being a rancher's wife. With a twinkle in her eye, she delights in the telling of a poor Christmas where all the girls received dolls from an uncle. Another favorite story is one about a farm winter when she and a dog spent three days around the clock in an ice storm, shepherding a herd of turkeys to keep them from being killed. All the neighboring farms lost most of their turkey herds.

At 85 Laura is the proprietress of the Lee Motel in Murdo which always has the welcome sign out for any road-weary motorcyclist passing through South Dakota. The motel, named after Laura's childhood nickname, began as an old house on Main Street with broken windows and doors. Laura and her sister Gertrude bought the old place and with the help of Gertrude's husband they turned it into the H Motel which boasted four rooms. Later she bought out her sister and began to expand. First a local building was dismantled and rooms added from the materials and later she bought a six room-motel in Pierre and had it moved to Murdo to add rooms. She had to crawl under the motel in Pierre and dismantle the plumbing and pipes herself. All this moving and adding-on makes up the Lee Motel of today.

Folks around Murdo think a lot of their two wheelin' octogenarian. Theresa Osterberg, a former student, who had her in the second grade in '46, still thinks fondly of her and remembers that, "she was stern but we learned." Barbara White Buffalo, who works at the Triple H Truck (and biker) Stop says, "She's pretty special to everybody."

Apparently you never know what to expect from Laura. Locals tell stories that range from her showing up at Christmas in a Santa Claus suit at the truck stop to being there, right on cue with her moped and Harley paraphernalia, when the annual pilgrimage of bikers began their scheduled stop at the Triple H for coffee, donuts and fuel before rolling into the Black Hills.

When asked about the bikers, her face lights up and her eyes sparkle like polished Black Hills crystals. Around 18 years ago she discovered how much fun two wheels could be. Two years before, her fella bought each of them identical mopeds and hers sat in the garage until he threatened to sell it. So, she learned how to ride and discovered that it was a lot more fun and faster than that old gray mare she used to ride. Since then she has worn out three motorbikes and accumulated her share of road-rash, mostly from sand. Says Laura, "Riding is the most enjoyment I've had in my whole lifetime."

The Triple H is a traditional stop for The Run To The Fun ride from the upper midwestern states and the ride gathers many numbers of bikers joining in along the way. The truck stop manager, Doris Convey, who is also a HOG member, invited Laura to show up on her little bike about 10 years ago. One of Laura's motel employees helped her to put together an outfit of proper 'biker regalia' and a new tradition was begun.

Since the beginning she has led the groups who stop back to the highway where they parade thunderously by her on the last leg to the rally. Sometimes she puts on her outfit and rides in other town parades as well and is easily Murdo's most notable character. She has been filmed by national news teams following the bikers to Sturgis and everyone wants a picture with her at the stop. Sometimes called, "The Motel Queen," she always welcomes the bikers at her motel, and many, including this writer, make it a point to stop there for a night either going to the Rally or going home. Any time a motorcyclist pulls into the truck stop and asks for directions to a good motel the staff will say, "have I got just the place for you." Those of us who travel the roads by two wheels on a regular basis can tell you just how welcome those words can be. If she has a vacancy, she cheerfully opens the office at all hours to rent rooms to the bikers.

At 85 she is still riding and as long as she is able she will be a part of the gathering at the Triple H on the way to the Rally. Each year the bikers try to talk her into going with them, even if they have to tie a rope to her moped and tow her to Sturgis. Maybe this year she will make it.

In the words of local shop owner, Sherry Dykema, "She is a very unique person. She is probably the most unique person in the county. She works hard and plays hard. She has a lot of fun, no matter what she does."

Laura Heyden could just maybe be considered Murdo's

best goodwill ambassador, or maybe the town's best asset, or maybe even the best all around person in general. What she is for sure is a tiny, white haired, ball of fire and sunshine, who loves the bikers that stop in Murdo on their perennial pilgrimage to or from Sturgis. Once you meet her she is reason enough to make Murdo a scheduled stop.

Eat your heart out Laura Ingalls Wilder.

The spirit of America is ever strong and stands proud in the examples set by its women, historically and of today. No better definition can be said than these words, which are among the last written by Amelia Earhart on her famous but illfated around the world flight.

"Please know I am quite aware of the hazards...I want to do it because I want to do it. Women must try to do things as men have tried. When they fail their failure must be but a challenge to others."

-Amelia Earhart in a note to her husband George while enroute on her last fateful flight before vanishing without a trace, July 2, 1937-

The Machines

"Come ride with me, ride with me,
Take me to the places that you wanna be"
-70s era motorcycle ad theme-

The popularity of the dime novel and theatrical productions, such as Buffalo Bill's Wild West Show, had firmly implanted the image of the American cowboy in the minds and imaginations of people in the eastern United States and western Europe. Everyone with a little adventure in his spirit and a good imagination was dreaming of going west and becoming a cowboy.

The first years of the twentieth century brought moving pictures to the masses and everyone could see their favorite hero or heroine larger than life. This new medium was all that was needed to finish firing everyone's imagination.

By the turn of the century most real cowboys had, with the exception of a few to tend herds, been replaced by mass transport to the cattle markets via the railroads. The industrial revolution had taken hold and between the construction of machinery and those goods and services needed to make them work we had evolved into the industrial age and the era of the Robber Barons.

Trains had been followed in short order by motorcars and the legendary success of Henry Ford. Simultaneously two wheeled motor vehicles were as natural a development as was pie from apples in America, and so was the love of riding them.

All this was closely tied in with our emerging cowboy star phenomenon from the dime novels and movies. A person living in the cities could read about an American Hero and ride a motorcycle and suddenly he was Tom Mix. He was no longer seeing him on the screen or reading about Buck Taylor; he was there. Along with these times came a machine developed by four guys and called by a combination of their names that was to become as synonymous with the term American as riding the wide open spaces and loving apple pie. The machine was called the Harley-Davidson Motorcycle.

This motorcycle was to be the only American made machine left in production by the latter half of the twentieth century but it was not the only one ever produced in the States. We will discuss briefly the numerous others to come into existence and their demise then return to the evolution and legacy of the one and only Harley Davidson and its phenomenal and unprecedented success, which has led to a resurgence of motorcycles produced in America.

Now at the risk of shattering anyone's dream, I have to say that the Harley Davidson folks did not have the first motorcycle. In fact there were lots of them that came before. Most credit the one patented August 29, 1885 by Gottlieb Daimler as the first "serious and practical," gasoline powered motorbicycle. (Grolier) This bike had a 264 cc engine that produced a half horsepower at 700 rpm. This machine also had training wheels.

According to the Grolier Encyclopedia, Daimler used the four stroke concept developed by Nikolaus A. Otto for the engine design. Daimler decided that this was not a practical means of transportation and went on to develop cars which evolved into the Mercedes Benz of today. I am told that Daimler's first bike caught fire on it's maiden voyage.

The Daimler was not the first because a British design was patented in 1884 by a man named Edward Butler.

Grolier's Encyclopedia also credits British motorcycle manufacturers for the development of such features as steel chain drives, friction clutches, fuel injection, shaft drives, multigear transmissions, telescopic suspension, overhead cams/valves, and disk brakes. All of these innovations, which have only become standard in the latter twentieth century, were developed from 1900 to 1918.

This first Daimler was not, however, the very first motorcycle. The first ones were steam powered and the first documented one was built right here in the USA around 1865-69. This machine was built by a man named S. H. Roper roughly the same time as the French came out with a Perreaux steam engine fitted to a Michaux Velocipede. Both the American and French machines were dubbed as "Boneshakers" and examples can be seen at the Smithsonian Institution, and in France at the Robert Grandseigne Collection.

Only pictures exist from times previous to these machines being developed, but it is likely that since steam powered carriages were in use in the 1820s perhaps a motorcycle was as well. An 1831 picture had too much accurate detail to believe that the artist had not drawn his vehicles in the painting from life.

The first actual picture of the concept of motorcycling was seen in an 1818 cartoon and called a *"Velocipedraisiavaporianna."* Try saying that after two plates of barbeque and a six-pack. Supposedly this contraption was based on the hobby-horses of the time and was tried out April 5,1818, in the Luxembourg Gardens in Paris after being developed in Germany. No one knows whether it actually was built or if it even ran.

A man from Philadelphia, L. D. Copeland, constructed a motorcycle the same year as Daimler. (Olyslager, 4) This machine was an <u>American Star</u> bicycle fitted with a steam engine.

Trike fans will be happy to know that the first motorcycles were tricycles. There are references to "several steam-propelled tricycles produced from the 18th century onwards, but reliable records of these pioneers are virtually non-existent." (4)

Copeland is credited with producing the first production run with a steam powered tricycle. It was reliable enough that a run of about 200 were successfully manufactured.

Some steam powered motorcycles were still constructed into the 1900's, such as the Barr Steam Motorcycle, constructed in Middletown, Ohio. Its engine had a boiler made from a 75 foot pipe 1/4" in diameter and fired by kerosene.

According to C. F. Caunter in his book, <u>Motorcycles A Technical History</u>, the first commercial production of motorcycles was by the Hildbrand brothers:

> What was perhaps the first internal-combustion-engined motorcycle to be produced and sold commercially was designed by the Hildebrand brothers, Henry and Wilhelm, of Munich. In 1892, with the assistance of Alois Wolfmuller and his mechanic, Hans Greisenhof, they made a small two-

117

stroke petrol engine, and in the following year they produced a twin-engine four-stroke horizontal petrol engine. This was at first fitted into a safety pedal bicycle, but as this proved to be too weak, a specially designed machine was evolved which they called a "motorcycle" ("motorrad"), thus originating the name by which this form of vehicle has since become known. This design proved to be sufficiently practical to warrant a comparatively large production in both France and Germany. (5)

It seems that motorcycles received a bad press from the very start. In addition to a hostile press, public opinion, "held the motorcycle to be dangerous, dirty, and noisy, without considering that it was also, like the motorcar, a social development of considerable potential utility." (28)

On a humorous note, the early 1900's produced a British NUT motorcycle which featured a JAP V-twin engine. See, there' nothing new under the Sun.

The Encyclopedia Of The Motorcycle lists, as of its publication date in 1995, 180 motorcycles confirmed as made in the United States, with 158 additional ones listed as unconfirmed. That is a lot of motor companies.

The world of motorcycles in America has been a colorful one. In the United States as in Europe motorcycles seemed to get a bad rap but hung in tenaciously for quite some time before being eliminated down to one marque. Harley-Davidson.

Based on notoriety and existing records it seems as if there were four brands from the start, which dominated in popularity. These were respectively Excelsior, Harley-Davidson, Henderson, and Indian.

There were many many others, however and some had quite interesting names and were built almost everywhere. Some of the more interesting examples of company names are the Badger, Duck, Doodlebug, Eagle and Greyhound, are taken from the animal kingdom. Some names are kind of imaginative also like Puddlejumper, Ner-A-Car, the Whipple for soft toilet paper fans, and my particular favorite, the Flying Merkle. Between 1911 and 1920, TV sets, stereos, and lawnmower engines were predated by Briggs & Stratton and Montgomery Ward motorcycles. Sears also had a motorcycle believed to be manufactured for them by the

Excelsior Cycle Company. (Not the Excelsior Supply Company) Some of the more outrageous motorcycles were the car/motorcycle combinations such as the Bi-Car in 1911 and the V8 powered Bi-Auto-Go in 1913. This experiment in massive power on two-wheels was never put into production. In 1990, however, the Boss Hoss went into production with a V8 powered bike which worked well and, as of this writing, is still in production. Many of these machines are seen on the road today and are at all of the major rallies.

The corker of them all has to be the Militaire, manufactured from 1911 to 1919. This machine was intended for military use and even the most seasoned antique cycle aficionado might just shake his or her head at the sight of this bike. It looks like a stripped down Massey-Ferguson tractor, with two Model-T Ford wheels fore and aft, and handlebars. For the coup de grace this motorcycle (and I use the term loosely) had training wheels and wooden spoked main wheels.

Just a year after the turn of the century began what was to become the legacy and symbols of the American spirit. These would be the motorcycles of choice that would transport our entity in the form of millions of two wheeled riders across the American landscape. In 1901 George Hendee and Oscar Hedstrom joined forces to began the Indian Motorcycle company.

Two years later two other young men would join together to build a motorcycle. They were William S. Harley and Arthur Davidson. These two best friends were soon joined by Davidson's brothers Walter and William and the Harley-Davidson company was born.

Between the Indian and the Harley-Davidson America was to realize a dream of mobility for which its spirit had thirsted since the first boat of colonists landed. Motor cars were being invented and developed simultaneously but they were not quite the same. Cars did not provide the independence and the connection with nature. Horses provided the free feeling, as did bicycles, but something was lacking. With the motorcycles came a feeling of power and control not possible with horses and bicycles. Combined with the sense of freedom, there became a connection and a lifestyle between man and the machine. That connection remains today and is still the primary reason men (and women) ride.

Indian and Harley-Davidson quickly established themselves as the major machines to have. Even though many other makes would be developed there wasn't that intangible something which captured the imagination and heart of those filled with the American spirit.

Four years later another would be designed and step up to take its place in line with the other two big bikes. This would be the Excelsior manufactured in Chicago. Although started by the Excelsior Supply Company, by 1911 the motorcycle was bought by the bicycle manufacturer Ignatz Schwinn.

In the interim another machine, manufactured in 1912 in Detroit by Tom and Bill Henderson, made its debut. By 1917 this company would also be bought by Schwinn.

Within two years the Henderson brothers left Schwinn, moved to Philadelphia, and designed a new high performance bike called the Ace.

The Ace was a four cylinder machine and designed similar to the Henderson and was successful in concept and production. Success was not to be for the Henderson brothers. By 1922 Bill had been killed in a motorcycle accident and by 1924 the company was decimated financially. Michigan Motors continued with a limited production of the machines for a couple of years and in 1927 Indian bought the rights and used the design for their four cylinder model. As soon as the Ace machines were sold out Indian redesigned the entire motorcycle and in 1929 released the model 402 for a whopping $445.00. (I wonder if I could find a few still around for that price.)

Harley-Davidson had been steadily growing as had the Indian and the Schwinn machines Excelsior and Henderson. Sometimes known as the "Big Three", these companies dominated the motorcycle market in the States and their future should have been bright.

The three companies had made many milestones over the years, winning races, developing better and faster engines, and improving the frames and suspension systems. A rivalry had developed which was initially a friendly competition but would have a cutthroat element from time-to-time. Schwinn made a major coup, by bypassing the bidding process, to make a deal under the table with the California Highway Patrol. All three companies had been planning to bid, and this act by Schwinn left a surprised Indian and Harley-Davidson smarting.

Disaster struck in 1929 with the great depression and the motorcycle business like everything else plummeted. Most makes went out of business entirely and the "Big Three" suffered but managed to hang on to survival. Indian seemed to suffer with greater difficulties than Harley-Davidson. All were hurt but mistakes and ineptitude in the executive office at Indian seemed to doom the company. According to author Harry V. Sucher, 1930 brought resuscitation in the form of two men. Hap Alzina was generating an infusion of money on the West Coast and then E. Paul du Pont in the East bought controlling interest in the company. For the time being Indian was saved.

1931 would be a year for surprise in the whole world of U.S. motorcycle production. The industry was shocked when Schwinn announced that his company was leaving the motorcycle business and the Excelsiors and Hendersons would be no more. This left Indian and Harley-Davidson alone to battle for supremacy.

On a side note, the engine for what was to be one of the most popular airplanes ever built, the Piper Cub, was developed in a corner of the Indian plant.

The 30s and 40s saw Indian enjoy a lot of notoriety through movies and promotion by Indian dealer, Floyd Clymer. The H-D brand also received some significant promotional benefits during that time from the film industry.

World War II would provide a market for both Harley-Davidson and Indian and the factories geared up for wartime production. Harley-Davidson had a clear advantage having not suffered the amount of damages as did Indian during the depression. A large French order for 5000 Indian bikes was to help greatly and a chance to develop shaft drive cycles for the military seemed to make for good things to come. Harley-Davidson was also attempting to develop a shaft drive version but shaft drive orders were canceled for both companies when the Willis Jeep was developed. This agile utility vehicle with a much better ability for getting into places almost inaccessible by motorcycles, and the greater passenger and load capabilities, became the prefered production choice.

Both companies would survive past the war. Harley-Davidson on its own and Indian through a series of ill-fated attempts to get the company back to its former popularity and sales figures.

In 1945 du Pont sold the company to Ralph Rogers and the new owner began making valiant attempts to get the floundering company up to its former position in the industry. Between wrong directions and innovations before their time, and plain old mistakes Indian was not to make the cut. Rogers tried everything, including a grab at the practicality of British designs with a transfusion of English money. Nothing Indian attempted worked as anything but a Band-Aid fix. Bad decisions and just plain old bad luck choked the life from the company and in 1953 the last chief sang his death chant. In the words of Tod Rafferty from his book on the history of the Indian motorcycle:

> These were perhaps the most American of motorcycles. To the uninitiated, Indians and Harley-Davidson were indistinguishable, both just big V-twin-powered machines with few differences. Indian enthusiasts, you may be sure, do not feel that way. The indefinable element of distinction, some unique sign of character or personality. Not, in other words, just another motorcycle.
>
> Of course all genuine enthusiasts feel the same way about their favorite rides. Indian riders simply display their allegiance with a bit more intensity, hold the banner a little higher, and demonstrate the unwavering devotion of the true believer.
>
> Indian, after all, was America's Pioneer Motorcycle for more than fifty years. And will remain so forever. Amen.

Post war America was good ground for Harley-Davidson. The Motor Company had the factory facility and infrastructure to take advantage of the country's need for bikes. The American spirit had come home from war and had an itch for freedom to satisfy. After all they had just won the war of all wars to free the world. According to the book, 1903-1993 Harley-Davidson Historical Overview, 1948 was a banner year for the company. The most sales in forty five years and changes were happening at a fast pace. Bigger engines and improvements in other areas and a changing of the guard marked the progress of the company. The last of the original founders died in 1950 leaving a "new generation of Harleys and Davidsons" (72) to run the Motor Company.

By 1954 the company found itself the only survivor from what had been an incredible number of companies manufacturing motorcycles in America since the turn of the century.

The 50s and 60s were a magical era for America and in spite of the negative image left on the American public by the movie the Wild One, Americans took to the road in droves. Many of them on Harleys.

The factory invested in fiberglass by opening the Tomahawk plant and the company came out with such new machines as scooters with automatic transmissions and golf carts.

In the early to mid 60s Willie G. Davidson joined the company as design director, land speed records were set, and Harley-Davidsons started being equipped with electric starters.

In addition to electric starters, the company went public in 1965. By 1969 it had merged with the American Machine and Foundry Company, AMF (yes indeed, bowling pins and fishing rods) and began rapid expansion.

The assembly plant was opened in York, Pennsylvania where the production run could take advantage of a huge overhead conveyor system for assembly. There is a wonderful museum there and tours are a regular feature.

In June 1981 a group of company executives bought the company back from AMF and the Motor Company was once again privately held. The motorcycle market was deluged with imports, mostly from Japan, in 1982. This situation was in a declining market prompting the company to petition the ITC to provide relief in the form of tariffs on imported machines of 700cc or larger. The following year, President Reagan imposed five years of additional tariffs on Japanese bikes with engines over 700cc.

The Harley Owners Group (HOG) was formed in 1983 to involve riders more closely with the company and its dealers. Today this organization is world wide and is the largest motorcycle club in the world.

1985 found the company sponsoring more charity events raising $250,000.00 for restoration of the Statue Of Liberty and the introduction of the 883 Sportster to reenter the under 1000cc class of bike.

In 1986 the company went public once again in order to raise capital and in a modern day, only in America, Cinderella story, began a meteoric rise unparalleled in our country's history.

New models and innovations and machines which appreciate almost on the showroom floor have been the hallmark of the Harley-Davidson legacy in the 90s. Names such as Fat Boy, Softail, and Evolution became household words. People who would have never considered riding at an earlier era were now fashionable only if they had a "Harley" and the popularity was so great that commercials which would have considered it the kiss of death to have a reference to Bikers in them now felt that they had to show them. (a sample list is in chapter 2)

In the movie industry even robotic heroes from the distant future have to ride a Harley-Davidson while they are here. It used to be that only the bad guys would have been the ones on bikes.

The transition from the 80s to the 90s found Harley-Davidson number one in America and by the middle of the decade second only to Honda world wide. A breakdown of the statistics demonstrates the position of the company half way through this decade and also its position as we finish the century.

Honda Motorcycles led the United States and the World in 1995-96 with a 29.3% market share. At the end of its fiscal year the company had net sales of 5.5 billion dollars selling 189,000 new motorcycles in the United States with their dealers retailing 168,500. The rest were kept as inventory. These sales generated 614 million dollars in US sales of motorcycles and related products. The factory sponsored motorcycling organization, Honda Rider Club, had 120,000 members in the United States in 1996 and by 1999 has grown to 130,000.

Harley-Davidson's second place market share, and total net sales in 1996 of 1.53 billion dollars, places these two well ahead of all other competition. Harley-Davidsons are the most popular, however, and the factory sponsored club, Harley Owners Group (HOG), had 325,000 members in 940 chapters by the end of 1996 and now has 450,000 members in 1100 chapters.

The next closest competitor was Yamaha, with a 15.2% share of the pie.

How does this translate into a realistic market example? The subject itself is immensely popular and if we examine the market beyond just motorcycles and riders then the market becomes readily apparent.

Looking beneath the surface figures of the motorcycle market we see a slightly different picture than meets the eye at first glance. Although the Harley-Davidson share is only second place there are some very important reasons for the lower numbers. While Harley-Davidsons are the most popular motorcycles in the world, new ones can also be very hard to get, and the ones obtainable are as expensive as some very luxurious cars once were. They can sometimes cost in the twenty thousand dollar range for the higher end machines. Their popularity is so great that almost all of the foreign competitors have introduced model lines that are mirror images of Harley designs. In many cases the engines have been redesigned or cosmetically altered to resemble the Harley-Davidson's familiar V-Twin. Even to the extent, in some cases, of discontinuing good engine designs in favor of a Harley look-alike. This imitation led to attempts by some makes to develop devices to make their machines emulate the distinct Harley-Davidson sound. Harley responded by filing for patent rights on the sound in 1995 to stop the imitators.

The wait for a new Harley-Davidson has been known to take from nine to fourteen months for delivery after a purchase deposit is placed. Almost every Harley model is sold before it can roll off the assembly line. This sales dilemma has driven the used market through the roof, with used models selling for higher prices than new ones in some cases. The overseas used market will take almost any Harley, of any year, and in almost any condition. To meet the demand for new machines the factory is expanding existing assembly numbers and building additional facilities.

Returning to numbers beyond the 3.9 million motorcycles in the US, figures for motorcycle riders in America were 31,000,000 as of 1994 statistics compiled by the Motorcycle Industry Council, Inc. in Irvine, California. This figure includes owners, passengers, and riders who use other people's machines. There is no means of tallying the fans and buffs who collect motorcycle paraphernalia and memorabilia. This is one area where market sales are targeted.

Harley-Davidson's 1.531 billion in sales includes 90.7 million in general merchandise for 1996 and 31.1 million in trademark licensed items. These two categories are in addition to sales of motorcycles, parts, and accessories. The company estimates five to ten million in lost sales due to unauthorized Harley oriented merchandise and products sporting counterfeit Harley-Davidson logos.

The popularity of the American Biker image has spread to such a high level that there are stores and boutiques that specialize in Harley-Davidson items and collectibles. These stores thrive in high-rent locations such as major malls, and many motorcycle dealers have opened satellite stores which sell only motor clothes and general merchandise. Even major chains such as Wal-Mart now carry Harley-Davidson licensed clothing.

In addition to the licensed Harley products, most major department stores and other mall shops carry biker image merchandise from imitation biker leather jackets to belts and buckles. The list goes on and includes chain wallets, boots, and tee-shirts with all the familiar biker symbols and sayings. There is now a shirt for real bikers that says, "I have a Harley-Davidson, not just a tee-shirt." There is nowhere in the United States where you aren't likely to see a number of people who aren't riders, or at least Harley Riders, wearing a Harley or biker type shirt or sporting a decal or bumper sticker.

There are millions more wannabes, collectors, and the merely curious, than there are motorcycle riders. This secondary market, which is considerably larger than the primary market of actual motorcyclists, ultimately, may well be the area of greatest revenue from bandanas to book sales. Those are the millions who ride up and down the streets to look and wish during the rallies. They are the people who buy jackets, wallets, belt buckles, and tee-shirts and keep those boutiques and mall stores in the black ink as well as black leather.

There is a third, smaller but growing, European market as evidenced by the huge numbers of motorcyclists over there who buy Harleys at much higher prices than their American counterparts. Many work overtime all year so that they can vacation with their bikes touring the States and attending the big rallies. Many thousands ride other makes, but dress the part to look like American bikers.

It is not possible yet to have the 1999 and end of the millennium figures but financially and demographically a breakdown of the Motor Company's success as of the last annual report is as follows.

In 1997 the net sales rose from the 1.531 figure to 1.763, and for 1998 increased to 2.064 approximately. General merchandise rose over the two year period to 95.1 and 114.5 respectively. No current data was available for trademark licensing at this time but with the increase in popularity of motorcycling paraphernalia it could be expected to have increased proportionately along with the other categories.

Honda rose from a total motorcycle revenue of 5.5 billion to 5.814. which is a little over a quarter billion increase but a little less than Harley-Davidson's figures during the same period. All financial information here is taken from the annual reports of Harley-Davidson Motor Company, American Honda Motor Company, and the Motorcycle Industry Council.

No one can deny that the enormous and unprecedented popularity and sales of Harley-Davidson and the hunger for more bikes than are available has paved the way for the future. There is a new order in America and all driven by the American spirit. The 90s have given birth to new chic terminology and new lifestyles, and a tremendous growth of new motorcycle companies.

Where there was once only one name to remember, unless you were speaking of antiques or imports, now there are many. Some are based on custom Harley similar designs and some are new from the tires up and some which were formerly imported are now manufactured over here with American workers. Some as it happens are made here now and imported back to where they were originally produced.

Among the ones similar in appearance to Harley-Davidsons are a number of marques all made here in the United States. Each is somewhat different and is carving its niche in the market.

Not the least of these is Honda, with several models manufactured right here in the USA. American Honda Motor Company is located in Torrance, California, and the manufacturing plant for their motorcycles is in Marysville, Ohio. This plant opened in 1979 and the first day accomplished the task of building 10 motorcycles. In July 1996 the plant had built its one millionth Honda in America.

Honda's attachment to America and motorcycling goes back to Mr. Honda himself. Honda's success story is the American dream. A fairly poor boy makes one product and grows from that to be a giant in industry. Mike Corbin did that in the motorcycle industry and so did Honda before him and he had the dream while still in Japan.

Starting at age 29 in 1935, Soichiro Honda was involved with piston rings and from that point his involvement in motor technology grew.

He had already worked in automotive repair by age 15, and by 17 owned a Harley-Davidson. His love of motorcycles led him later to acquire an Indian. He loved building race cars and he opened his own repair shop for automobiles and motorcycles.

Honda was into casting wheel spokes and piston rings and developed a company which manufactured piston rings for cars, motorcycles and airplanes. This was the Tokai Seiki Company, Ltd.

At the end of W. W. II Honda sold everything to Toyota and after taking a year off came back to establish the Honda Technical Research laboratory. This new enterprise converted bicycles to motorized transportation using war surplus Tohatsu and Mikuni generator motors. (so the carburetor on my bike started out as the first Honda motor)

This new company became the first Honda Motor Company and began life in a 12 x 18 foot shed with 13 employees. The new company was joined by Takeo Fujisawa who's innovations coupled with Honda himself created the vast Honda empire.

Honda's dream was the American Dream, that is where he was headed, and headed there with a motorcycle by the same name. In 1955 Honda became the largest motorcycle manufacturer in Japan and by 1959 was the biggest in the world. Honda's dream was *America* and he set about to make it come true. Ignoring warnings that the United States would be a poor market and knowing he would have to overcome the stigma of "made in Japan" he came here anyway. He brought a motorcycle over here which had a look like a miniature Harley with dresser type fenders and a 300cc engine. Honda and Fujisawa knew that it would not compete with the big bore motorcycles already here and that if they reached acceptance in the US they could build on that. Once accepted in the States, the international market would be an easier nut to crack. By the end of 1959 American Honda had 15 dealers and sold 1,732 motorcycles. At the close of 1960 the company had 74 dealers and climbing. September 1979 saw Soichiro Honda's American dream come to fruition. Honda motorcycles made and sold in America.

At the close of the century and the millennium this poor boy from a far away land, has a success story which is one of the most significant achievements in the 20th century, and Honda's American plants today employ close to 7500 people, turn out more than 1.5 million units and export from America to over 60 countries around the world.

As the century closes some radical changes exist in the motorcycle industry. The popularity and success of Harley-Davidson has given inspiration, and at least indirectly, the birth of a whole new phase in motorcycle manufacturing over here in the colonies. A number of new marques have sprouted and appear to be flourishing.

A description and history of the more well known, and most similar to Harley-Davidson, motorcycle companies is in order here. They are presented in alphabetical order so as to show no partiality.

In as much as these manufacturers are fairly new there is not the lengthy historical documentation as is available for marques like Indian and Harley.

Almost all of these are using a variation of engines developed by S&S Cycle of Viola, Wisconsin. All of these companies seem to be using very fine parts and accessories and are dependable in workmanship and all are American made.

First on the list is *American Eagle* of Hollister, California. Located on Technology Parkway across from Corbin Saddles, this company, founded in 1995 offers a variety of models with names like Maverick and Mirage. The plant is spacious and clean and has an assembly room of very large and clean proportions. There is a showroom with displays and it's well worth a visit if you are in the Hollister area.

American Iron Horse of Fort Worth, Texas, is a company spoken highly of by some of the other makes. They build a variety of models including a new touring bike. Model names reflect the biker image with titles of Slammer, Outlaw, and Bandit among the six they offer. In business since 1996, the company has an impressive catalog of apparel and sports wear available.

Big Dog Motorcycles of Wichita, Kansas, has been in exist-

129

ence since 1994. Founder, Sheldon Coleman, (of camping gear fame) began the company and named it after a rock band he was once part of called Dewy and the Big Dogs. Although there was a possibility of a trademark problem with similar named companies, all was smooth sailing and Big Dog came to be, after requests that he build a couple of custom bikes for friends.

After opening in 1994 the company did well and was forced to expand to larger digs. They build a good product and the models offered sell well. Each bike is custom constructed to the customer's specifications and guaranteed delivery within 60 days. According to Rick McCrary, everything is either designed or built in house, or by the best builders in the industry. In an interview he said each bike is an, "...individualized performance oriented motorcycle, custom built to compete in today's world."

The company is working on a bike targeted for women for the year 2000 models. This will not be just a lowered men's machine but one designed from the ground up for women riders.

The facility now has 110 employees and has spread into six buildings. Big Dog spokesperson Willie Shew said, "Since day one our growth has been far beyond our expectations. We have now outgrown the present facilities, but the problem is there is no building here in the middle of town big enough to hold us. We might end up in the outskirts of town with a new building."

Bourget's Cycle in Phoenix, Arizona is a bird, or bike, of a different color. With patented frame designs, one of which uses the frame as an oil tank, and in house wheel manufacture this company is at least innovative. Roger Bourget started the shop, June, 1993 in a three car garage. At the start he was only able to turn out a couple of bikes a month, then went to a couple a week. They are at a comfortable, and maintainable, level of six per week with 90% sold through dealers.

Production now is out of a 15,000 square foot building owned by the company, has a building at Sturgis, and is building one in Daytona. Except for shows and events Bourget's no longer advertises, preferring instead to use word of mouth or repeat business. Brigitte Bourget, wife of the owner, says they are, "a little bit wild - a little bit different."

130

California Motorcycle Company in Gilroy, California, has one of the most impressive reputations in the industry. In addition they have recently merged with Indian and have produced the special 1999 Limited Edition Indian Chief. While the new Indian looks like an old one somewhat, due to the classic Indian fender skirts, the rest of the bike is state of the art in accepted performance equipment. From Progressive Suspension to the Corbin Saddle it promises to be a fun machine to ride. Company President Murray Smith says, "We had no interest in creating a replica - we wanted to create a bike for the new century." The 1999 Limited Edition has a look of the old Chief with skirted fenders and all but with the low chassis, and S&S engine, the bike is strictly 'Now' and high-tech. A good marriage of classic style and the best of new. Word has it that there is an all new specifically Indian engine in store for 2000 and beyond.

California Cycles has been known for quite a few years now as a top-of-the-line builder. Usually a new machine from their shop takes six weeks or less with full dealer customer support. Motorcycle Industry News described them as the most efficient operation they'd seen. Most well known for custom bikes like the replicas of the Captain America bike in Easy Rider, they have the humorous slogan, "You can have the bike of your dreams — without the pile of parts in your garage."

New location, new merger, and new Indian, what a combination!

In the spirit of the West, is *Classic Motor Works'* line of motorcycles. Located on, wouldn't-ya-know-it, Deadwood Avenue, in Rapid City, South Dakota, this company has been around for about seven years. Originally a company which manufactured custom parts, they now have a production line of bikes.

Riders who are accustomed to doing their own modifications are familiar with this company's products, such as fenders, taillights, dashes, and side covers, and have been purchasing them through mail order houses such as J&P Cycles for several years.

With the slogan, "American Owned, American Made, American Parts", Classic has for the last two years expanded to building custom bikes and now has a base model line of ten machines. The manager, Ron Zufall, chuckles and proudly says, "And all under one roof."

One roof is right. The company is nestled at the entrance to the Black Hills, in an impressive expanse of continuous shop space, which actually houses six separate business entities under the umbrella of Classic Motor Works. Three of them are devoted entirely to motorcycles and parts. The three others are automotive in nature, and this takes us to the earliest beginnings of Classic Motor Works in a story which could rightfully be titled *From Hot Rocks To Hot Rods*.

The Classic story begins with Ron's wife Rebecca, to whom Ron gives the credit for being the driving force and major influence over the business.

Known to her family and friends as Becky, her interest dates back to her college days some 20 years ago. Becky is the daughter of Dr. Spencer Macy who was a prominent physicist and mathematician, and was with the School Of Mines in Rapid City. Later he would work for Delco, which required travel all over the US. The family ended up finally in California.

Ron and Becky met in 1975 in Santa Barbara, where she was earning a degree in geology. She was attending UCSB and working a variety of mechanically oriented jobs to pay her way through college.

Among the variety of temporary occupations in which this energetic lady became proficient was the printing industry where she was a bindery operator and mechanic. Another was construction which is where Ron enters the picture. He owned a construction company, was advertising for workers, and Becky applied for a construction job.

Ron says Becky is very natural and her own person, and taking no passive position. He explains, "Rebecca has always managed to step outside her gender stereotype and do it with ease. She can stand her ground, make her point, and not be abrasive about it."

She had won several awards and is one of the few women to become an ASE (Automotive Service Excellence) Master Technician. This means she is certified on all systems.

Ron's story is a bit different. He is a "child of the 60's", who was raised in Southern California, and received his education through a combination of classes at Pasadena City College and Santa Barbara Community College. He even had a brief attendance at UCSB. The curriculum ranged from psychology to marine technology.

He worked in painting and home building to support himself and pay for his education and liked the work, so there he stayed.

Construction always had the stress of being feast or famine and Ron had an artistic side and an interest in custom hot rod cars with his main drive being the challenge of designing and creating and restoration. Once teamed with Rebecca the result of being where they are today was a natural evolution.

Eventually they quit the construction business and moved to Becky's hometown of Rapid City and into the automotive world. Starting with just a mechanic shop, they quickly progressed to custom assembling and restoration, and became nationally known in the automotive field. A love for motorcycles led to creating bike parts and then evolved into custom bikes.

The transition from parts to whole bikes was over a short two year period and incorporated the techniques used in the automotive industry. Ron coupled fiberglass and metal refinishing techniques that he developed with his head R&D person Pete Haines to complement PPG's global system. The company's system is set up for a complete and even proper cure. The facility will maintain a climate controlled atmosphere at 80 degrees, even in 20 degree below South Dakota weather.

Classic Motor Works has grown since its concept seven years ago to a team of four with 18 additional employees. Jerry C. Heberlein began by working with Ron in construction and after Ron left for automotive pursuits, decided to join the husband and wife team about a year later. Jerry brought with him to the CMW table a great deal of business expertise and local interest.

The team of three was recently joined by Ron Plender who had over 20 years with Harley-Davidson Motor Company before coming over to Classic. The company hierarchy from the top is Jerry functioning as CEO, Rebecca as Vice President, and Ron managing the business. With Ron Plender coming on board

133

there will be some restructuring and Ron Zufall will move entirely into research and development. Plender will assume Zufall's position as manager.

The company has a somewhat different philosophy than some of their contemporaries. Rather than taking a shot at Milwaukee, they see themselves working in a more additive vein. Says Ron, "The reality is that Harley has been through several battles and come out strong and respectable. If it hadn't done its job and done it well, we wouldn't be here. None of us would be." They will always have a hard-core loyal group of buyers. Ron sees CMW as specializing in taking the customer from stock factory options to full custom, giving the client a variety of choices and design input from start to completion. All this at a price affordable to the typical motorcycle buyer in today's market.

All-in-all, Classic Motor Works has a good background, facility, and team which should make for a great future.

Way down yonder in Luzianne just a wee bit no'th of Nawlins is the town of Abita Springs which just happens to be the home of *Confederate Motorcycles*. A bit different in looks and theory from the usual, this bike company is out to do everything to the nines. With 1999 model names like America and Hellcat this company with its radical appearing machines may be out to change the face of motorcycling.

Formed in 1991 Confederate was located early on in the San Francisco area but in 1994 relocated to Baton Rouge. Much of the first four years was development and perfecting design of the motorcycles and their performance features. Company objectives were to perfect a motorcycle of immense strength and durability in the chassis which would handle well and produce an inordinate amount of power to the rear wheel. This they achieved.

The frames on these motorcycles are not only of superior strength but double as the oil tank. Holding six quarts this tank configuration allows more room to nestle the seat low in the frame. The company's mission statement dedicates the intention to stay in this field and produce motorcycles of uncompromised and unparalled quality and design.

134

For a new twist on the old there is *Panzer Motorcycle Works* in Canon City, Colorado. This manufacturer states that it is not trying to compete with the other companies making bikes similar in appearance to Harley-Davidsons. The Panzer bike is a real hardtail and sports the familiar Panhead valve covers to give the look of an era gone by. The reliability of the machine is much better than the original in as much as all of the components on the bike are the latest state of the art technology.

Titan Motorcycles are also located in Phoenix, Arizona and have established quite a record for sales and quality. Advertising that they were born from the cult of the big all-American v-Twins, they have made their presence known throughout the industry and the world.

Titan dealerships began in 1994 and are now located in several countries including Japan and Australia. Claiming symbolic kinship to the spirit of the modern American West, the company was started with the father and son team of Frank and Patrick Keery. Patrick was possessed with a vision of producing the finest machine possible and equipped with no less than the finest components to be found in the industry. This was to be a dream they would make a reality in the short space of five years.

The Titan philosophy is simple. One man - one bike. In other words the tech who starts the assembly is the one who takes it through until it rolls out of the factory. This concept means that the likelihood of pride in workmanship will be stronger than if an assembly line person just stands and bolts on the same part daily. Titan outgrew the original digs and moved into a new 60,000 square foot facility in 1998. What began as six bikes has grown to become a sales volume which will reach 2500 this year.

Bikers Dream Inc. is a manufacturer, distributor and retailer of *Ultra Cycles*, quality-built American heavyweight cruiser motorcycles. Headquarters and manufacturing operations are located in Mira Loma, California in a new 56,000 square foot complex. Chairman and CEO of Bikers Dream, Herm Roseman, has said, "The manufacturing and headquarters complex provides the ability to more than quadruple our previous production capacity to meet the high demand for our Ultra Cycles brand of heavyweight motorcycles." The move will also provide facilities to support the launch of their new e-commerce web site."

The company has announced an alliance with Easyriders, Inc. and, coupled with Easyriders, they will have access to a large percent of the market in the motorcycle field. Easyriders on the other hand will have access to the Bikers Dream outlets to distribute products and services they offer, including an extensive clothing and accessories line. The combined efforts will double the size of outlets.

In addition Ultra Cycles have signed an agreement with Speedvision and as such was a TV sponsor of the annual Kyle Petty Charity Ride for 1999. This alliance is expected to work out a multi-faceted marketing program to advertise and build a greater awareness of Ultra Cycles.

Heading back Northeast from the sunny climes of Arizona and California takes us into Minnesota and a short hop from Milwaukee to find two entirely new production machines stepping into the market to take their share.

Minneapolis based Polaris hit the road in July of 1998 with the *Victory Cycle*. Manufacturing of the bikes is in Spirit Lake, Iowa, and Osceola, Wisconsin, and thus far have shipped over two thousand bikes to its network of dealers. They have around 300 dealers and goals for 1999 are to ship 5000 before years end.

Polaris feels that, with the infrastructure and manufacturing facilities already in place, the company will have no problem meeting the market demand for the tens of thousands of bikes expected to sell. Plans are for expansion into the international market as well as the North American motorcycle arena.

The parent company, Polaris, is the largest snowmobile manufacturer in the world and one of the largest makers of personal watercraft and ATV's in the US.

Polaris has an impressive legacy, with its products commanding a fanatical loyalty from the owners of their recreational machines. The company feels that motorcycles were the logical next venture after snowmobiles, ATVs and watercraft. (could a sport airplane be next?)

The company history goes back to 1954 with the invention of its the snowmobile by Edgar and Allan Hetteen and

David Johnson to make it possible for trappers, and others working outside, to get around during the harsh Minnesota winter months.

Initially the company was let by Edgar with Allan taking over in 1960. Allan carried the leadership of the company for eight years, then sold it to Textron in 1968. In a similar vein and preceding Harley-Davidson's history, Polaris was bought back and turned into a super successful company by a group of investors led by W. Hall Wendel Jr.

Now Polaris has entered the lucrative American motorcycle market. They were smart in the testing and examined most of the competition to find their weaknesses and try to eliminate them in the Victory. They put the bike on the road as early as possible and proved with the 1999 Kyle Petty Celebrity Ride, that the machine could go across America. That is the way to convince the average American motorcyclist that a machine will go the distance. Just do it. It is precisely the way the big three did it in the early 20th century with riders like Cannonball Baker.

In the 45 years since going into production the Polaris company has established a solid reputation in the production of some of the finest quality products in its field. Who knows where that field will end? From the brink of bakruptcy to tremendous success over the past 20 years is an prestigious record so they must be doing things right and now have taken a leap of faith with the production of the Victory motorcycle.

Whether it is short lived or lasts a hundred years as Harley-Davidson is about to do in 2003, the Victory by Polaris will go into the 21st century, and the history books, as the first American mass production motorcycle since the demise of the Mustang in 1965. An impressive feat to say the least.

The long awaited entry of Minnesota based *Excelsior-Henderson* into the market is a milestone in the motorcycle world. With a new factory and, like Indian, this is a resurrection of a grand old name in the industry. This new/old marque brings back to life in a new form, the only cycles to seriously challenge Harley-Davidson and Indian in those glory years before the depression. Affectionately known as "The Big Three", these companies dominated big bike performance and sales. This would be the case until out of the blue, the face of the motorcycle business in 1931 was to change, when without warning, Excelsior and Henderson were unceremoniously shut down. And then there were two.

There never seemed to be the camaraderie after that as the Great Depression had American industry in a dog-eat-dog rivalry for mere survival. Excelsior and Henderson would be followed twenty two years later as, a weary and worn down by corporate mistakes Indian, sadly died away.

Like Lazarus rising from the dead the names Excelsior and Henderson are alive again. This time not only owned by one company but attached to one motorcycle.

The original Excelsiors, Hendersons, and Indians had a lot of fairly big named riders in the colorful past of North American motorcycling. Henry Ford and Charles Lindbergh rode Hendersons, while Poncho Villa had an Indian. Not so typical people at best as motorcycling grew in spite of the general public's jaundiced eye and opinions.

The Hanlons, Dave, Jennie, and Dan, your not so typical Minnesota farm country folks, have launched Excelsior-Henderson with a big splash in the industry as well as a big spot on the rural Minnesota landscape.

The trio worked at assembling a viable business plan in the Fall of 1993 and incorporated before the end of the year. Putting their own money into the company to get started they looked for a name to be the marque. Nothing seemed to fit until discovering that the trademark on Excelsior had run out and the name was available. According to Dan Hanlon, "For us it was like finding the lost city of Atlantis. The name was exactly what they were looking for and had the nostalgic sound of history behind it. Excelsior-Henderson was born, or to be exact reborn.

The task of finding capital to really launch this endeavor was needed. Rejecting the loss of control which comes with venture capital, they set about finding investors which would be able to understand and identify what they were attempting, and the marketing of a new entrant into the world of motorcycles.

In the Spring of 1994 the Hanlons were able to move into offices and by 1997 the company went public. The three were able to make a great impression on the type of people needed to fund the company and get behind them and demonstrated that they, and their new enterprise, was a sound investment with a livable risk factor.

Once capitalized they began to acquire the management team and staff needed, to run such an undertaking. Pulling from many directions, within and outside the motorcycling industry, they surrounded themselves with an assembly of good people with expertise in the various areas of business necessary to control such a massive undertaking.

Working toward production of the machines, and a goal of taking advantage of the present trend of growing popularity in cruisers, the Minnesota threesome plans annual numbers of 20,000 by 2003. The company has also produced a full line of clothing and accessories with Jennie Hanlon heavily involved in design and function.

Having been successful businessmen in the first place, Dave and Dan knew well that you don't sell the steak, you sell the sizzle, and the sizzle sells the steak. Once the company was committed to going ahead, the Hanlons (which includes all three) began to turn the splash into a tidal wave of advertising and promotion. With magazine ads, billboards, and aerial banners, America has watched as the new company grew from a vision born in a hotel room in South Dakota to a state of the art manufacturing facility in Minnesota. A facility producing an all new, all American, machine of the roads.

Looking into the future, to quote a well worn phrase, is like looking through a glass darkly. It is not possible to know which companies will survive well into the 21st century and which will not. Only time will tell and time can be a benevolent benefactor and it can also be a cruel taskmaster.

It is entirely fitting, that, as this century comes to a close, those marques which were so much a part of the beginning of it, should have the breath of life breathed back into them once again.

The Long Riders - A Love Affair
With The Road

"I'm as free as the breeze and I ride where I please."
-Marty Robins-
Saddle Tramp

There are some of us who prefer the long ride and have developed an attachment for seeing the country this way. This chapter will give some insight into some of those individuals for whom two wheels and the wind in your face are necessary ingredients for the fulfillment of life.

Among those are Dorothy Schmidt who is the only woman, that I know personally, with as many miles on one motorcycle as myself, and my friend Fritz Voight, who may have crossed the US on a motorcycle more often than anyone else alive today. In addition readers of Easyriders Magazine will be familiar with the author of the regular feature, Rip's Run. Rip is featured here as is Malysa Wyse, of Titan Motorcycles, and Jim Trotta, The Ice Cream Man From Hell.

In this author's not so humble opinion, this is the only way left for anyone to really see America or get the feel of the open road in anything like the primitive setting or circumstance of those pioneers who preceded us. Possible but no longer practical, I suppose it could be done by horse or bicycle. However you couldn't cover as much of it.

The earliest record of anyone crossing the country on a motorcycle points to George A. Wyman, who Left San Francisco, May 16, 1903, on his way to New York City. This epic journey was the first motorized vehicle to successfully cross the continent.

I can only imagine the thrill of being the first man to do this feat. I must say that having crossed it a few times on two wheels, the thrill never goes away and grows stronger with the telling of it.

Most probably no one has done more long-distance record setting, than Erwin G. "Cannonball" Baker of Indianapolis, Indiana. He was called "Bake" by his closest friends.

He won his first big race as one of four competitors in the Ten Mile National Championship of 1909, which was the first race conducted on the site of the forthcoming Indianapolis Motor Speedway. In 1911, Baker won the July Fourth "Presidents Race" at Indianapolis, and afterwards received the personal congratulations of President William Howard Taft. Baker is the only known motorcycle racer to be afforded this honor.

Indian president George Hendee, hired Baker to conduct a goodwill tour of Cuba, Jamaica, and Panama in order to boost sales in the tropics. Baker ended up logging 14,000 miles of riding, and this was the first of many Indian assignments. For the next several years he would continue to complete many unwritten deals made over the handshakes of George Hendee and subsequent Indian negotiators.

In 1916, Baker completed an Australian tour for Hendee. After completing his run, the leather suit had become so dry and stiff that it had to be cut away from his body.

In 1917, at the Cincinnati Speedway Cannonball set a new 24-hour record of 1,534.75 miles over the board track, using an Indian Powerplus. Baker set many records and logged countless miles on a variety of bikes but mostly Indians.

Baker would make his last coast-to-coast ride in 1941 to test the viability of using one of the rotary engine designs in a light weight motorcycle. He is honored today with the running of the annual Cannonball Baker Sea To Shining Sea International Trophy Dash. This is an event which begins in New York City, and ends up in Long Beach, California. Several movies have been produced that were based upon this event including the Cannonball Run films starring Burt Reynolds.

RIP, as he is known to the public, is a journalist with Easy Riders Magazine living in California for the past forty years.

He was born in Florida, and grew up three blocks from the Everglades, which became a play ground to the area children. With nothing much happening in the area for recreation he and his playmates built air boats and swampbuggies. They played out in the Everglades and then on Saturday nights they would go to the stock car races which was a little track called Mesolee and it was the infancy of NASCAR. The thing to do on a Saturday night, was to go learn to drink beer and go with relatives so they could buy you a beer and you'd sit there and cheer the local folks on.

In high school RIP motored around on a '48 Indian, a yellow and black chief, that all the girls loved and wanted to ride. Said Rip, "I was very popular; you know how the attraction is with women and motorcycles so I got to get all the pretty girls and take them for rides."

Before becoming a journalist RIP had a shop and painted bikes, cars, appliances, etc. He ended up in California and eventually associated with Easy Riders.

Lou Kimzey, aka "Spider", Joe Teresi and Mel Blair were the original founders of Easy Rider Magazine, in 1971. Rip's involvement in Easy Rider began in 1976. RIPS RUN is a monthly magazine feature, the preparation for this article: Rip's been traveling one trip per month for thirteen years. RIP goes a lot of different places and likes to experience what is indigenous. If in Maine he eats lobster, and in Louisiana, Cajun food is called for.

When RIP retires he wants to work for the American Diabetes Association. June 13,1999, saw the second annual Rips Bad Ride, Bikers Against Diabetes. RIP has diabetes.

RIP has several Harley-Davidsons, but his 1988 FLHS is his favorite. RIP has named it, "Baby". His favorite places to ride are Western Montana and Baja, California. Earlier in 1999, he was in Phoenix, Arizona and had the privilege and honor of being a recipient of The Silver Spoke Award, which is a prestigious wall hanging plaque for the media. He received it for all the work he'd done for the biker nation.

RIP has by his own admission logged a million or so miles and advises riders and members of clubs alike to go and see America rather than just go to one place from one place. Rip says, "Go to Montana, Washington State, The Rockies, Denver, Maine, and New England... Go see it!" This was his opening and closing theme in Phoenix and this author agrees with him.

Way up north in Minnesota, lives Dorothy Schmidt, who says she is your typical girl next door from the 50's. She was brought up with three brothers, the oldest being 6 years older than herself. Interest in bikes came from her brothers and father. Said Dorothy, "I learned to ride a bike when I was 14."

She married early and has had three children and one husband. Returning to school when her youngest was three years old, she earned a Bachelor's Degree in Accounting.

Dorothy says that, in January, 1993, she woke one morning, looked at her husband and asked, "How about if I buy two Harleys, a bigger for you and something smaller for me?." He inquired as to the state of her sanity then replied, "Absolutely not, Don't you dare, and stay away from the Harley shop. "Well, after a day or two of thinking and mulling it over, she decided it must be divine intervention (owing to the fact that she had not recently thought that much about cycling and had no clue of where this idea had come from) she decided to just look, after all, what could it hurt? She felt her marriage was not a match made in heaven. They had spent little time together so buying two Harley's seemed like an opportunity to spend enjoyable time together. Quote, "Oh well, so much for together time. Honestly, the more I thought about the idea, the better it sounded. So I did the only thing I could, I called and ordered a bike and charged the down payment to my Visa card."

Dorothy Schmidt says, "The Harley arrived in early September. It was love at first sight. The day they called, my grandson and I went and looked at it as, I thought I could change my mind. I rode it around the parking lot while the shop watched my grandson. I traveled as part of my employment so unfortunately I was out of town the first 6 weeks that I owned the bike. I am from MN which means our weather is questionable that time of the year. I had 1000 miles on the bike within 2 weeks.

People asked her if she was having a mid life crisis. Her answer was, "Not really, perhaps the Harley is a piece of an empty nest syndrome, but I don't think I'll have a mid-life as long as I have a Harley.

Ms. Schmidt has logged 175,000 miles in five summers. She wrenches her bike as much as possible, doing maintenance and many repairs. Her Harley Dealer will photo copy instructions from a manual when she purchases the parts from them.

Dorothy says, "I am still a strong, independent woman who

can barely look at a map of the United States without getting the *I want to/need to go there feeling*, I look back at the girl who married young and find it hard to believe that I am the woman I have become. I am able to look at fear, feel fear, touch fear, make a rational decision and know that the best is yet to be. I Have changed careers, started my own company and am very pleased with life."

She has been all over the United States, mostly by herself, due to the fact that it is difficult to wait for anyone to find the time to go along. She has started out from Melbourne, Fl at 7:30 PM (Eastern Standard Time) in the evening and arrived in Beaumont, TX. at 7:30 PM the following evening traveling 1100 miles and only stopping at that point due to a terrific lightening/thunderstorm which was just beginning. She has ridden from Minnesota to Boca Raton, Florida for Lunch, Minnesota to Maine just because, Minnesota to Prince George , British Columbia. She has ridden her bike down the mountain from Telluride in September when six inches of snow had fallen, praying all the way.

She says she has always stopped and read road side plaques and historical markers. She's been to churches where French, Spanish, English and German have been spoken. She has ridden with many and with few and by herself. She has ridden to every state but Alaska, Hawaii, and Virginia. No matter where, there are always wonderful, unique, interesting, friendly individuals to meet. Whether they be other motorcyclists, men, women, children, grandmas who give you the thumbs up signal, families on vacation, individuals who always wanted to ride, did ride, didn't ride, will never ride, who want to share their experiences with you. No matter where she travels she always comes home having met people who will stay in her mind forever. She finds that when you go about the country by yourself, people are not intimidated by you and they open their yards, garages and hearts.

She enjoys packing up her tent and sleeping bag and going on an adventure. She says, "I love the feeling that I'm free. I can stop when I like, where I like, as long as I like. I have slept under the starry skies and under brilliant gorgeous moons. I have slept in tents when the wind has blown so hard I thought for sure I would blow away. I have learned that even when it looks like rain all it takes is a little patch of blue to stay dry. I will be 50 in the fall and expect to visit 50 National Parks the summer of my 50th year.

I do not want to grow old saying " I wished I would've or "why didn't I?" So I try to take the best advantage of the opportunities presented in my life."

By the way, she has 3 daughters and 5 grandchildren, and her employment has always involved computers. She attends events as part of her business. Currently using a professional grade digital camcorder to record motorcycle events and the lifestyle concentrating on the nontypical image of biking and the surrounding events using nonlinear editing equipment to document the motorcycle lifestyle. She intends to dispel those myths people still harbor regarding the suitability of motorcycle events for grandmothers. She has been involved with women's riding groups as road captain, as well as HOG (road captain 3-4 years ago). She's always had an attitude brought about because of the positive upbringing she'd had in which she never knew women couldn't/ weren't allowed to/wouldn't be proper to do what a man was given the opportunity to do. Dorothy has never flaunted this like as "an attitude" but more as an inbred/ingrained confidence.

The longest distance rider I know is Fritz Voight. Fritz presently owns several motorcycles and spends considerably more road time than static. Fritz is a first cousin to a will-o-the-wisp. I have been sitting by a hotel pool in the middle of nowhere and have seen him ride in. An amazing fellow to all the "few" who really know him. All agree if you are going to be on the road with anybody, Fritz is the one to be with.

Fritz was born with with the help of a midwife on the edge of the Dismal Swamp in a shed, in February in 1947, in Witchduck, Virginia. Although his legal name seems to have been inadvertently listed, due to a clerical error, as Albert Jr., his name is actually Fritz. He was named after a German professional boxer, Fritz Brugger, by his Grandfather before he was born. He's Fritz to his friends regardless. Fritz's Dad was a Veteran and working as an Oysterman.

While still a baby, a thunder and lightening storm destroyed part of the shed house where his family was living. The storm turned to snow and came in the damaged area. He was exposed and covered in snow and almost died from the exposure.

When Fritz was about age three, the family was forced to move into a Banks Ave. print shop with his grandparents in downtown Norfolk. From there his family lived in projects until he enlisted in the Marines.

When the governmental reclamation of some of the swamp land was in progress, Fritz, at age 11 or 12 was employed in a peculiar job. He was one of a number of kids who would camp in the swamp and catch and remove poisonous snakes threatening the reclamation workers. (where was OSHA back then) Fritz's method was to take a couple of W.W.I bayonets and slice them up from a row boat and bring in the heads for a bounty. I'll bet job related insurance on that one today would be a pip of a premium. He says that the older boys somehow ended up with the money, even though he caught the snakes.

One fascinating story he tells is about a time when the other boys left him in the swamp for a couple of days and he was bitten twice by Black Widow spiders.

Growing up Fritz was fond of hanging out at a local motorcycle shop and listening to the old guys talk about bikes and there he formed the opinion that a motorcycle is a more feasible means of two-wheeled transportation than scooters and says Fritz, "I always thought it was the best means of motorized transportation."

Fritz rode his first motorcycle on a dare as a teenager. The bike was an old Sportster and he just took to it as a natural thing. The bike owner was sent to prison and left word for his friends to let that kid Fritz ride the bike and take care of it while he was away. He learned to be proficient with the bike and to maintain it himself.

He enlisted in the marines in the early sixties and when he was discharged, returned to Virginia and motorcycling. Because of the early age he had started riding, he earned the nickname 'Young Old-Timer" by some of the older veteran cyclists.

Fritz describes himself as one with neutral prejudices. Said he, "Anyone with class has my respect."

He bought his first bike while still in the Marines and stationed at Cherry Point Marine Base. This was a 1954 Harley Hydra Glide with a 1956 engine. His next machine was an Allstate and he describes it as the worst piece of Junk he has ever owned. He was able to sell both of these first machines at a profit. He was without a bike for a while and then bought a Honda Super 90. He and a best friend rode Hondas for a good while and as Fritz tells it, "All over Hell and back."

From then he has owned a wide variety of motorcycles and presently owns six of a variety of makes, which include three Harleys.

He rides all over America and regularly takes off on what his friends laughingly call "Sabbaticals" and can be gone for many weeks at a time. He'll ride anything on two wheels and has been known to cross several states on a bicycle. He waxes fondly about older, and what he calls, real motorcycles. For a short while he even raced bikes.

A most unusual character, he is unanimously known by his very eclectic group of friends as the one friend to have if you were allotted only one. An old friend of his once, while canvassing for a surprise birthday party for him, made the comment, "There are only two kinds of people who know Fritz: Them he's helped and them that ain't asked him." After knowing him the last 26 years I personally can attest to that statement, and I am the better off for knowing him.

Jim Trotta, 43, and wife Anna have been selling ice cream for 13 years, the old fashioned way, driving through the neighborhoods, in their Flagtown section of Hillsborough, New Jersey.

Jim decided to rebuild some old ice cream stuff, like a 1954 Chevy ice cream truck, push carts, peddle bikes and a Harley-Davidson ice cream bike. This added a little flare to compliment the cool equipment. In addition, Jim dresses the part of the ice cream man of the '50's; the red and white garb that Trotta wears while working is traditional garb. "The Ice Cream Man from Hell" is not a member of any motorcycle club past or present.

He's found fame by pushing his zany sense of humor on anyone who would listen. For a fee he will sell ice cream out of a specially restored Harley-Davidson at any function. He's done weddings, divorces, birthday parties, bar mitzvahs, anniversaries and even a funeral or two.

In addition to ice cream, the "Ice Cream Man from Hell" (a registered trademark) sells; frozen dog treats, T-shirts, comics, patches, decals and stickers.

During the '99 Bike Week event, the Hardest Working Man in Ice Cream, did any number of things, from video interviews, to spaghetti wrestling and wet T-shirt contests, and for the girls, his famous "All Male Buns review".

"My intentions have always been to make a living and have some fun", Trotta said. A tattoo on his forearm reads: "If they ever outlaw freedom, only outlaws will be free".

None of this is a coincidence or luck. It is a direct reflection of hard work, continuous action in one direction, processed though love and determination.

Jim, who many of us simply call Ice-Cream, is a familiar and welcome sight at all the big events with his Harley Ice cream wagon and long black cape-like vest and the familiar skull eating a popsicle. Always upbeat, if not outrageous, Jim, Ice-Cream, Trotta is one guy you are glad to see and he leaves you with a biker hug and an, "I'll see ya at ..."

Another person you'll see at most events is a lady with a warm smile and the kind of attitude that makes a person feel special. Even if it is only the second time you've seen her she remembers you and it leaves a warm fuzzy feeling with you after you've spoken to her and parted. Besides that she ain't too hard to look at either. This is of course Malysa Wyse whom I had the pleasure to interview and write for a national magazine, the following piece featured here. It began with the poem:

> There once was a girl named Malysa
> So sweet all the guys want to kiss her
> Tho she'd tell them nay nay
> They'd hide and wait anyway
> But Malysa was Wyse so they'd miss her.

Do the guys really want to kiss her? Silly question indeed, but as the high-profile spokesperson for Titan Motorcycles and Playboy, Malysa Wyse is all business and takes her position seriously.

The first thing you notice about Malysa is, well, the obvious. She is without a doubt gorgeous. Tall striking and blonde. After speaking to her, you go away with a really nice feeling. There is a genuine sweetness and the distinct impression that here is a person who is nice purely for the sake of being nice. This impression is further enhanced by the rare treat that she remembers you and is glad to see you again, even if it is a year later.

Malysa was born in Pensacola but raised in Barrineau Park, located between Pensacola, Florida and Atmore, Alabama, and describes herself as a regular country girl. A tomboy who grew up working by pulling weeds on the family's 26 acre and neighboring farms. Pay back then was 50 cents an hour. On lunch breaks they would all pile into a pickup truck and ride to a nearby country store where she would spend her just earned money to buy a pack of potato chips and a soft drink. After lunch the next stop was the river for a cooling and cleansing swim then back to work pulling weeds. Later would come working in her parents' gas station. Her mother also had a florist shop for twelve years and Malysa worked there learning floral design from her sister Holly. The whole family all pitched in to do what ever had to be done and where ever needed. Her Dad, Buck Wyse, also held a full time job with Monsanto, accumulating a 35-year perfect attendance record. Although she bears a striking resemblance to Barbie, she'll tell you quickly that she spent more time working with her brother Dennis in garages, than playing with Barbie Dolls.

Malysa in the mean time is keeping her feet on the ground, or rather on the pegs, as an avid motorcyclist. This is not a new fad for this lady of the highway who traces her two wheeling history back to age six or seven and her love of the sport is evident when she talks about it. Even though she is now a celebrity herself, she still speaks in childlike awe of meeting the famous Evel Knievel. She admires how even in his present fragile physical state he "still keeps going."

At an age when most little girls were sewing doll clothes, Malysa was working on motors and building her first bike. She earned the money to buy a $15.00 minibike frame and a $30.00 used go-kart. With her big brother's help she adapted the kart motor to the bike frame and thus built her own first motorcycle. When she was older she rode her brother's motorcycles.

She still has her first big bike, a 95 Nostalgia Harley-Davidson, but since then has added several Titan motorcycles to her collection which now numbers four.

She isn't limited just to driving on two wheels either. She has owned a monster truck and successfully completed a course at the NASCAR driving school where she excelled as a driver taking her rightful place with the men as an equal.

Malysa who had met David Mecey with Playboy seventeen years before had been planning to suggest to the magazine that they do a Biker Babe feature when she heard that they were doing just that. She was enroute to Orlando with her dog Harley and her bike for a photo shoot when the photographer called to tell her that Playboy was at Daytona shooting for a Biker Babe feature.

She went to Daytona to try out and discovered that David Mecey was also there and that she was the only girl competing who actually rode her own motorcycle. As luck would have it, she was still carrying Mecey's business with her after seventeen years. The magazine called about a week later and with the support and encouragement from her mother she was on her way.

Once picked for the feature she evolved into her present relationship with Playboy and Titan and is the first woman in several years to be selected from a pictorial to go on tour like a Playmate. Malysa is featured as the four-months of 1998 bonus in the new Playboy and Titan sixteen month Biker Babe calendar and is also March of 1999. Wyse doesn't mind letting you know that she is very happy to have her continuing relationship with Playboy and Titan.

Malysa has been on other tours as well, such as being the Iron Horse Girl with George Strait and Skoal Music, and the Autorama-World Of Wheels-Championship Auto Shows. She recently added the sponsorship of Logan Coach and their Silver Eagle line of trailers which are among the finest in motorcycle trailers. She has been on Hard Copy, Entertainment Tonight, Cops (Sturgis Segment), and the MC for WCW Wrestling. She has been in music videos for Hank Williams Jr., Travis, Tritt, Tracy Lawrence, Roy Orbison, Marty Stuart, and Mick Fleetwood. Magazine credits in addition to *Playboy* are *Life, People, Sturgis, Entertainment Weekley, Country Weekly, Hot Rod Bikes,* and now *Bikes & Spikes.* She participates in competition deep-sea fishing, has had her cooking featured in magazines, and hopes these accomplishments will open doors for other women to follow suit. Above all, she is a vehement advocate of women becoming more involved in motorcycling.

Plans for the near future include a product line (she loves marketing), and establishing a home on a recently purchased eleven acre tract where she will raise beagles. She presently has three dogs. Two beagles named Mylo and Harley and a catahoula named Ru-Paul.

Also in the works is a foundation, to be called The Lindsay Foundation after her mother's middle name, to benefit homeless children. "After all," she says, "children are our future." Malysa is firm in her belief that, as we get older, we will need a generation of children who have been raised with care, love and nurturing.

Malysa has a fan club located at Wyse Enterprises, POB 5942, Metarie, LA 70009

Finally this 35 year-old Libra freely admits that she needs her alone time, peace and tranquillity, and dearly misses her mom with whom she was very close. Her mother passed away about a year and a half ago. She is a fair-play extremest who is more comfortable being a cheerleader for others rather than blowing her own horn. She says her hero is Linda Vaughn, with Hurst Shifters, and her advice to all women is, "to think more seriously about their place in society."

Presently Malysa is home based out of Atlanta, but a base for this lady is simply that. Her home is the road and her heart is in the wind

Her friends say that she has a heart as big as Texas, but you know, all-in-all that just may be too small a comparison.

Regardless of which side you take personally, if you ride you will sooner oe later end up in a discussion of helmet laws. This is the one topic among motorcyclists on which there seems to be no nutral ground. For the record here, mandatory personal safety laws for consenting adults, called "nanny laws" by Assemblyman Tom Woods of California, are violations of the US Constitution.

Likewise the first rule of economics in a free market society is the obligations of society to pay for certain things not affordable to those who are economically disadvantaged. This is a social welfare obligation. Every student of the history of economic thought learns this, or should. Therefore the argument for mandatory safety regulations in order to lessen the financial burdens on society does not hold water.

Third point, in this digression from biker biographical sketches, is the apparent push behind helmet laws of the insurance lobby. Insurance companies are not benevolent organizations whose intent is to help you. They are for-profit companies who are concerned about the bottom line and no more. This is true inspite of the good neighbor and good hands advertising. Like any business they are entitled to make a legitimate profit. However, being able to manipulate legislature to this end is not their right. We are forced to have insurance almost as a necessary evil. Because of this the insurance companies have even less right than other types of businesses to manipulate legislation. This borders on the base structure of our system and has a kinship to the protection of the criminally accused due to the huge power posessed by the state, but that is another book. Bottom line is that the insurance lobby gets a law passed for the benefit of company profits which in itself is a violation of your rights under the constitution. Then your tax dollars go to pay for the enforcement of the violation. Double jeopardy I'd say or at the least insult to injury. This is not an issue of safety here, pro or con, just a right and wrong thing affecting motorcyclists under the Constitution.

Having said all that, which is a sneaky way of soapboxing and leading into our last rider bio, we come to David 'Deacon' Phillips, who was quoted earlier in chapter 4. Deacon is an interesting rider and has a long history of motorcycling and a variety of its aspects not the least of which is his involvement with ABATE in California to protest mandatory helmet laws.

Deacon seems to have an affinity for motorcycles since he was a small child. At age ten he was hanging around a guy with a motorcycle and the bug bit to ride. He was old enough (15) in 1956, when able to consider getting a bike he found an old Indian in a garage covered with dust, and bought it for $100.00. His father arranged to turn in the Indian to his Uncle, the manager of Philadelphia Harley-Davidson, who gave him a 1949 1200 Harley on his 16th birthday. Although an older bike, the engine was new and he rode the bike all through high school.

Life for him was one of living a split existence between biker and preppie. In the era of white bucks, khaki pants, and crew necked sweaters, biker leather just didn't fit.

He was planning for college in Philadelphia after graduation, but there was a program offered by the Navy making it possible to go to boot camp in the summer and return to school for the last half year of 12th grade. He attended the boot camp, but upon returning return to school, found he just didn't fit in. Deacon applied for active duty and finished high school in the service, returning after two years to Philly and his trusty iron steed. He married and found jobs scarce. He met a Policeman who gave him the idea to try for the department. In the back of his mind he felt there might be a way to get into the elite strike team of the department called the Motor Bandit Patrol (now called the Highway Patrol Division).

Deacon walked a beat, and worked a car,until finally there were some openings on the Motorcycle Squad of the Highway Patrol. After being accepted, he revelled in the fact they would give him a brand new Harley Davidson and he could still do Police work.

Deacon really believed he could make a difference on the streets. But ultimately, after several years he became disillusioned with Police work, and went into the private sector. Always with his old Panhead as his primary source of transportation.

He was divorced in 1966 and his ex-wife moved to Florida. It was after a visit there, that he decided to move to the sunshine state. (liquid sunshine) It seemed to rain every day.

A friend wrote to Deacon and extolled the virtues of California. He discussed the move with his son and with his son's understanding, Decon moved on to California.

One day, he was in a place called the Rock Store with a lady, when by coincidence the Police decided to rid the area of all the "undesireables". They raided the place in full force writing all kinds of bogus tickets for everything from open containers to spitting and crossing the highway. This was on Private property, and the nearest cross street was a mile down the road. Deacon was apalled. One of the Officers cited his ladyfriend for "intent to smoke in the canyon". She had an unlit cigarette in her hand.

This incident began his involvement in Motorcycle rights advocacy. He had all the tickets collected and had them heard at the same courtroom. In addition he had flyers printed, contacted polititians, and aquired information on the laws they used for the raid. The end result was that all the summons' were dismissed.

After that court date, he was contacted by a rep from a motorcycle rights group and asked to join. Deacon joined and worked for them.Over time moving to a high position in the group.

153

Easyrider Magazine was sponsoring an organization called A Brothrhood Against Totalitarian Enactments (ABATE). The board of directors for California were dissatified that the California organization had'nt even been registered as a business, let alone a service organization. ABATE approached him with an offer to be their State Director, and get them going.

After a lot of soul searching,he decided to go for it. He wanted a democratic organization run BY and FOR the membership. With no money and a lot of old bills Deacon was able to find people who agreed with the dream and who would help finance ABATE in California.

After the bills were paid, he turned to the name ABATE . He presented several alternative names to the then smalll membership since "totalitarianism " was a difficult word to use to politicians. The membership decided on the name the American Brotherhood(sisterhood implied) Aimed Toward Education of California Inc. As a founding member, he looks back over the last 22 years with the satisfaction of knowing he was a part of the fight for freedom that still goes on and on and on. He still rides the old Panhead, and after 41 years it still is his primary transportation.

These folks here discussed are a mix, an eclectic bunch, and some a bit excentric, as are we all. All have one thing in common and that is a love of this life, and a heart full of the spirit which makes America unique, and all prefer to express and enjoy that spirit with our faces in the wind. The words from a poem written by South Dakota's poet Badger Clark come to mind and are appropriate here;

> "No, when the waning heartbeat fails
> I ask no heaven but leave to wend,
> Unseen but seeing, my old trails,
> With deathless years to comprehend."

154

Clubs, Organizations, And Angels With Wings

*" In no country in the world has the principle of association
been more successfully used or applied
to a greater multitude of objects than in America"*
- Alexis de Tocqueville - 1835

No other symbol of motorcycling causes more emotional reaction than the image of a group of bikers, "on a run", all wearing the familiar vests with some insignia on the back. This insignia, usually in the form of a large sewn-on patch called "colors", can create in the minds of those who encounter them, reactions that go from fear to admiration.

From the smallest of the outlaw clubs, (outlaw to mean not AMA sanctioned) to the 450,000 member Harley Owners Group, these membership organizations abound in America and have spread overseas in ever growing numbers.

This chapter explores the world of the motorcycle organization and the fierce allegiance and reasoning behind their existence. Almost a contradiction of terms in a world of individuality, these clubs, as they prefer to be called, attract both members and opposition alike from the public, authorities, and even other organizations. This paradox in the lifestyle covers as thorough a cross section of society as do the individual bikers themselves.

Clubs have been around longer than motorcycling itself, and are another of those areas which are more indigenous to America than other parts of the world. Much of society thinks of them as gangs, which by definition implies criminal activity, but they are no more gangs than any other group which has a legal intent to it's charter.

Club rivalries are unfortunately a matter of historical fact and occur in all segments of society. They happen between any opposing forces from athletic fan clubs, and rival work groups, and yes, even motorcycle clubs.

Much motorcycle rivalry can be traced to the depression when the rivalry between the factories of Harley-Davidson and Indian became fierce and the many clubs associated came at odds within their allegiance to the marques. Harry V. Sucher addresses this depression era problem in his 1985 book, Harley-Davidson, The Milwaukee Marvel.

He says that the factory rivalry was detrimental to motorcycling as a whole, but in particular, to the many motorcycle clubs inadvertently caught up in the problems between the factories. In the text he says:

> Many such organizations their numbers already decimated by the growing depression, were forced to disband. As the owners of the two rival makes now refused to meet or ride with their opposite numbers. In some instances, one make splinter groups were formed from former members of formerly congenial clubs. Fights often resulted when they encountered their opposite numbers at race meets or even along public roads. Many thoughtful riders deserted motorcycling in disgust and the public images of the sport, already somewhat tarnished, hit a new low. (120)

This work begs to differ with the public impression and reasoning and presents the argument that the lifestyle of motorcycle organizations are not very different from any organization in our society. There is perhaps a standoffish attitude among biker groups and the factors which have shaped their attitudes come from fear of them by the public and from political exploitation by the authorities. States such as South Carolina and California have spent millions of dollars in attempts to harass and eradicate their existence and even place them in the same level of threat to society as the Mafia.

Looking at these clubs on an individual basis would require a separate undertaking, but explaining on a non-judgmental basis, showing some history, and the focus of their make up is possible here in a short space. Society has, by its own actions, fused these organizations into tight-knit inner communities by refusing to accept them even though some are as beneficial to society as any group in America. Let's examine this strange world which has a fanatically patriotic loyalty, and rules of its own, which are far more stringent than the society which despises it.

The definition of a club is, "A group of people organized for a common purpose, especially a group that meets regularly." (AHED) On the other hand the first definition of a gang is, "A group of criminals or hoodlums who band together for mutual protection and profit." (AHED) Looking further down in the dictionary reveals other definitions, all of which are in the pejorative.

I believe that the public at large has been watching too many movies of the <u>Stone Cold</u> variety. Since my first involvement with motorcycles in 1964 I have never encountered a club of cyclists who had in their charter that the stated purpose for the club was robbery, rape, and pillage. I can just see the election of officers. OK Fred is running for Road Captain in charge of ride by shootings, lets see a show of hands for Fred. Most cycle clubs have rather mundane list of officer titles. Titles such as President, Secretary, and Treasurer. The same old usual names.

I would never suggest that everyone on a motorcycle has a halo and carries a harp strapped to the sissy bar. I can however attest that the percentage of bad apples in the biker barrel is certainly no more prevalent than in any other segment of society. It is true that most of us do not look exactly mainstream society and march a little out of step with the wooden soldiers of the status quo. We are possessed with a spirit which tells us that it prefers the cool clean air of a winding mountain road, or a wide open space, nose to the wind, rather than necktie bound in an air conditioned office. Sometimes we band together as a brotherhood to form a club of like minded individuals.

Pure and simple it is an American thing. Alexis de Tocqueville visited the United States in 1832 and wrote what is considered to be the most accurate and detailed observation of America and Americans ever put to paper. It seems that every other work in print missed the mark, and some were written by the very finest writers of their day. A look into Tocqueville's intent is found in the introduction:

> Although Tocqueville writes about a nation and a continent, his overwhelming concern is for the individual. Haunted by a well-documented fear of the power of democracy to frighten and submerge the individual, he was

a prophet—even an inventor—of individualism. The very word "individualism" first entered our English language through Reeve's translation of Tocqueville's *Democracy in America.* "Individualism," Tocqueville observed, "is a novel expression, to which a novel idea has given birth ... Individualism is a mature and calm feeling which disposes each member of the community to sever himself from the mass of his fellow-creatures, and to draw apart with his family and friends." (ix)

Motorcycle clubs, like motorcycle events, provide a place for a group of like minded individuals to be together, and not forfeit the American spirit of individualism. We are all different yet together in that individuality. We are aware of ourselves, and our entity as a collective. It is a pledge of unity without relinquishment of freedom.

It is another of those peculiar things which are here, and specific to us, and in the assortment things that make the American spirit different from anyone else's. Being in clubs and organizations is an American thing.

In his book on <u>Democracy in America</u> Toqueville wrote his observations on this subject back in 1835:

As soon as several of the inhabitants of the United States have taken up an opinion or a feeling which they wish to promote in the world, they look out for mutual assistance; and as soon as they have found one another out, they combine. From that moment they are no longer isolated men, but a power seen from afar, whose actions serve for an example and whose language is listened to. (109)

At some point a club or for that matter a gang goes beyond being a club and becomes a group and larger than that is a society. We have clubs in existence today which out number whole town populations of a time past. Societies resent individuals or groups which are different. If they fear them then they feel they must take some action. A preventative measure of sorts. The rationale is that we must eradicate the menace before it gets a chance to do us any harm. Society has that attitude at times toward bikers whom they fear. After all they have seen it in the movies and read about it in the papers so therefore it must really be a threat. This sort of mentality is what Tocqueville was warning Americans to beware of.

Historically there are many instances of terrible consequences meted out to people who's only crime was to be different and perceived as a threat.

Textbook commentary on this subject tells us:

Social Cognition refers to the ways that individuals gather, use, and interpret information about social aspects of their world. It is concerned with the ways that cognitive elements, such as attitudes, beliefs, and values, shape our social behavior.

Groups exert a strong influence on their members to go along with the crowd. The tendency to match one's behavior to that of others is called conformity. People conform by adopting the social norms or customs of the larger group. Changing fashions in dress and hair are illustrations of conformity. (Benjamin, Hopkins, & Nation, 594)

Bikers and bike clubs get a bad rap and always have to be Peck's Bad Boy in the news and the movies. When the bad guys come after Stallone in Cobra they come on bikes. The guys who do all the foul deeds in 48 hours are bikers.

This image perceived by the public leads to a prejudice. This attitude of prejudice toward a stereotype leads to harassment. According to the book:

Prejudice is defined as a negative attitude toward members of particular social groups. When prejudice is expressed in behavior, it is called discrimination. Prejudice is maintained in part by stereotypes, mental images in which specific mental, physical, and behavioral traits are uncritically attributed to members of a group. (599)

Perhaps my memory fails me but I can't recall seeing the Love Ride featured in a film, or a toy run, or a scene where the CEO of Harley-Davidson is handing Jerry Lewis a check for a million dollars raised by club activities for Muscular Dystrophy research.

Earlier accounts of motorcycle club activities speak of the vast amount of public service performed. During emergencies and disasters local authorities have called upon motorcycle clubs to do a wide range of public service such as getting needed supplies, medicines, blood, and communications through to areas impassable to automobiles.

During W.W.II a general in the Army was asked, after some spectacular feat of warfare, "Where did you find such a splendid gang of men?" He replied, "Oh, I just asked if they ever owned and rode a motorcycle, then I took those who said, 'I did.' " (The Motorcycle Book, 78)

There are two mainstream clubs which have made a tremendous mark on society, and represent motorcyclists to the public at large. There are a host of others, smaller in number which cover the spectrum of the world of motorcycling. Women's clubs, for instance, are becoming prevalent as more and more women take to the road on two wheels. This is not a new thing. One of the oldest clubs in America is the famous Motor Maids of America. We will address some of these clubs here, Alphabetically.

The American Motorcyclist Association is probably the most representative of collective organization in motorcycling. Established in 1924 the AMA closes the century having been a part of it for 75 years. An impressive tenure to say the least. With 234,000 members the AMA is the second largest motorcycling organization in the world and has worked since its inception to protect the rights and interests of motorcycling and motorcyclists.

While the idea of having a representative organization is commonplace, if not expected, this day and time it was a relatively new concept at the time. The AMA was formed from two pre-existing organizations, the Federation of American Motorcyclists (FAM), and the Motorcycle and Allied Trades Association (M&ATA).

Even before FAM there were clubs and one of these was the New York Motorcycle Club. In 1903 the NYMC was concerned that New York City was enacting a law requiring the registration of motorcycles as motor vehicles. The club was of the opinion that a national organization be formed to represent motorcyclists. The meeting to form such an entity was held at a clubhouse in Brooklyn. With 93 attending this assembly voted to form the FAM. One of the attendees was George M. Hendee, founder of the Indian Motorcycle company. Hendee brought with him 109 pledges of support for the new organization from the New England area.

The other ancestor of the AMA, the M&ATA was formed in 1916 and was more like a trade union rather than a club or political organization. Membership gradually lessened in the FAM and the organization failed to survive.

The M&ATA began to absorb those functions previously handled by FAM. These included supporting the Gypsy Tours, registering clubs, and handling competition events. The competition committee of the M&ATA was chaired by the editor of Motorcycle and Bicycle Illustrated magazine. He wrote in his magazine that it wasn't truly a rider's organization but its registration of riders would be the foundation of one which would be an M&ATA affiliate.

The AMA, true to the prediction, came to be May 15, 1924 from those registrations. As for the M&ATA: it merged in 1969 with the West Coast Motorcycle Safety Council and is the Motorcycle Industry Council of today.

Even before it was official the AMA had adopted the slogan: "An Organized Minority Can Always Defeat an Unorganized Majority". This was printed May 20, 1924 in the Western motorcyclist & Bicyclist, as was the announcement that the AMA would build to become a live and active fighting organization. The intent was that lawmakers would have to fear trying to put anything over on motorcyclists. The wisdom of this stance and of forming an organization of such power would become apparent in the 1960s when attempts would begin to ban motorcycles, pass mandatory helmet laws, and other forced regulations.

After 75 years of existence the AMA remains the only national organization devoted to serving all of the motorcyclists in America. The organization has prepared itself to step into the new millennium continuing to watch over the rights of motorcyclists and stand ready to protect their interests. It is in fact the live and fighting organization as predicted 79 years ago.

There are several Christian motorcycle clubs with chapters around the country and literally thousands of members. Among the ones most seen at major events are the Christian Motorcyclists Association, Sons of God, Laboring Few, Tribe of Judah, Heaven's Saints, and the Bond Slaves. These clubs do a tremendous amount of work in the way of ministries and at most events are offering services such as free water to everyone. Always willing to discuss their perspectives on religion with passers by, this author has never known them to be pushy or overbearing in their presentations. Except for the nature of their mission, and the wording on their patches, they look no different than any other bikers or club patch holders.

Corporate America has known for a long time that forming a customer club is good business. A concept supposedly developed in Germany where the development of such programs was a necessity.

> German law is extremely restrictive and make it almost impossible to give different customers or customer groups different prices and discounts simply because they are members of a customer loyalty programme. In most other countries, customer loyalty programmes are nearly entirely price based and offer their members special discounts and prices. German marketers, in contrast, were forced to develop customer clubs. (Butscher, 6)

A customer club is not just a discount program to get customers to be loyal on a price basis alone. That would work only until someone else had a lower price. A customer club is a communications union of sorts between the customer and the organization. It must be managed by the organization in order to be in contact with the customer on a regular basis as well as be able to offer a package of benefits with a high perceived value rather than one of price and savings alone. The goal of the organization is to establish an emotional relationship which will activate the customers and increase their loyalty.

These are not just value oriented programs in as much as they must do more than say a Sams Club or a music or book club, which offers savings as an incentive for becoming a member. There are special criteria which apply to customer clubs that are as follows:

- Customer clubs are initiated, planned and managed by an organization and not by the customers themselves.
- Customer clubs offer real and perceived value to their members by optimizing the combination of financial (hard) and non-financial (soft) benefits.
- Customer clubs provide opportunities for members and the sponsoring company to talk to each other.
- Customer clubs can collect data which will help other departments of the sponsoring company improve their performance.

Customer clubs aim to activate customers by encouraging them to buy or recommend a product, communicate with the club and so on. (6)

Perhaps no company has ever put together the structure of a customer club more successfully than has Harley-Davidson with the Harley Owners Group. (HOG)

It is not known as of this writing whether the concept was a stroke of genius on the part of management at Harley, which coincided with the German concept, or if it was something Germany passed on to Milwaukee. It makes no difference and it worked well. The Germans developed the concept in the early 80s and the Harley Owners Group was formed in 1983.

In its first year the new club was to attract 33,000 members and began a steady growth upward. As the popularity of the Motor Company soared so did HOG membership. It is a factory policy that whenever a new motorcycle is sold a first year, free membership is included, providing an incentive to test the waters of participation. Each new Harley owner is presented his or her new machine, accompanied by a warm welcome and an invitation to go on a scheduled ride. There is a lot of incentive there. Riding with your new found comrades in the wind, there is safety in numbers and readily available brotherhood. Everyone will make the new guy welcome and make sure his mistakes aren't too costly.

Generally HOG members are entitled to discounts at the home dealership on parts and accessories and there are a number of other perks and benefits for members. Not the least of these are club rides and sponsored events. The HOG state, regional, and national rallies offer entire weekends of fun and usually there is a chapter ride to major events.

After an incredibly short period of time dealing with growing pains, and working out structure and direction, HOG has seen steady growth in membership annually. The present world wide club roster has membership numbers of around 450,000 in 1,100 chapters. The club has chapters in 100 countries with about 60% of the chapters remaining in the US. Female members are able to hold regular memberships with as much input as the men, rather than riding behind the old man on his 'scoot,' with a property of Zeke patch on her back. As an additional benefit, they can be members of "Ladies Of Harley". HOG has about 65,000 members who are women or roughly 14% of the total membership.

Since 1985 the mean average of women (not mean women bikers) owning Harley-Davidson motorcycles has risen from 2% to 7% with the median age of both genders going from 34.1 to 44.4 years old. The average of men to women motorcycle owners has dropped in men and risen in women, while the married to single ratios have gone from 54% to 69% in married owners, and singles have dropped from 29% to 16%.

While these numbers arguably are in motorcycles purchased, rather than a direct connection to membership, they can be argued logically that the demographics are indicative of a pattern of ownership changes. These changes may directly correlate to the rise in the popularity of HOG and the increasing participation of married couples and families in motorcycling through HOG membership.

Ladies on bikes are nothing new or even recently popular in spite of the more larger numbers of them now taking to the road. In 1907, Clara Wagoner won an endurance race from Chicago to Indianapolis and finished with a perfect score. Because she was a female (remember women would not have the right to vote until 1920) her performance was declared "unofficial" and she was denied her trophy. However, "Her fellow riders were somewhat more enlightened and appreciative of her accomplishment. They took a collection among themselves and awarded her a gold pendant to honor her accomplishment." (Hollern, 13)

The point of the previous example is once again to present the reality that women have been riding motorcycles as long as men and in fact as long as there have been motorcycles. In addition, historical research shows that the forming of clubs for both men and women goes back to earliest colonial times and was a specific point mentioned more than once by Tocqueville.

There are at present a number of women's clubs and some have been in existence for quite a long time. A few should be mentioned here to example currentness, history , and variety of purpose. The common denominator is as always motorcycling.

Leather & Lace was founded 1983. The goal of the club was to change the image of lady motorcyclists. Husbands and boyfriends are kept involved by making them honorary members called Dendaddy's and Big Brothers. They provide support and encouragement for the women in their activities. The club members acknowledge that the men support them 110% in all that they do. The children are involved with club functions and activities and even have their own divisions and a newsletter. Little girls 0-12 are Future Lace, 13-15 Teen Lace. Their bi-monthly newsletter is titled "Future Lace Tails."

The women are family and career oriented. They, in the words of their website information, "also share the feel of the rush of the wind in their faces and the excitement of the rolling thunder and the raw power beneath them as they ride."

Each chapter has a project involving children. An annual run is held, called the "International Run for Children." This is somewhat different in scope than the typical motorcycle run. The run is of a 150 mile duration and held at 10:00 a.m. on the 3rd Sunday in September. In the words of the club:

> Each member of Leather & Lace starts her engine. She could be a member of a chapter or the only member in her area. As she turns the key on her machine and it comes to life to begin the 150 mile ride, no matter the weather, wind, rain or snow, she knows in her heart that she is not alone...because all over the world her sisters are riding with her. It is an incredible and awesome feeling; the thriving spirit of *sisterhood* that resides within Lace. Women working together to better their own futures (and yours) by helping today's children. All of the funds having been raised through sponsorships (much like a walk-a-thon) are forwarded to a local charity. (L&L website)

Leather & Lace is headquartered in Daytona Beach, Florida and holds only one national meeting per year. All members are required to attend this meeting which takes place the last Friday of the first full week of March at Leather & Lace National headquarters. The ladies say, "It's a full week of pure camaraderie."

One of the oldest clubs in America, and dating back to the 1930s, is the famous Motor maids Of America. Organized by Verna Griffith in the 30's, chapters of this organization were formed in many of the larger cities of the country and immediately gained recognition as an officially chartered AMA group. While most were organized as auxiliaries to already established AMA clubs, a few chapters were organized as independent entities.

165

The founder, Verna Griffith was a Harley-Davidson enthusiast, and her cohort and later perennial National President was Dorothy Robinson, the wife of the Detroit Harley dealer, Earl Robinson. Therefore much of the Motor Maids organization was largely oriented toward H-D machines. Some of the women rode Indian motorcycles and there appears that there was no prerequisite as to brand of motorcycle beyond personal preference and peer pressure.

The ladies wore smart uniforms and appeared regularly at club outings, Gypsy Tours, and holiday celebrations. Much attention and comment was generated from their ability to handle their heavyweight mounts. A petite 100 pound rider handling a 600 pound motorcycle still attracts a bit of attention.

Another and somewhat smaller club is Raw Silk. This is an all women's clean and sober motorcycle club. The club officially began in August 1989 with 4 founding members and over the years has gone from the original 4 members up and down to as many as 8. What is important is that the size of the club makes no difference. It is the brotherhood or in this case sisterhood, and they have formed, "a strong group of "Sisters."

The Jackpine Gypsies Motorcycle Club started in 1936, with an official AMA charter in 1937. AMA began promoting the club's racing events; which started the rally in Sturgis August 14, 1938.

The average age for a motorcycle club is three years, yet after sixty-two years, this club is still running strong, with over 150 members living all over the United States and abroad. Jackpine Gypsies owns all the property on which most of its club activities take place. The Jackpine Gypsies are a non-profit organization, donating heavily to the local food bank, the high school, the Zonta club of Sturgis and the Chris Motorcycle Association.

A final note is needed here regarding those clubs and organizations normally referred to as "Outlaw Clubs" or "One Percenters". I have received no real information from any of those clubs and perhaps may include them, if possible, in later revisions of this book.

Many of the club names are known or at least familiar when seen at an event by the rest of us. I have friends in quite a few clubs and out of respect will not print material from news media or police files. I am a journalist and historian, not an investigative reporter.

Out of respect, I must, however, give credit where credit is due. It is only proper here to acknowledge that the very style of the clothes we wear, and the insignias upon them, date back to the Outlaw Clubs. These codes of dress, or a biker uniform as it were, have been established long ago by clubs such as The Booze Fighters, Hells Angels, and many others.

The Great Events

"Buy me some penuts and Crackerjack,
I don't care if I never get back"
-Jack Norworth - 1908

Every year, beginning in March, it's a whole new ballgame, as massive numbers of motorcyclists take to the road like geese flying home after the winter. With numbers in the hundreds of thousands, they converge upon a number of areas for some really grand events and they are doing a lot more than watching a game and buying penuts and Crackerjack.

To only briefly tell the story of the great events that happen yearly across America, one for over seventy five years, may actually do them an injustice, but it is a great subject in itself and so must be at least touched upon here.

Beginning with Bike Week at Daytona Beach, Florida, a person with a year to just ride, could cover a winding route around the US from event to event which would actually end back at Daytona for Biketoberfest to finish the season. If we take a look at the stops he or she would visit along the way we'll be treated to a look at nine of the events and their history. Stopovers are at Laughlin, Nevada, Myrtle Beach, South Carolina, Laconia, New Hampshire, Washington, DC, Hollister, California, and the most prestigious event of all Sturgis, South Dakota. These events now typically draw participants from all over the world, and some have an attendance of over three hundred thousand annually. They are not just part of an annual occurrence but have become legendary in reputation and scope.

Before the discussion of the annual events we should mention that there have been some non-annual events which drew immense attendance. The 85th, 90th and 95th anniversary party rallies Harley-Davidson threw for itself in 1988,1993 and 1998 in Milwaukee. Details were not available for 88 and 98 in time for this writing but the 1993 one was a corker.

The city of Milwaukee turned out in its finest to welcome over 100,000 bikers on Harleys coming home to the place where their machines had been born. The billboard entering Milwaukee read, "Ever Seen So Many Twins In One Family?" Every hotel within a hundred mile radius was filled for this event.

The big party was at the Lake Front Festival Park on the shore of Lake Michigan. To get there the participants rode in a seven mile parade across Milwaukee on I-94 which had most of the over 100,000 participants riding 60,000 bikes four abreast. For the first time in history an Interstate was closed to all traffic but motorcycles. All other traffic was routed around the city or through city streets.

Another parade was led from the airport by Willie G. Davidson making a collective 75,000 plus bikes going to the party.

With Harley staff and factory workers volunteering to be hosts, the revelers were treated to an awesome good time. Besides the usual eats there were a number of celebrities wandering about and the entertainment was non stop. A quick rundown of talent gracing the various stages and the Marcus Amphitheater in addition to local and regional bands were Marshall Tucker Band, Little Feat, and REO Speedwagon. Headlining the evening was Z Z Top, and Jay Leno from the Tonight Show was the MC. Amid the festivities and Leno's humor there was a surprise guest of honor in the personage of Jerry Lewis, there to receive a huge check from Harley and HOG for Muscular Dystrophy research. What a party night.

The information and following histories are pretty much as furnished by the events upon request. Information will be updated as received in future editions of this book.

For some reason or perhaps a combination of sand, cycles, and racing, Bike Week at Daytona has been a tradition since 1937. It was first held in conjunction with the inaugural running of the Daytona 200 Motorcycle race. This race back then was raced in part on the hard sand of the beach. According to the event literature:

The first race took place on a 3.2 mile beach and road course, located south of Daytona Beach. Ed Kretz of Monterey Park, CA was its first winner, riding an American made *Indian* motorcycle and averaging 73.34 mph. Kretz also won the inaugural City of Daytona Beach trophy.

The 1937, race course ran approximately one and a half miles north on the beach; through a ¼ mile turn where the sand was banked, and then onto the paved, public roadway portion for the trip south

The race, which had starting times dictated by tide tables, was nicknamed by the press as the "Handlebar Derby" and were run from 1937 to 1941. Racing was discontinued from 1942 to 1947 because of the war and fuel rationing, but the cyclists continued to attend anyway and it was unofficially given the name Bike Week.

Back in those days local citizens were asked to open their homes to the bikers because of the shortage of hotel rooms. (Hmmm, wonder if that would work now?)

In 1947 the racing was resumed and the promoter was Bill France who created NASCAR. In 1961 the race was discontinued on the beach and moved to the Daytona International Speedway.

According to the official history the event has always had a "flavor of its own" and things got a bit rugged for a few years which had local citizenry and authorities very unhappy.

The 1986 event was the worst year to date and since then has, with some restructuring and control measures in place, become a huge and exciting event. Presently the event is a 10-day adventure which spans most of the county. Most of the festivities are still in town and Daytona's Main Street is one of the main attractions with wall-to-wall bikes, bikers, and many vendors.

While we are on the subject of Daytona we may as well tell about the event which closes the season each year which is Biketoberfest.

Biketoberfest is relatively new as events go having begun in 1991. Each year motorcyclists and non riding visitors alike come from around the world to Daytona Beach to enjoy the festivities of this annual motorcycle gathering. The event is held each October, and features championship motorcycle road racing at Daytona International Speedway. Since Daytona is a popular vacation spot many attend Biketoberfest as a family event to take advantage of both worlds.

Of course Main Street & Beach Street have rally exhibits, vendors, shows & music just as does Bike Week in March. One of the best perks of this event and one thing making it grow in popularity is the weather. October in Northern Florida is usually very nice and mild.

The event originated in 1991 when the Daytona Beach Area Convention and Visitors Bureau (DBACVB), hired Janet Kersey, a life-long Daytona Beach resident with an extensive background in promotions and marketing.

Her job was to create special off-season events to attract visitors. Kersey's first assignment was to organize a biker event similar to Bike Week, around the AMA annual fall races, held each October at Daytona International Speedway. The event has continued to grow in size and popularity and has every sign of continuing to do so.

In April each year for seventeen years the annual Laughlin River Run has been held in Laughlin, Nevada. This event, the West Coast's largest motorcycle event, is a real bash which features nine resort casinos, top name entertainment, motorcycle displays, factory demo rides, trade show exhibits, a custom bike show and a lot more. Official registrants receive a commemorative ride pin, bandana, breakfast ticket, and drawing tickets for some super prizes. New trucks and new bikes are prize examples. There are many smaller prizes to make the event a rewarding experience for everyone.

The Laughlin River Run has been in existence since 1983, and motorcycle enthusiasts have made the annual trek each April to what has become the largest motorcycle event on the West Coast. At this desert oasis there are typically over 50,000 participants gathered for three days of fun at the banks of the Colorado River. With the event located just 100 miles south of Las Vegas, a participant would have to bring misery with him to keep from having a good time. This is one place with cooperative weather most of the time and some beautiful riding areas including some of the last remaining mileage on historic Route 66. Other things within easy riding time are Hoover Dam, the Grand Canyon, and London Bridge in nearby Lake Havasu City, Arizona.

A tale of two events in one city that happened fifty years

apart in a little town in Northern California is as much a part of motorcycle history as anything mentioned in this book. Near Santa Cruz, is a little valley town in the heart of some of the best farming country South of San Francisco. Located 14 miles from The Garlic Capitol of the world and down the road from one of the West Coast's most famous old missions is Hollister. This California town, will forever have the reputation of being the site of the most famous and infamous motorcycle rally in history. This event took place on the Fourth of July 1947 and turned into a media feeding frenzy which made such a stir that the whole nation was shocked. While nowhere near the riot presented in the news, this event forever crowned American bikers with the reputation and public image still believed today.

The 1953 Stanley Kramer movie, <u>The Wild One</u>, was based on this event, creating much of the mistaken public impression, and making stars of actors Marlon Brando and Lee Marvin. The actual circumstances surrounding this event and its impact were minor compared to the hullabaloo in the press. A Gypsy Tour and races with a few rowdies gained more notoriety than any event in motorcycling has done since then.

There is more mayhem at a typical British soccer game than happened at Hollister or any other biker event ever held. This event revisited the town of Hollister in 1997. This was the second rally ever held there, commemorating the original event, on its 50th anniversary. The rally was organized by Corbin Saddles which has since relocated its manufacturing facility to the little valley area. The event is new, but it's a good one, and now after its third annual gathering, appears to be a growing yearly favorite.

Held in late September, a new but exciting event, is becoming an East Coast fun favorite. Titled the Steel Horse Stampede, this rally is not centered around racing, but typically is attended by some of the motorcycling NASCAR drivers.

The event is short by rally standards but is packed with entertainment and rides, including one on the first day from Music City to the Jack Daniel Distillery. (sorry no samples are given out)

From Thursday evening to the conclusion on Saturday night there is solid entertainment and things to see and do. All activities take place at Riverfront Park and are walking distance from all of the places and clubs which have made Nashville's fame as the music capitol of the world, including the Grand Ole Opry.

The Steel Horse Stampede is an event organized and hosted by professionals in the field of promotions and also are motorcyclists. This event is all fun and as good as it gets to enjoy the transition from Summer to Autumn in the Tennessee hills.

The event with the most serious purpose is Rolling Thunder. It began in 1987, when two guys, Ray Manzo and Artie Muller, met just before Veterans Day and formed a plan for a motorcycle run for the POW-MIA issue. "Many American Prisoners Of War were abandoned and died in POW Camps after WW II, Korea and the Vietnam War", states Artie Muller.

The first run was in 1987 when about 2600 bikers rode Rolling Thunder-I, through the streets of Washington, DC; to the Viet Nam Veterans memorial Wall. Over the past twelve years the event has grown in size, scope, and dedication, and in 1999, Rolling Thunder-XII, saw over 350,000 brothers and sisters gathered at the Pentagon.

The bikes gather at daybreak the day before Memorial Day, and assemble to leave at noon in a parade through the streets of Washington, DC to the memorial.

The 1999 event was the largest ever with much TV coverage and a parade in excess of 250,000 bikes headed for The Wall. Before they pulled out on the parade route the North Pentagon Parking Lot was overflowing. Miles of bikes were backed up south of the Pentagon and thousands coming in from two other directions had no where to park. Tens of thousands of bikes were parked in Washington, DC that came to the event, but didn't ride with the main pack. Many that don't ride lined the streets around Washington, DC and The Wall to honor men and women whose names are on The Wall, as well as the Veterans of All Wars that have given their lives for this country!

The goal of the event is to bring the issue to public notice world-wide, that POW-MIA's do exist! To demand a complete accounting of all POW-MIA's as accurately as possible! To bring home All Live American POW's still held by Foreign Countries! To protect our future veterans so they will be "guaranteed" that they too will not be left behind! That is the purpose and mission of Rolling Thunder.

Incorporated in 1995, Rolling Thunder, Inc. has worked on getting a POW-MIA stamp approved, assisted with funds to send search teams into Southeast Asia looking for POW's & MIA's and helped a POW family looking for their father in North Vietnam.

In addition the organization has worked on the Missing Service Personnel Act of 1995 and 1997, got a bill passed to make it mandatory to fly the POW-MIA Flag on main holidays on federal buildings; on the Vietnam & Korean Memorials in DC, major military bases, and to fly it over all US Post Offices.

The event is generating the support to assist with S-484, HR-1926, the Bring Them Home Alive Act of 1999, with another bill which will be introduced very shortly.

Rolling Thunder helps veterans in need and goes to the Veterans Hospitals in each area. They bring food (dinner), clothes, personal items and brotherhood. They provide the Vets in the VA Hospital with a Bar-Be-Que in the summer and a Christmas Party every year. If you love to ride then this one is the parade of parades with the Nation's Capital to play in, and all the while supporting a wonderful cause.

Sometimes known as the Spring Rally, the Dealer's Rally, or Bike Week at Myrtle Beach, is another sun and fun event at a major beach resort and similar to Daytona. The Rally is held around the middle of the month of May and sort of kicks off the tourist season there. This event is promoted by the combined Harley-Davidson dealers of the Carolinas. With about a 100,000 attendance, in size this rally is just slightly behind the Big Three. (that title keeps coming up in motorcycling for some reason)

Myrtle Beach is a very popular beach area, with an enormous amount of entertainment, dining accommodations, and sporting endeavors such as golf. With all there is to do and see, to have an unhappy time at this rally, you have to work at it.

After 76 seasons, the Laconia Motorcycle Week, in New Hampshire, is the oldest of American motorcycling's "Big Three" events. The racing is and it has always been one of the biggest attractions. While all three of the really big events were started around their races, Laconia's racing was first.

Racing does not have to be your interest to enjoy this event, just motorcycling. Laconia is nestled in the heart of traditional, New England. Easterners have for all time sung the praises of this part of America, and the riding is worth the trip.

Not far away from the event are Vermont and Maine and any excuse for an excursion is a good excuse. A major part of the heart of the American spirit steeped in the history of our nation is there, and those who have attended all say it is something easily sensed. Motorcycling around New England brings with it at once a peacefulness as well as an exciting time while you are there.

With parades and activities, coupled with the riding and races, if only a few events must be chosen during the riding season, Laconia must be among the few.

If there be magic anywhere in America then it is in the Black Hills. Ancient and sacred to Native Americans, it has also been for the motorcyclists who make their annual pilgrimage from all points of the globe to attend. For the last 58 years motorcyclists have treked to this event just as their ancestors did before them for a variety of reasons. This year will make the 59th and close both the century and the millenium.

The first gathering was held in August 1938 in a big tent behind Clarence and Pearl Hoel's Indian Motorcycle shop (Hoel's Motors) on Junction Avenue. According to Pearl, who still lives near Junction, there were about 200 in attendance for the first event. They made coffee, sandwiches, and donuts for everyone then they all just had a good time talking motorcycles and travels.

For the competition there were 19 racers at the half-mile track. Besides the racing, the event featured such stunts as board wall crashes, ramp jumps and head-on collisions with an automobile. Johnny Spiegelhoff from Milwaukee, Wisconsin won most of the prize money - $500 put up by four local businessmen. The two-day event did not feature any tours.

Clarence, better known as"Pappy" Hoel, was one of the originators of the event. He and some others met in his garage and formed a club named The Jackpine Gypsies Motorcycle Club. They then formed a corporation, the Black Hills Motor Classic, Inc. to develop the event.

5,000 spectators watched in 1940 as 150 racers ran the Sturgis half-mile. Later like many other events the one at Sturgis would be suspended during the war. Many rallies were not held during World War II, because so many people were involved in the war effort, and because of rationing.

175

Gradually the rally attendance increased during post war times and days were added, with activities to fill up the days. The 1947 event saw 400 riders participating in the A.M.A. Gypsy Tour and races.

Pearl Hoel remembers well some of the events which took place at Sturgis during the Rally. One contest she laughingly recalls was the suitcase race. Like some modern day bike games several riders ride to the end of a field where there is a suitcase full of ladies clothes. The rider must stop, get off the bike and put on the ladies clothes from in the suitcase and ride back. First one back is the winner. (and has a new rep to live down) I'm not sure I'd want to win that one. Maybe it will resurface and knock the weenie bite contest out of popularity. Nah!

There was an event or perhaps a surprise exhibition with an outhouse. It seems as if some rider would ride in pretending to be drunk and wobbling on the bike. He would then crash into a fake outhouse, which would collapse and a guy would run out waving a roll of toilet paper as if interrupted while taking care of business.

Tours, with lunches provided, were added to the line up of things to do. The participants, most of whom were families and traveling in side car rigs, would travel through the black hills and be treated to the same sites riders enjoy today. The ride would arrive at Custer by lunch time where some of the women would be waiting with lunch already set up. (food was a part of the event right from the start - see the end of this chapter) Pearl Hoel and Joann Cruchshank made the dinners in advance and would leave so as to be at Custer ahead of the ride and set up to serve. Lunch was all you could eat for $.65. On another note, Pearl's companion was the first girl in Sturgis to ride her own motorcycle.

Once on the Needles Road the women serving the lunches, came across a man in a car with his radiator boiling over. He was desperate for water for his car, but there was none close by and the ladies saddly informed him they had nothing but five gallons of iced tea if he could use it. The tea worked and he went on his way. Later in the day as they were entering Deadwood this same man pulled up beside the women and yelled, "Ladies, that was the best damned iced tea I've ever had."

By the mid 60's the event was growing and attendance

reached 1000 in 1965. The lunch was now a Barbeque hosted by the Sturgis Chamber of Commerce in the city park, which included a beauty contest for the queen of the classic. An award was given for the person and couple traveling the longest distance – both in and outside of the US, Awards were also presented for the longest-married couple, best-dressed man and woman, and oldest rider.

The Gypsy Tour to Custer now had three hundred thirty riders participating and had become a two-day event with an overnight stay. The 1965 event lasted five days and was claimed to be the "biggest in history."

Pappy Hoel along with motorcycle racers and Sturgis residents, developed a hexagonal monument in 1981 listing the White Plate Flat Trackers. The white plate is a designation given to motorcycle racers fast enough to earn the distinction. The monument is located on Junction Ave. near the local hospital.

The 45th year of the classic was dedicated to Pappy Hoel. South Dakota Governor William Janklow dedicated the entire 1985 event week to Hoel "who earned national respect and fame because of his years of devotion of friends, family and community." During the event, Pappy Hoel kept his cycle shop open all night before the races so that the racers would have a place to work on their bikes. All were welcome and worked side-by-side, regardless of type or manufacture.

A news article about the event suggested that "regardless of what type of motorcyclist you are, you should take a minute while attending the 45th Annual Rally to pay silent homage to a man whose love of motorcycles helped make the event grow into one of the largest motorcycle events." Clarence "Pappy" Hoel unfortunately passed away in 1989 just short of seeing the event he created become the largest and most popular motorcycle event in the world. The attendance at the 50th anniversary event in 1990 was four times the previous attendance record.

After the 1990 rally, attendance dropped to previous numbers but has steadily increased until the 1988 rally figures were just slightly less than the 1990 event.

In 1991 Sturgis Rally and Races, Inc. was formed to 'plan, organize and promote' the rally and races and to return significant tangible financial benefits to the residents of Sturgis. The new group represented the residents of Sturgis, the business commu-

177

nity and racing organizations.

The Black Hills Motor Classic name was changed to Sturgis Rally and Races in 1992. Most people knew the event as Sturgis. The organizers wanted to emphasize the historical basis of the event – racing. Therefore the name change.

The present event lasts seven days, and still has racing and touring at its core, even though Main St. has become the visual image. Four blocks are closed except for motorcycle traffic, and it is an unbelievable photo opportunity.

Neil Hultman has been involved with the event since 1947. He was the first paid coordinator of the event and was in that position until stepping down to turn the event over to Sturgis Rally & Races. Neil speaks nostalgically of the earlier events when all the vendors could fit in the Armory and motocross races were held out at Bear Butte Lake. He laughingly says he learned when he was coordinator that he was not a politician.

People attend from all fifty states and a variety of foreign countries. One of the places to see in Sturgis anytime but especially if attending the rally is the National Motorcycle Museum And Hall Of Fame which is located in Sturgis, and is now open in its new building on Lazelle Street.

The name Sturgis continues to hold a magical attraction to motorcycle riders everywhere. The annual event has become a pilgrimage, and has more than once been referred to as being to motorcycling what the Indy 500 is to Auto Racing. The yearly return is like Christians returning to Jeruselem.

Ever Sacred to Native Americans, riding the Black Hills has become so for bikers and is like no other place on Earth. The scenery is breathtaking and being there almost healing.

The Rally is a time for rejuvination and to renew ties to friends. and meet new ones. A place all who ride motorcycles feel they have to attend at least once. Sturgis cannot be simply described. Those who have tried end with "you just have to see it!"

In concluding this chapter, one final area of event participation must be addressed, which is not about motorcycling. This part of the chapter was researched at The Sturgis Rally, but the subject matter is indiginous to all of the great events and as far as that goes, all major events in the US, regardless of locale or time of year. It is as much American as is apple pie and in fact, apple pie is a part of it.

It's easy to think of bikers in terms of oil, gasoline, paint, and chrome. Most people might even add beer to the list. Well there my friend, one attendance at any of the major motorcycling events will show otherwise.

Although a great deal of expense goes into the paint and chrome and the bikes run on oil and gasoline; the bikers themselves run on gastrointestinal delights. Whew! Historically, what a mouthful, and a mouthful is what you'll see there.

At every major event and especially at Sturgis, among the rows and rows of gleaming motorcycles are an array of vendors. Second only to parts and tee-shirts is food. After all, that biker-beer-belly look in the tee-shirts needs something to keep it filled 'out'. Second only to riding, bikers love to eat, and we do it a lot.

One of the tee-shirts reads, "Remember when Sturgis was about motorcycles and not a fashion show." That looks good on a shirt and probably expresses the feelings of many of us die-hards but it isn't an accurate statement.

Most of the people who attend events want vendors and they want lots of them. Shoppers want choices and wide selections and Biker shoppers are no different.

Historically this phenomenon is as American as hot dogs, apple pie, and well, Harley-Davidsons. All can be found in abundance at Sturgis Rally and Races every August.

Vendors have always peddled their wares in America from settlements, to gold discovery sites, to military encampments. They would have been common at Sturgis, or what would have become Sturgis in the mid 1800s.

In the way-back they were called "Sutlers," and followed the major people movements all over the country, well in fact, like motorcycle events. Military troop movements were followed all over the country during the 1800s and bases like Fort Meade even had permanent ones.

Not unlike today's vendors the sutlers primarily sold items that were not readily available to the troops. Things not issued by the military, soap for example, were very popular. Some of the most popular were the very rare things. Examples then were newspapers from back East, canned peaches, and canned smoked oysters.

179

It is easy to make a modern Sturgis comparison. Many of the things we buy are only available at the big events. Only there can you purchase that rare or specialty item by walking into a shop or tent. You cannot get a Sturgis Ride Bell at Wal-Mart, or old bike parts at the local NAPA store, and food is one of the big three.

A quick scan of the list of vendors at the 1998 Sturgis Rally reveals 88 tattoo setups, 92 vendors selling leather, and 94 selling foods. This places food vendors behind only parts and accessories and tee-shirts. There were 169 tee-shirt vendors. These numbers do not count the permanent establishments. A few good examples are, Philtown, Bob's with the $1.00 pie and ice cream special, Easyriders, and of course the infamous Road Kill Cafe.

On an ordinary day back home you can't get Ostrich on a stick at Mickey D's, or Amish Maid ice cream listed among the traditional 31 flavors.

At Sturgis you might just get your Billy Bob Teeth fitted at the rally, then try some of Big Red's Cajun Cooking, or one of Grandma's Indian Tacos.

A short stroll down Lazelle Street would have taken you to where you <u>can</u> have a bowl of Amish Maid Ice Cream and if it's Ostrich your taste buds were crying for, well Sturgis had at least two locations. Maybe a simple carry-around snack was more to your liking. It would have been difficult to find some Cheyenne Mountain Buffalo Jerky at the C store back in Peoria.

For a real meal to satisfy a biker's appetite, nothing beats the steak sandwich at Famous Dave's. I can't imagine a great event week without a couple of visits to Porky's for a huge pork chop or some tenderloin. A great way to end any riding day is to cap it off with your ridin' buds and you stopping in at the Road Kill for a late night burger or omelet.

Yessir, seeing Sturgis on your stomach is my favorite way to enjoy it and if something simple, ordinary, and familiar is what you crave - there was plenty of that there too.

The Power Brokers

"I feel the need...The need for speed."
-Tom Cruise & Anthony Edwards-
Top Gun - 1986

Human beings have always loved competition and speed. Ancient Greeks valued runners among the most favored in the Olympic games. From foot racing to horse racing to Soap Box Derbys for kids we love racing. If it moves we will find a way to make it race against something if only the clock. Quiz shows look for the fastest answer, while greased pigs run at county fairs. Lumber Jacks chop logs and frogs try to out jump one another in Calaveras County.

In North Carolina one of the oldest folk legends or haunting stories is of a horse race in colonial times, where one member of landed gentry who was determined to win, demanded that his horse take him over the finish line first or take him straight to hell. The story goes that he whipped the horse to all out speed and running as if the devil were after him. Suddenly the horse ran up to a large tree and stopped as suddenly. The rider was thrown into the tree and killed instantly. Thus the horse obeyed his master's command. Legend has it the horseshoe tracks are there to this day and chickens will not eat grain there, (somehow chickens eating grain are always used in these old stories to detect the presence of the devil).

The point here is what ever it is that makes Johnny race is in everyone and everywhere. And, motorcycling is no different.

The quest for power and speed sought by many bikers and the manufacturers who supply the demand for more performance is among the strongest human drives. From rural home shops to major players this quest is pursued 365 days a year across America. This has led to large companies, who for decades have been the major force behind performance for street and track in the automotive industry, to add divisions devoted to the same pursuits in the motorcycling world. Large performance equipment developers such as Crane Cams and Edelbrock are two examples of traditional speed equipment providers who have become synonymous now with two wheeled power. New on the horizon are companies which are producing whole motorcycles with super engines, some actually fabricated from V8 automobile engines.

The major players have risen to prominence and recognition in the motorcycle community. Companies such as Jims, Barnett, and Carl's Speed Shop, have made giant names for themselves, exclusively in the production of awesome power from motorcycle engines and drive trains, are intertwined in the history of the speed industry and where the future seems to be headed both for street and track is more or less anybody's guess. One thing is for sure, if there is a way to extract one horse power from an engine or squeeze out a single second from an ET it will be discovered sooner or later.

Among the earliest records of motorcycling are races. The first race, at what would be the Indianapolis Motor Speedway was a motorcycle race and was won by Cannonball Baker. As early back as motorcycling history takes us there is racing. Many famous names are connected with the fierce competition between the various motorcycle companies. Records were being set on and off the tracks. Prior to W.W.I Motorcycles were raced wherever they could be. Anywhere was fair game for a race, and you'd find events ranging from board tracks (paved lengthwise with wooden 2x4s) to hillclimbs. Endurance races from coast to coast and from the Canadian border to Mexico were held to set time and distance records. After the war a new commitment to competition was voiced by Indian and Excelsior and Harley-Davidson officially reentered racing with an awesome team eventually nicknamed, "The Wrecking Crew." Under the direction of Bill Ottaway and R. W. Enos the H-D team pioneered the precision pit stop setup and routines, publicized as so much a part of successful auto racing today. Pretty much all of the marques had teams and fought ceaselessly to set records and win races. Gypsy tours and the major events, like Daytona, Laconia, and Sturgis, all were started around or to promote races. Through the years racing, and much of it motorcycles, have given us names like Cannonball Baker, Red Parkhurst, and probably the greatest champion of all, Mike Hailwood. Tourist Trophy Races (usually abbreviated TT Races) were popular world wide and the American factories would compete overseas against European and Japanese entries. All the competitive factories raced at the Isle of Man, in the Irish Sea. A race conceived in 1904 by Lord Raglan, the Governor of the island. The actual first race was May 28, 1907.

Even Honda would learn that a win at the Isle of Man would produce more sales than a World Championship otherwise.

Drag racing appears to be at the peak of popularity in America. So with no intent to short change round tracks and road racing, in the interest of space limitations, detailed examples here will be from the world of motorcycle drags.

Just how basic is the quest for speed and competition? Every August at the Sturgis Dragway a race, only held there, draws a large contingent of entrants. This event is called the Sturgis FLASH Race. The American Heritage Dictionary defines the word Flash in part as:

> **flash** (fl²sh) *v.* —*intr.***1.** To burst forth into or as if into flame. **2.** To appear or occur suddenly. **3.** To move or proceed rapidly. —*tr.* To communicate or display at great speed. —**flash** *n.* A split second; an instant. —**flash** *adj.* Happening suddenly or very quickly.

Flash now has a new definition and it incorporates all of the above definition and more. Flash now stands for <u>Fastest Legal All Street Harleys</u>. This is a relatively new motorcycle drag racing class and it's taking off in a flash. Pun intended. Brought to life from a concept in the mind of American Iron Magazine's publisher, Buzz Kanter in 1992, this racing class is now drawing contenders from all over the country. For a race only held at Sturgis during Bike Week, FLASH racing is growing in numbers and popularity. Record crowds at Sturgis annually watch as approximately forty bikes and riders compete, sometimes as fiercely as the big guns, for good money purses and trophies. The racing, albeit not as fast, is exciting and spectators seem to loved it. The best part of all is that the show is good and the bikes are not all that much slower than some of the big guys.

Staff members open at 10:00 a.m. and began to check in bikes and have them tech inspected. Tech is a little different than in most categories of racing. Remember the definition of flash is Fastest Legal All Street Harley. It's those three words in the middle that are the rub. Each Bike must be completely streetable and legal to ride as such. This means mirrors, gas tanks, street tires and lights.

This is reminiscent, to us old Road racers, of a time when Sports Cars were, by definition, vehicles that could be equally driven on the road or track. A good driver and tuner could drive to the track, compete, and really have a chance to win. Now days it takes cubic dollars rather than cubic inches to be a front runner.

From Maine to California the Flash racers come and their resources vary from best of everything to peanut butter budgets. Their reasons are all the same. To whet their appetites for that thrill that can only be understood by those who lust for something a little more on the edge than mere existence. That one moment when human and machine become one and, as if propelled by a giant catapult spring, suddenly they are hurled along a race course at breath taking speed.

The late Steve McQueen once said something to the effect that, "to a racer this is life and everything else is just waiting." The waiting is over at Sturgis for competitors who get this thrill at no other time, and it is time to live.

Registration wraps up about noon and all registrants have to get ready for qualifying. Now qualifying in FLASH racing is a little different than in other classes. These bikes and riders must prove that they are streetable by doing just that. Going out on the street. Things get underway with a ride to prove that each bike could go out for a Sunday putt with no trouble. For the Sturgis races the ride is to somewhere like Belle Fourshe and back. If any bike is built with non streetable equipment or tires or even a fuel tank that will not last as long as an average stock Sportster between fuel stops, then it is disqualified. The average shakedown ride can be up to one hundred miles.

In short, you must complete the run in order to run and you, "run what you brung."

The bikes end up back at the track and are impounded until

race time later in the evening. No changes or modifications are allowed at this point. No one can swap carbs or clutches or change anything. Minor things can take place such as fine tuning. Perhaps some repairs on the order of minor necessities are allowed in the interest of safety or preventative maintenance. Mirrors must then be removed for track safety.

Each year's round of racing draws quite an eclectic field of competitors. They range from school teachers and tattoo artists, to top performance bike builders.

The individual stories of some of the contestants are as varied as motorcycle riders in general. A sampling of the 1995 line up is a good example of the variety.

Jerry Holdeman of Sacramento, California, rode his FXR to the event and said that to compete was a dream come true. He said, "I've been reading about FLASH for two years. I believe more people can relate to this class."

Meg Jackson, who hails from Belfast, Maine, is one of the first woman racers in the class as is Linda Elliott from Colorado Springs, Colorado. Meg loaded her bike and then she and her daughter piled in the family truckster and headed west to go racing. Meg incidentally is the legislative contact for United Bikers of Maine and representative for the Motorcycle Riders Foundation. She has been riding motorcycles for 23 years and has had her own Harley for ten.

Verl 'Smitey' Smith was enroute from Oregon when his truck broke down for the second time since leaving home. He left the truck repairs to his companions, unloaded the bike, and determined to race, he rode to Sturgis from Gillette, Wyoming. Proved his bike is streetable I'd say.

Smitey is sponsored by one of the nicest dealers in the Harley dealer network, Doyle's in Eugene, Oregon. Doyle and his staff are the kind of folks you hope to be near if you have a problem on the road. They share the spirit of kinship with all who are traveling by two wheels.

At race time engines and nerves are at a fever pitch and all ready to go. Always a couple of bikes drop out due to mechanical difficulties.

The Sportster Amateur Class opens the Ball. Round two is the big twins' turn and they put on quite a show even though they

185

are not quite as quick as the lighter sportys in the 1/8 mile.

The final showdown is the Lightning FLASH race, where the fastest of each class goes against each other. All in all the racing is great and the spectators enjoy some real excitement and racing entertainment. FLASH racing is, in and of itself, refreshing. It's a competitive class that has room for the little guy to have a chance. It's a class that can grow in size and popularity because it means that some folks who would otherwise only be able to watch, may now win. Perhaps FLASH racing will not be just a "flash in the pan."

A few years ago there was a team that just seemed to have everything fall into place. They called themselves Flying V Racing and led sort of a charmed existence for a brief couple of years. Sometimes everything comes together just the way its supposed to, and that seems to be the way things are at Flying V Racing. Just buy all the right parts and bolt them together and go win. Well, maybe that's stretching things a bit.
While it's true that all the pieces did fit and fit well for this record breaking Cinderella drag racing bike and team, there's more than met the eye.

This black and polished aluminum bad boy just seemed to disappear at the Christmas Tree and suddenly reappear at the finish with Wayne Pollack lying along the top of it. Usually its broken a few things along the way, such as track records, national records — the sound barrier. From time to time it even breaks hearts and parts.
This machine, looked about as harmless as a Black Mamba, and catapulted itself and the Cinderella Team into the record books over a period of time that is almost a record itself.

Starting three races late in the season in 94 at Piedmont in Greensboro, North Carolina, the bike broke its engine mount and its first record. Right off the trailer and being ridden for the first time ever, the bike streaked down the 1/8 mile with Wayne stretched along its length like Superman's cape, to blister the asphalt with an ET of 5.85 @ 117 MPH. This was on the first pass and four MPH faster than the previous record. It started out the 95 season at Houston by doing the same thing.
So what makes this fire breathing dragon so special? To answer this question we have to get down to the nuts and bolts of the matter — literally.

This machine began as a 108 cube hopped up street engine and an off-the-cuff remark to Ed Fornwalt, owner of Durham Harley-Davidson. Wayne said he was kidding around when he said to Ed, "If you give us the motor we'll do the rest." To his surprise Ed called the next day and said OK and Flying V Racing was born.

Wayne and partner Jay Barker had been best friends for about thirteen years and building custom bikes for ten of those years. Their friend Mike Schulz joined in from the start and helped build the bike.

The guys freely admit that without Ed's faith and financial support there would never have been the success they've had. Following Ed came the Durham HOG Chapter and then other individual sponsors. Wayne said, "I was smart enough to realize that I couldn't afford to put this effort together on my own."

The x-ray view of this monster revealed a breakdown of parts which began with a Bonnie Truett frame to wrap around the engine.

The dragon's front legs are Ceriani and are shod with Dunlop. Power to the rear is through an Auto 5-speed connected to CDL/Bandit clutching and hit the ground via Goodyear rubber. Both wheels were RC Components and the rear struts custom fabricated by Flying V's crew.

Things that go fast must also be able to stop quick and this was accomplished via a combination of Performance Machine and Flying V brakes.

At this point almost everything on the bike was custom fabricated or modified for this machine, but Pollack and Barker both have been heard to say that if they had it to do over, they'd have started with a clean sheet of paper rather than try to modify a street engine.

When finished the engine had cost them about twice the man-hours and cash that a power plant from scratch would have. In its final state everything in or on the engine had been replaced or reworked.

Once the guys discovered that they couldn't coax the horses out of the motor in a reliable fashion they began to build and rebuild.

The main problem was that the same modifications that make fast street horses don't necessarily do the same for all out

187

radical track power.

Starting at the heart with welded and re-machined stock Harley cases, S&S flywheels, and JIMS rods, the Carl's modified heads are pumped up to power by Arias pistons custom fabricated to Flying V design specs. The mixture being compressed is breathed in through a reworked S&S D over Baisley valves and fired by a Dyna 4000 ignition.

The JIMS lifters and blocks are sitting atop a modified Crane bumpstick to make sure that those enormous valves open and shut right on cue. The bike first came to life with a 4-speed tranny and Carl's cam but over the two seasons it ran, the Truett frame became altered to better distribute the weight, and the cam and gearbox were changed.

I might add one tiny little note at this point. This was the first successful attempt to run with a big twin engine in Pro-Modified, instead of a Sporty power plant.

So, where's the magic? Luck-of-the-Irish maybe, but I don't think so. Wayne, who freely admitted a liking for living on the edge, has ridden everything fast since age eight but Motocross. He says it's too bumpy. Now this sounds strange for a guy who spent a season as a pro Bareback Bronc and Bull rider. He was a good chauffeur but that's not enough. Nobody joins metals together better than Jay and Mike but that didn't do it alone.

Ask the guys and they unanimously would tell you that it was the *Team*. Jay says, "The secret is that there's no secret. There isn't anything magic. We were a team and we worked well together." He went on to say that they were a dedicated high maintenance team and all devoted to the bike. Each guy knew his part and did it. "No one had to say do this or do that," said Jay, "we all just did what ever needed to be done." "Check, check and re-check everything," was a lesson learned from an older more experienced racer. They constantly tested everything and looked for areas that needed attention, even if everything was running good.

Never stopping short of giving credit where credit is due. They heaped praises on James Haithcock of Raleigh, NC, for the lessons on bike building and machine work he'd taught them. They acknowledged a huge debt of gratitude for the help provided by their friends in the AHDRA. Pollack, who shifted by sensing and feel rather than using a tach or shift light, said they owe much of their success to their intense desire to understand machinery and the lessons learned from their friends.

I'd say they learned well because the bike has set thirteen records to date and was the first modified gas bike to go over 120 MPH in the eighth and 140 in the quarter. During its first season and much of 1995 it was never outrun under power. Whenever it's lost there was some kind of mechanical failure. All the right pieces were there and they all fit just right. Not just the parts on the beast itself but everything and everyone involved right down to the smallest contribution.

There are many great jockeys in the world of motorcycle drag racing but none so "colorful" or quite so interesting as Patricia Sexton Nied. This is a high-speed grand mother who goes by the nickname of Peppermint Patti. Her story is at least unusual and at best exciting. Not a Harley girl, however, she is just afflicted with two-wheel-itis and the go-fast flu.

Peppermint Patti grew up on the south side of Chicago. She was a tough city girl with a strong sense of, in her words, "righteousness and justice." Introduced to the world of motorcycles at age 14, she rode off on a 90CC Honda Scooter in Wisconsin, which belonged to a friend of her father, and she was gone for several hours. Upon her return, the two men, although worried, had a good laugh over how well she handled the scooter.

On her 15th birthday, her dad bought her a 1965 CB160 Honda and Mom threw a fit. According to her mother, "Nice girls didn't ride on the back of motorcycles, let alone on the front of them," so Dad sold it to an uncle, who still has the little 65 Scrambler.

By age 17 she was married and the mother of identical twin girls. Shortly after high school she bought a used 1968 350 Honda for $500 from an assembly line foreman, where she worked bottling salad dressing. Unfortunately the little 350 Honda was lost in a garage fire set by her then husband.

Patti's second husband, a motorcycle mechanic, instilled in her an interest in the art of motorcycle maintenance and repair. (That is <u>Art</u> not <u>Zen</u>) By age 21 she had 3 children about the time her son was 2 years old, she was seriously involved with motorcycles again. Within the next year Patti was racing in motorcycle Pro Stock Drags, on a 1013 KAW.

189

In 1975 she was doing more street racing than most of the guys. Patti became, "the one to beat." This 108 pound lady showed no fear whatsoever. Token offers of sponsorship for track racing came and went.

In 1980 she received her first serious sponsorship. At the time Patti was racing a 1980 GS 1100E. A few slight modifications made it extremely fast. An aging member of a Chicago motorcycle club, named Swanny, promoted her under the name of Peppermint Patti, because her attitude reminded him of the peanuts character. With him as her promoter they secured sponsorship with A&P Custom Cycles in Chicago.

In 1984 she married again and this time to George Nied, owner of Star Chrome, a metal finishing shop in Chicago. Patti ran Star Chrome alone very successfully for 2 years, while George was in pursuit of other business avenues.

Over the course of her life's adventures she has been through 18 bikes, participated in dozens of drag races, won multiple trophies, even been in a few TV spots, and had a heck of a lot of fun!

She quit racing in 1980 preferring to step down rather than go down in a wreck. Said Patti, "I figured I'd had a good time and a lot of guardian angles. God had let me have my share of wins, and I didn't want to push it. By 1980 I was ready to leave."

Recently she has packed up everything she cares about and moved to Sedona, Arizona. Climbing mountains, lying in rushing streams and recharging in waterfalls. According to Patti: health, energy, and beauty, abound in God's landscape. In recent correspondence Peppermint Patti said, "I guess it was true all along. I was BORN TO BE WILD! And I'm loving it!"

She likes working on making the bikes look pretty, and now rides a 1981 GS1100E. This machine has been customized by her and she showed it in the 1999 World of Wheels Show. Patti says it is the prettiest bike she has ever owned. These days she rides the breath taking Red Rock Canyons of Arizona and enjoys just stopping to write poetry whenever and wherever she wants. What a life!

Of the many names which loom large in today's world of motorcycle drag racing none is able to strike more favorable comment than Hall of Fame inductee Ray Price.

Step through the doors at Ray Price Harley-Davidson, in Raleigh, NC, and you are greeted by the not atypical showroom mix of boutique and machinery familiar to all who frequent the dealerships on a regular basis. If you stop in, at a time when he's there, you might be greeted by a man of medium stature, with a distracted look on his face, but a smile and handshake for everyone who comes in close proximity.

The distracted look is for real for he is always planning and working on new projects. In addition, he is constantly being tugged, pulled, or directed from one thing to another, and having to answer questions or make decisions.

When you stop in, and do see the fellow described, his head will most likely be tilted, lending an ear to his even shorter, but equally nice dispositioned wife of 40 years, Jean.

Should you encounter any or probably all of these criteria, you have met the very atypical Harley dealer, Champion Harley drag race pioneer, and Motorcycle Hall Of Famer, Ray Price.

The Ray Price brochure says, "What does a guy do for excitement at age 60? ... 1/4 mile in less than 7 seconds!" At 61 he is still doing it and still winning.

His interest in motorcycles hasn't been there all of his life. It didn't start until around age seven or eight.

Ray grew up as a North Carolina farm boy and as a child had a bicycle. One of his friends had a scooter and this friend's uncle had a real motorcycle, an Indian with an inline four cylinder engine. "Now I thought that was cool," says Ray.

His first actual motorcycle ride wouldn't come until much later while serving in the Air Force.

While in the service two major milestones were to take place in his life. He rode his first motorcycle, which was a Triumph, owned by a fellow serviceman, and September 20th, 1958, married his sweetheart from home in Smithfield, Jean Wood.

Ray's love for motorcycling was to hold strong but not yet become his career. It remained a hobby for the next thirteen and a half years.

Since discharged, Ray went to work again in the electronics field.

Ray's love of motorcycles never waned during those years and he purchased his first bike in 1963. It was a used 1953 Harley-Davidson K-Model, which was followed by a 1954 K-Model and then a 59 Pan Head. These motorcycles only whetted his appetite and led to his eventually leaving his job to begin a new career in the motorcycle industry. This life change decision was to be the birth of a legend.

Riding with his wife's brothers on Sunday afternoons was his beginning as a racer because the Wood brothers both had Sportsters and the Sportys were quicker than the Pan, so he began a series of modifications to compete with the quicker bikes and satisfy a thirst for innovation which is unquenched even today.

After about a year the Pan had lost it's saddlebags and all unnecessary accouterments and the bulky front end was replaced with narrow K-Model forks and suspension. The bike was much like the Superglide which Harley would eventually put into production.

Though the bike was now more competitive it was still very hard to shift the bigger machine quick enough to beat the Sportsters. He realized that if you can't beat 'em join 'em so in the Fall of 1965 he tried to trade the Pan. The dealer wouldn't accept it so he restored it to stock and went to another dealer and traded for a new 1966 Sportster.

He still has the accessories from that Sportster as well as a K-Model, and plans to restore another Sportster like his first one. (When time permits - Ha Ha.)

His racing, modifying and testing formation of Precision Cycle, housed in an old gas station, was his first venture into self employment. Sound familiar?

Precision Cycle did well as a custom and performance cycle shop and in about three years moved down the road about a mile into digs four times as large. He operated there until 1982 when Precision Cycle was moved to the present location of Ray Price Harley-Davidson. He had bought the building and the dealership in 1981 and changed the name but operated the two separately for another year. Precision Cycle can still be seen on the side of the building.

Unforeseen by Ray, this move and consolidation of the two entities was to be the beginning of the end for the racing as demands for his time with the dealership conflicted with the time necessary for the racing effort. This conflict caused his racing to gradually dwindle and 20 years of competition came to a close with an unplanned retirement.

The previous years of racing had seen Ray Price set records over and over again and pioneer many developments and engineering advances in the machinery itself. All of these factors lead to his induction into the Motorcycling Hall Of Fame in Sturgis, South Dakota.

From those early drag races with his wife's brothers and the purchase of his first XLCH, he continuously modified and built faster and faster motorcycles in an unquenchable thirst for ever faster speeds and elapsed times.

Sunday afternoon hours of cruising gave way to rides of seconds as the Sportster evolved from a street machine to a racing bike. The first modifications were in the form of a frame-mounted custom aluminum seat and solid struts replacing shocks. Outings were now consisting of spending the day at the dragstrip.

As the Sportster made its way from street bike to all out dragster, so did Ray's reputation, and his collection of trophies grew. Much time was spent on backroads with friend Bobby Turner working on racing technique and elapsed times. Time well spent that paid off big.

In the early days all classes of bikes were lumped together. Said Ray, "back then they didn't have the modern sophisticated timing systems and mostly would run everyone heads-up. Sometimes they would spot someone but not often." With most of the entrants being street bikes with an occasional modified showing up, spotting was a way to even the odds by placing disadvantaged machines in front of the more powerful ones at the start. Ray successfully ran that Sportster, now an all out dragster, until 1972.

Ray ran his first professional race and made a good showing in August 1968 at Atco, New Jersey. (see endnote) From then on it was professional racing in C-Modified class. He set the record in C-Modified in 1968 and held it until 1973. During that period he repeatedly broke his own records and at times held the ET and speed records simultaneously.

That first race at NJ was under the old Mid Atlantic Motorcycle Association which gave way to the American Motorcycle Drag Racing Association. Following came the National Motorcycle Racing Association, the Drag Bike Association, and finally the International <u>Drag Bike Association</u> which is still in existence. To-day Ray races under the sanctions of the <u>International Hot Rod Association</u> and the <u>All Harley Drag Racing Association.</u>

In the early 70s, Ray was approached by Roy Strawn (see sidebar) to build a bike to follow the popularity of the 'Funny Cars' in automobile drag racing. These were cars which grotesquely re-sembled street cars but had little front wheels and giant rear ones and made a lots of smoke while going very fast. Ray enlisted Danny Johnson, who was already racing fuel bikes, involved in the project.

With Danny's help Ray pioneered the first 'Funny Bike' making a stroker bike look somewhat like a street bike, but with the exaggerated proportions of the 'Funny Cars' seen on the tracks. Some of the modifications included a fiberglass shell resembling a stock tank and solid struts machined to look like rear shocks. A small front wheel followed by an Avon 4" slick in back finished the setup. The bike made its first pass down the track in an exhibi-tion, running on gasoline and using only the top three gears. Ray and Danny went back to the pits and changed the carburetion and gasoline over to fuel and Ray ran the bike again down the track in high gear for his first time ever on nitro. The Funny Bike class was born.

Ray was booked to run this bike in exhibition runs because it would smoke the rear tire all the way down the quarter mile. Four inch rear tires grew to seven eventually, as competition de-veloped. With better traction, instead of smoking the quarter mile, the front end was carried the whole way in the air. A new class was now racing these bikes and called, for image considerations, Pro Fuel. Eventually the class would, under Ray's urging, be re-named back to Funny Bikes. The third and final configuration of this pioneer bike is on display in the Motorcycle Hall Of Fame in Sturgis.

Over the years Ray has invented or played a significant role in the development of many innovations and inventions in modern motorcycle drag racing. Two prominent examples are the wheelie bars, which keep the bikes from flipping over backwards, and a design used in the special two-speed transmissions on many drag bikes.

After retirement in 83, Ray and Jean spent the next thirteen years building the dealership into one of the largest in the Southeast and have a very active HOG chapter.

Building his Harley-Davidson dealership has included buying the adjacent buildings and real estate on both sides of the original 10,000 square foot building. The business has expanded and all are now being replaced by a brand new 56,000 square foot building which will take over the whole area. The new shop motif is indicative of Ray's love of drag racing and the new floor was recently launched not with Champagne but with burnouts by Ray and many of the top contenders in the drag racing world today who came with their racing bikes as a show of friendship. The appearance as you enter the store will be of looking down a dragstrip complete with a Christmas Tree timing device.

Participating in this ceremony were Jim McClure, Bill Furr, John Russell, Jamie Emery, Jay Turner, Bob Spina, Tony Mattioli, and Pete Hill. This was held during the annual RPHD customer appreciation day.

Even during the years of not racing the spirit was in his blood and never far from his heart and mind. Attempts to satisfy that thirst by building, fielding, or sponsoring bikes for others to ride were numerous and unsatisfactory. Even the satisfaction of helping others with the same itch become winners was less than his own appetite demanded and a hollow thrill at best. In January 1996 at the AHDRA 1995 awards banquet, Ray announced that he was coming out of retirement and returning to racing. The latter half of 1995 he had climbed back into the saddle on three different occasions and discovered that even at age 58 he could burn up the quarter mile with the best of 'em.

Since that announcement in 1996 Ray has consistently shown well. In 1996 he finished fourth for the season in points, second in 1997, and third at the close of 1998's season in two different racing organizations. Does he love it? September 20, 1998, marked Ray and Jean's 40th anniversary. Jean was working at a rally and Ray was in Virginia racing. He did, however, send her a big bouquet of flowers with his love to the rally. Forty years, a good track record for the both of them, at home as well as on the dragster.

What does a man do for excitement at age 60? At 61, Ray Price is still racing and now he has created his own dragstrip inside the new dealership.

Editor's note: An amusing incident happened to him at his first major race away from his home area. Ray had modified his Sportster to the point that it was really strong and a friend of his had recently been to the professional drags at Atco, NJ and knew that Ray had quicker times than the strokers running there. He talked Ray, reluctantly, into going with him to New Jersey to race. This track had all the modern timing equipment and was a first for Ray.

Ray ran with quicker times and beat all the local champs with their stroker engines, until the last pass when he messed up at the start and was beaten by a big block engine. Coming back down the return road he was stopped by a huge guy who looked to be about seven feet tall who told him they needed to see him at the start line.

Ray rode over there elated thinking they were going to congratulate him for doing so good, only to be shocked that he was being protested by the track for being illegal. With the track doing the protest he wouldn't even be compensated for the teardown, and were showing a pretty angry attitude toward him.

They took the heads off and a local tech inspector measured everything right there at the start line with everyone watching. Then the guy looked up said to everyone but Ray, "guys it's legal." No one believed it and they ordered it done again. This happened a third time and the tech inspector stood up and apologetically looked at the others and said, "I'm sorry guys but it is legal."

Ray left really puzzled at why a country boy from North Carolina would draw so much attention from all these professional racers. The organization director who protested was Roy Strawn, and he felt so bad about the attitude and the way Ray was treated, from then on they have been good friends.

It turns out, however that Ray's pal had been going around with his chaw of tobacco instigating all of these guys by making comments to the other riders like, "you ain't gonna let that country boy come up here and beat your stroker with that pretend legal engine are you?"

On the way home he let Ray in on what was going on. He was getting the local boys fired up enough to bet on whether or not Ray was legal and after the protest results he went around collecting his winnings. He did, however, split the take with Ray.

Motorclothes And The Aftermarket

"I see by your outfit that you are a cowboy.
These words he did say as I boldly walked by."
-Marty Robins-
-Streets of Larado

Chrome horses need chrome, and fancy saddles, and the riders must have appropriate outfits to ride them. In this chapter the market for accessories is examined. In 1996 Harley-Davidson had net sales of 121.8 million dollars in general merchandise and products licensed for sale by stores other than Harley dealers. A trip through any mall in the US reveals stores which wouldn't have shown a motorcycle oriented product a decade ago now displaying racks of cycle style leather jackets, boots, belts and other paraphernalia.

Making a logical transition from The Power Brokers, this chapter examines the aftermarket and its role in the image that has gone from one of disdain to everybody has to have at least a tee shirt. Aside from the boutiques and department stores there are dozens of companies producing everything for the machines themselves, from seats to custom painted parts. If it can't be chromed, painted, or polished then it is covered in leather.

Let's address this market by examining some of the larger companies like Corbin whose patented saddle designs have enjoyed a world wide market, providing comfortable seats for most of the worlds more popular motorcycles. The chapter includes the accessories companies, many of whom are crossover companies which produce both speed and dress up parts to fit the bikes.

The aftermarket keeps growing yearly and seems unstoppable as more and more new companies are starting up each year to help catapult this American phenomenon into the next millennium. We'll explore this part of the market both now and its projected growth for the future. More modern day cowboys are showing up on the streets and in the corporate offices now that the image has become acceptable. This chapter examines the market that is ready and waiting to outfit these new age cowboys who in their minds are still riders of the purple sage.

Before examining things in the way of leather and metal parts there is one catagory of item which neither goes on the bike or the rider but often goes with him. More likely to be found with the biker riding the porcelain horse than the chrome one, are the magazines which cater to the motorcycling industry. These are some of the most publicly visible aftermarket items in as much as they adorn almost every newsstand in America.

The magazine industry has been with the motorcycling world from the very early days and are still a very vital part of the industry. From the magazines we learn about the latest inovations and the best roads to travel. We learn how to do it ourselves and do it right. We are encouraged, entertained, and enticed and all the while we are able to live vicariously a life on the road riding in our minds with those who write the articles and take the pictures.

With names like *Easyriders*, *American Iron*, *American Rider*, and *IronWorks*, we have the distinct image of this being an American biker oriented form of literature. There are others which are geared toward performance such as *Hot Rod Bikes* and *Hot Bike*, and event directed like *Sturgis Rally News* or *Motorcycle Events Magazine*. Some are primarily for the ladies with names like *Bikes and Spikes* and *Asphalt Angels*. A variety of tabloids are also to be found among the average biker's reading materials. Representative are *Iron Biker News* in the East and *Thunder Press* in the West. If you are fond of straddling a motorcycle at all, there is a magazine with your interest in mind.

In the early days of motorcycling there were riders and racers just to broadly lump everyone together. You might have a mechanic at the races but often enough you had to run what you brung and this sometimes meant you had to be the mechanic also. I have no statistics here so the statement is a surmise of this aspect based upon my own early years of Sports Car racing. I can say however that if you were touring you'd likely as not, have to be mechanic and driver. Susie Hollern's book, Women and Motorcycling has a photo of two women having to work on their 'side hack' by the side of the road in 1925.

References have already been made in this writing as to the popularity of the image and the shopping mall paraphernalia and cheap biker attire. I'm not sure I would want to go down in a $60.00 jacket even if it did have a designer label in it. The real aftermarket makes clothes for riders who have either a practical use or a cosmetic connection to the motorcycle. For example, high compression engines need a heavy duty starter, such as Spyke, and an all weather, all season, rider would do well to purchase an Aerostch Roadcrafter (yes the spelling is correct) all weather riding suit. These suits are simply the warmest and driest riding attire available.

If your specific look or need is leather then there is a wide variety of makes you may work with. Among the best are Brooks, Hein Gericke, Leather Gallery, or any of the one sold by cycle specialty accessories dealers. Motorcycle manufacturers brand names are pretty much reliable as well. After all they don't want you getting skinned up in that eventual inevitable slide down the asphalt.

Things like engineering boots or cowboy boots used to be available only from stores which catered to blue collar workers or boot shops but now are regular designer items in motorcycle specialty catalogs and the boutique area of cycle shops and dealerships.

Stop in any typical motorcycle dealership this day and time and you will notice as much space devoted to motoring apparel as motorcycles. In many there is considerably more space devoted to trappings than transportation.

In the old days the parts on the bike would be removed and replaced by the owner, often with a trip to the chrome shop in the process. This market is off a bit says Sandie Papierski, of Atlantic Coast Plating, Inc.

Her shop produces some of the brightest and most well-done chrome plating in the industry. It seems to be the trend, however, that as more and more Americans are able to buy custom bikes directly from the builders, and factories, such as Harley-Davidson, are offerring chromed out machines as part of the product line, fewer people are removing parts and sending them to be chromed. There are also other factors coming into play. Many ready to bolt on chrome accessories that have been produced cheaply overseas, are available at dealerships and after market shops. This is a popular alternative as stricter EPA pollution and waste disposal regulations have driven prices up and have driven some plating shops in the US completely out of business. In addition, ever striving for greater levels of uniqueness, people are turning to alternative finishes such as paint, polishing, and powder coating on parts that wouldhave traditionally been chromed.

To make your bike ride better, re-fitting with a Corbin Saddle and Progressive Suspension are things that a rider with average mechanical skills can do. The things a true enthusiast will usually do first are improve the ride and do it with those items he or she can do herself.

When it comes to performance there are gray areas as to whether a do-it-yourself type could or should attack the desired situation. Many things are critical and should only be attempted by a skilled mechanic or an owner with considerable knowledge and experience. Learning the hard way on today's motorcycles can be a very costly experience.

The cost of a mistake might be as simple as ruined chrome or some skin. It could be at the other extreme a $4,000.00 engine or your life. A creative warning I particularly like is in the instructions from Custom Cycle Engineering. This company manufactures some of the finest motorcycle control parts in the industry. Items like the parts which keep the wheels and handlebars connected to one another.

The most worrisome part is the loose nut connecting the handlebars to the seat and so there are cautions accompanying the parts to be installed and one warning is that if you do not possess the skills do **not** attempt to **do-it-yourself**. My favorite from them is at the end of the directions where they are cautioning the owner about bolt torque specifications and excessive strain. The warning states, "The extra stress could cause the bolt to break which might provide an exciting, yet unpleasant experience." At first reading I had a really good laugh at the creative wording of the warning. Then the thought of having the front end come apart, at say 75 miles per hour, was chilling.

Many of the items that riders replace on their machines are for reliability or to produce the power to efficiently haul around those of us who are of a more rotund or portly persuasion. (I can remember how insulted I was once at the suggestion I consider buying a coat in the portly department)

Power train items should definitely be left to the experts for installation. For durability and reliability Jims is a very safe bet and any engine modifications from Carl's Speed Shop will produce a drastic increase in horsepower. Upping the compression with Wiseco pistons and adding any of the several streetable Crane Camshafts will give your engine a boost. On my own bike I have also added an American Wire Wheel to the front for safety and durability as well as looks. There are several really great carburetors available on the market but for performance in power, economy, and for negotiating the extreme fluctuation in altitudes where I ride, I have fitted the bike with a Mikuni.

Everything which is taken apart on my machine goes back together with James gaskets. While I am expressing my opinion here as to equipment: It has been my experience with the way I ride that I get the most mileage with Continental tires.

My opinions here are from my own experience in riding over 110,000 miles on the same bike and for extreme durations. Many people have different experiences and I only know what works for me. I am in no way making competition or all out racing recommendations. I gladly defer to the experts.

An item which is relatively recent as accessories go, but is fast finding favor with those of us who prefer the long rides is the T-Bag. This is not an item for brewing a beverage by the side of a stream. It is a device which will greatly improve the aggravation of packing and keeping dry those designer clothes and leathers we wear while riding to be in style. Lets face it, if you have ever been caught in one of those frog-strangling rainstorms, which seem to follow motorcyclists around, and you have your formally dry things packed in a conventional manner. Well hey, no need to change. Everything else is as wet as you are.

The T-Bag solves the problem nicely. It sits behind you strapped to the bike and keeps everything accessible and orderly. Did I mention dry? The bag is available with a truly water proof liner. There are a variety of sizes available and it rides behind the driver providing a nice backrest for cruising America at length. The T-Bag will also ride on the luggage rack should you want to take a passenger.

A few of the aftermarket suppliers are as much all American success stories as motorcycling itself. Three of these companies example the American Dream and are proof of the American ideal. There are many but these are among the most shining of examples.

Few bikers do any modifying or accessorizing without sooner or later adding something from Barnett Tool & Engineering, S&S Cycle, or a Corbin Saddle. These companies did it by the numbers exactly as we were taught in grade school that it is supposed to work. Forget the George Washington and the cherry tree story. These tales are true.

Charles Barnett, known to his friends as Charlie or Corky, was the typical unruly American teenager. Possessing more brass (figuratively) than most he quit school in the 8th grade and hopped a train for California. This was in the late 30s. Already it is easy to see a part here played by James Cagney.

Charlie lied about his age and enlisted in the Navy. His mom discovered his enlistment and contacted the government and Charlie was unceremoniously dumped by Uncle Sam back into civilian life. He did not return home, however , but remained in California.

Charlie Barnett was a brusque character but a straight shooter. According to his son-in-law, Mike Taylor, "You always knew where you stood."

In the 1940s he worked mostly in machine shops and learned to be a skilled machinist. He started out riding motorcycles as basic transportation because he couldn't afford a car. Being a machinist he made parts for his own bikes and those of his friends. This was the start of his future because his focus was in making practical items. Things which wore out, like cables and clutches. He eventually opened a store which imported parts for sale but soon began to make the parts for sale himself, but with improvements. A major part of his initial manufacturing was to make clutch inserts for British bikes, Harley-Davidsons, and Indians.

Honda entered the market of high performance bikes so Charlie made a Honda friction plate. His plate worked so well that Honda officially authorized dealers to use the Barnett plate as a warranty item.

Barnett bought a Chevy wagon, (sounds more American

as we go along) would close the shop, and haul his family around to call on dealers and distributors. Gradually he built the business to the reputation it has today.

Charlie was a bear of a man but didn't take care of himself. He ate poorly and was a heavy smoker and in his 30s had a heart attack. Regaining his stamina, he plunged back into the grind and continued to make great products. Charlie failed to take care of himself as well as he did his customers and the inevitable happened. In his 50s he had a huge stroke. At this turn of events the doctors informed his family that he couldn't live.

Charlie fooled them all and with his wife Afton and daughter Colleen at his side, worked hard and recovered. Barnett survived another 20 years and lived into his seventies after two incidents which would have killed a lesser man. Charlie Barnett finally passed away in 1996.

Mike Taylor, who is truly one of motorcycling's nice guys, married Colleen Barnett in 1967 and a year later joined the company.

Mike was raised in Los Angeles, and while in the Navy became interested in motorcycles. Having an avid interest in the machines, it was a natural progression to work in the company with his new family.

Mike and Colleen have been running the business since the early 70s and they eventually bought out her parents about five years ago.

Continuing the business philosophy started by Charlie has been the way of Mike Taylor as well. The business continues to produce some of the finest cables and clutch parts in the industry and providing good service for their customers in addition to superb quality. The company has recently moved the facilities from Los Angeles to Ventura, California.

Among the most visible of the aftermarket "Big Three" (back to the big three again) is S&S Cycle begun in 1958 by George Smith and Stanley Stankos.

George was born on the dirt tracks of post W.W.II Chicago. Smith as an adult had been an army pilot and attempted auto racing, but motorcycles, however, were his first love.

George and a friend, Stanley Stankos, officially started the company in 1958 in Blue Island, Illinois, naturally named S&S

Cycle.

A 1939, 61 inch Knucklehead was the first recipient of the Smith performance formula (more cubic inches = more power = more speed). Refining the Knucklehead to go faster, Smith discovered nitromethane. Adding the volatile liquid to internal combustion engines would produce instant and massive amounts of power. Thus a way of converting their motors into fire breathing monsters – and making it a simple transformation. Other ingredients, such as alcohol or gasoline were added to the concoction to produce the most power, yet still maintain a combustible mixture.

Smith became crowned the "Fuel Wizard" by Harley-Davidson in 1970. Furthermore, Smith continuously felt machining operations could be done differently to produce a better product and make overall fitting problems minimal. He also questioned the casting design and alloy used.

A year later George and his wife, Marge, purchased Stanley's interest in the company and began to run it out of the basement of their home. Her maiden name was also Smith. Company literature says, "It was destiny the company's name stay just as it was."

Together, they nurtured and built a business that would become the world's most well-known performance company in the Harley aftermarket.

George and Marge found a countryside home with farming and ranching. This was among other passions they'd had. The Smith family home is located in a wooded valley just outside Viola, Minnesota. It became the site of the S&S Ranch as well as the new company headquarters for S&S Cycle.

In 1979, George Smith Jr, along with his two brother-in-laws, Samuel Scaletta and Robert Grueneberger, joined the company, thus making it a true family operation. August 1, 1980, George Smith Sr., father of the long stroke V-twin, passed away. The family pulled together with Marge's directing to take S&S Cycle into the next decade. Today the company continues along the same principals that have made it the premier manufacturer of high performance parts for Harley-Davidson motorcycles for over 34 years.

The first product the company offered was lightweight aluminum pushrods, followed by the stroker motor with flywheels and connection rods. Soon there were performance carburetors, followed by big-bore cylinders called Sidewinders and matching pistons.

Today S&S is known to Harley riders around the world for the broad line of high-performance motors, the product line offers thousands of individual parts and hundreds of high-performance kit combinations for Harley-Davidson and Buell motorcycles from 1936 to present.

Testimony to the popularity and dependability of S&S engines is in the fact that the majority of the custom builders in America use S&S engines in the production of their machines. This includes the foreign made Knucklehead which has an S&S case and internal parts.

The company motto is, "Proven Performance.", Once new parts are developed, they are "battle-tested" on the Bonneville Salt Flats, where S&S has set numerous new land speed records.

The company's line of Super carburetors with the distinctive chrome teardrop air cleaner cover has been and is the industry's most popular carburetor.

The company employs 160 staff personnel, and a number of seasonal workers, varying up to 250 people at times.

To compensate for rapid growth, each area of the company has been expanded. Some operations like manufacturing and warehousing have been enlarged more than once. Currently, nearly 90,000 square feet of work space is under roof.

Motorcycling has become fashionable and gone upscale in the last several years, and the demand for parts has been explosive. S&S is keeping pace by adding computer-controlled machines that improve productive capacity on components that require precise dimensions like crankcases and cylinder heads. Currently, they are experimenting with the use of robotics.

To commemorate the advent of their 40th anniversary, they've come up with several special items, not the least of which is apparel.

One of the greatest all American success stories in motorcycling is the Corbin story. Irish Immigrant kid's grandson devises a single product and grows it into an empire. How much more American can you get?

Check with directory assistance for Hollister, California, and you will not find any listing for Corbin Industries or Corbin

Enterprises. If you ask your operator for Corbin listings, you simply get Corbin Saddles.

Corbin Saddles is an unassuming and simple name for an industrial giant which is diverse enough to design and manufacture a wide range of things from riding boots to electric cars. The Corbin showroom has all of the products on display. These include simple products like boots and leather cream, several Sparrow electric cars, a wide variety of motorcycles, and even a nose cone from a motorcycle -powered land speed vehicle. The main product, however, is the world's finest motorcycle seats.

It's hard to imagine any one in motorcycling who doesn't conjure some mental image at the mention of Corbin in a conversation. In fact, all you have to say is Corbin. No need to say a Corbin what, cause everyone will know anyway.

To a long distance rider it makes no difference whether you call this vital part of the bike a seat or a saddle, the meaning is the same. It is the second most important part of the bike, giving way only to the tires. If the wind is where your heart is, then the saddle is where you live. Corbin makes it a place to live in comfort.

Step among any group of bikers in a conversation and three major subjects will always be among the topics: rights & freedoms, travels & events, and accessorizing the bikes. One part of the latter will always be that someone either has or is planning to get a Corbin seat.

Why do these saddles invoke such popularity? Marketing, perhaps, and that certainly is a factor. More than that, these saddles work and are designed to be considerably more than something to connect your butt to the frame.

A tour of the plant quickly reveals a place where quality and customer satisfaction are number one. Much time is spent in the plant's state of the art modeling shop, where each new bike's stock seat, frame, and mounting are examined for form and function. Bikes are ridden with the intention of discovering where improvements can be made. Improvements can be in shape, ergonomics, or aesthetics, and in most cases, all three. Corbin will tell you, "Locating design flaws in stock equipment and improving are paramount."

Mike Corbin is an engineer and designer and holds many patents on the processes his company uses to create these unique cradles for two-wheeled tush transportation. He makes 'em do the job, do it well, and look great on the machines at the same time. But what about the man himself?

Corbin was born in 1943, in Gardner, Massachusetts, the son of a traditional first generation Irish Immigrant couple.

Mike's father Walter, a toolmaker in the furniture industry, and his Uncle Dan, who was an engineer, were to be profound influences during his early development. They were a guidon of sorts which led to the beginning of a love of design and engineering toward a predictable outcome. He credits his mother Mary for his inheritance of an acute attention to detail and neatness. He says with a twinkle in his eye and a smile, "Mom was a neatnick, and she taught me that everything had to be perfect."

In spite of the influences from others, Mike was an independent thinker and became interested in motorcycles rather than furniture. His interest in motorcycles didn't turn into an occupation until much later.

In school he made good grades but preferred to spend his time designing things, making models (really into remote control), working on almost anything, and attending science fairs. Even though he was a good scholar in early schooling he did not plan to go on to college right away, much to the dismay of his parents. He agreed to stay in school through graduation on the condition that his parents would sign for him to enter the Navy.

He entered the Navy as planned and saw the world, "Or as much of it as you can see through a port-hole," says Mike. It did, however, train him to be a Master Electrician aboard an aircraft carrier, which is very similar to earning an associate degree in electrical engineering.

After the Navy he returned to New England, married his sweetheart, and worked as an electrician. During this time he pursued a degree in electrical engineering on a part time basis, but never quite finished schooling for the degree.

Mike explains that he never wanted to follow his father's work ethic, but wanted to invent himself into being an entrepreneur. "Every one invents himself into the person and lifestyle he wants to have." he remarked pensively. He said, "My grandfather's goal was to get himself out of Ireland and to America, and my father took the concept one step farther with the goal of having a good job and a home on some land. The Irish love land, and he and my uncle built the house themselves on an enormous hand carried stone foundation." And, said Mike, "Mine was logically to be a success as an entrepreneur, and now my son's is to be a really big entrepreneur."

His interest in motorcycles began at age 14 when, after much modifying of bicycles, he worked on a friend's Lambretta scooter trying to get it running. It is safe to say, agreed Mike, that he was hooked from that point on. He bought his own first motor-cycle at age 16-1/2, a Triumph 250. He paid a hundred dollars for the bike, got it cleaned up and running, and since then has owned hundreds of motorcycles with a present stable in his possession of about twenty.

After the Navy, and while working as an electrician for Pratt & Whitney, he started his own business on the side doing more electrical work. By this time he was also raising children. He has four children, two boys, two girls, and his oldest works with him.

The love of motorcycles never waned and by 1968 he was riding a customized Norton Atlas. The seat was uncomfortable and being the designer he was, he constructed a custom seat which was a significant improvement over the stock one.

He rode this bike with its improved seat to the Grafton Rally where his new seat drew a good bit of attention. He was finally persuaded to sell it to another Norton owner, and rode home sitting on his folded jacket for a seat. (I don't know how far Grafton is from Gardner but I'll bet the ride home was a pip)

Mike wasted no time making another seat for his bike and this one attracted a friend with a Sportster who wanted one for himself. Corbin pleaded that he wasn't in the seat business and was too busy to make them for anyone else, but the guy persisted. They agreed finally that Mike would make one for the Sportster to settle a debt. This seat was shown to Sal Scirpo, the Harley-Davidson dealer in Hartford, Connecticut, who contacted Mike to order five more of the seats. These seats sold right away, and more were ordered, in spite of protests from Mike that he didn't have time to make seats.

In 1969 the movie Easy Rider came out and the motorcycle industry began to flourish and so did the demand for Mike's seats.

208

This showed him he could be a designer and have a career in the industry he loved, motorcycles. Said Mike, "This was the turning point, and I never looked back."

In the early 70s, during the fuel crisis, Mike branched out from just seats. He developed an electric motor conversion kit for VW Beetles, and designed an electric motorcycle. To prove the viability of these vehicles, he attacked the record books and eventually owned all speed records for electrically powered vehicles. He set the record on an electric motorcycle August 19, 1974, at Bonneville Salt Flats, and was featured in National Geographic's December 1975 issue for winning the MacArthur Award with this electric bike.

This electric vehicle business seemed to be a great idea and the conversion kits worked well, although the bikes did not gain the popularity that went to the Beetle conversions. Several thousand kits were sold, but the fuel crisis ended, and was followed by the recession so that the market dried up. It was a great idea that had arrived too soon. Someday collectors will probably bid highly for an original Corbin Beetle conversion.

Mike went back to what did sell well, which was creating his wonderful motorcycle seats, and that business prospered.

Corbin doesn't just make seats for bikes, he loves motorcycles and has them sitting everywhere. He collects Indians and has them all over his house as well as the plant. He laughingly says, "As my kids grew up, I replaced them with motorcycles."

His dedication to excellence shows in the quality of the product and the immense popularity of the brand. As soon as a new model of motorcycle is on the market, there follows rapidly, a Corbin Saddle custom-crafted to fit it.

When asked about his devotion to the creation of the new products, he speaks of his fast and efficient modeling and engineering shop. "Streamlining the modeling process means less charge to the customer, and less time to market." He waxed on this subject, saying, "We have a long-term commitment to the motorcycle industry. No fast buck here. We want to be in for the long haul. Customer support is very important so quality is critical to longevity in the industry. As soon as you make a long term commitment to the industry, you realize that the only thing which will insure that is quality. Journalists and business students visit the plant, and when finished, say surprised, "There's no secret here. Just good engineering and good workmanship."

Not content to sit on the success of his seats, Mike Corbin is a hands-on kind of guy. He gets up at four am every morning, jogs several miles, has a health drink for breakfast, and is at work before daybreak. Mike is an engineer who describes himself as a designer, not a manufacturer. He explained, as he worked on a new design for a BMW backrest, that it is a learning experience; watching him, you learn that doing this is a fulfillment of this man's dream, and that a motorcycle seat is considerably more than a soft cushion to put your butt on while riding your bike.

A family man at heart, you will quickly learn that the only thing more important to him than his business is his family. His eyes quickly light up as he speaks of his children, and he will play tirelessly for hours with his grandchildren. He describes his relationship with wife Bev as a great friendship. Said Mike, "We get along, and we never fight." They love their time at home in Monterey together with a Dalmatian named Freckles (Mike calls her Spot) and a jet-black cat named Licorice (Mike calls snowball).

His factory has a family atmosphere as well. Corbin is a fair man who has no prejudices in cycles or humanity. He treats his associates (he refuses to call the plant staff employees) as family also. A quick canvass of the work force reveals a group of contented, workers who like where they earn their living. The plant is clean and pleasant and well ahead of OSHA standards. Mike is gregarious and congenial; as he walks around the factory, he smiles and speaks to everyone he encounters, calling most of them by name. A good feat indeed since there are about 160 of them, but most have been there a long time and have no plans to leave. Mike says, "I love it when one of my associates buys a new house. That means it is working."

The plant has a great diner which is run as a separate business by the wife of one of the designers in the modeling shop, and this is not the only husband and wife team working for Corbin. The front of the diner has a life sized image of Johnny, the Marlon Brando character from the movie The Wild One. Inside, the decor is pleasant and the food is great. It is reasonably priced and known for generous portions. It's a great place to wait while your seat is custom fitted to your bike.

210

The present facility is only about two years old but plans are to replace it in two years with an even larger building. They are up to a production level of about 300 seats a day six days per week and in 1998 made seats for about one third of the 300,000 motorcycles sold in the US.

In the modeling and engineering shop are prototypes of classic auto related furniture, and a new Triumph powered land speed bike. The bike which is slated to go after a new record at Bonneville is named the Hollister Wild One for the Triumph Johnny rode in the movie.

Still passionately in love with electricity, and a fanatical environmentalist, Corbin has developed a zero emissions electric car called the Sparrow which will be in production in June, 999. His idea came while watching a freeway snarl in LA from a bridge, and thought there must be a better way to commute. The car is a single- person commuter vehicle with a range of about sixty miles. The little car is drawing a lot of national and worldwide attention, and is the hit at the auto shows. Plans are for a year 2000 production plant for the new electric cars in Daytona Beach, Florida.

Mike Corbin is a man who is living his dream. The classic American Dream. A small-town boy who grew up, and started with one simple product and made it a success. To quote Mike, "Lying around every failed business are unfulfilled beautiful dreams like the scattered pieces of broken porcelain dolls."

Most people think Corbin Saddles are building seats, but in reality they are building the future. Perhaps sometime in the mid-21st Century, when everyone is being transported on electric-impulse vehicles which defy gravity and travel laser-guided invisible highways through the air. You might look closely at your liquid polymer seat which automatically conforms to the contour of your body, and just maybe on the right seam you'll see a tag that reads Corbin.

The European Invasion

"No my friend,
unless you have seen it as I have,
unless you have seen it by motorcycle,
you have not seen my America"
-William G. Carrington - 7/5/94

It's a toss up over who is invading who. Ever increasing numbers of Europeans are making annual pilgrimages to the US to tour and attend major events by motorcycle. This part of the phenomenon is a curiosity and it is a little hard to explain why it is taking place and the real impact of this exchange of cultures.

Many of these people work overtime for months to be able to afford these trips, both in time, and finances. Some ship their motorcycles over here and some come in groups, preferring to rent the machines at dealers near their port of entry. This peculiar state of affairs demonstrates just how much influence the American biker image actually has over these invaders and how they in turn, take that influence back home in the form of attitude, image, and appearance.

The motorcycle market in Europe and Asia is growing. With fuel in shorter supply, and consequently more costly, the motorcycle is finally coming into its own as an efficient and practical means of transportation. The popularity of American made motorcycles is growing with this market and the image is following in step.

The infusion of motorcyclists annually attending events and touring over here is continually growing and they return to unleash our culture over there. This boosts the motorcycle market over there, making the case that Europe psychologically is being invaded by us, and that this invasion of our cowboy image across the pond is actually working as a de facto goodwill ambassador.

Tour Europe with your Hawaiian flowered shirt, camera, and itinerary, and you are the ugly American. Do it on a Harley and people come from their homes into the street to speak to you.

I have ridden many miles with bikers from Europe, most of whom could barely speak any English. They tell stories of the hours worked overtime to come to the US, with their own machine or a rental here. They wear the same leather and look like us, and proudly. They spend a fortune in time and money to ride our roads when they could tour the Alps or some other breathtakingly beautiful area cheaper.

Today America's cowboy hero is everybody's cowboy hero. Perhaps he alwas was. Europeans have gobbled up dime novel fiction about American Heroes from the beginning. Filson's story about Daniel Boone, published in his 1784 book Kentucke, sold well in Europe. Later in the 1800s and early 1900s writers found a hungry audience overseas for the dime novel westerns.

Our compadres across the pond are now able to go beyond reading about it. They can now come here, mount their own iron horses, ride with us, and take the spirit back home. After all, it came from there in the beginning and some of its relatives are still there.

To answer the question of "Who is invading who?", maybe there is no simple answer and then again maybe there is after all. The European biker comes over here because he or she has seen and read about riding the roads over here and something inside says tells him he has to do it. It's a related gene in the blood. They come here and catch the simplicity of it. It's a scent, a taste, it's something intangible. Catch it they do and take it back to Germany or Sweden or wherever and pass it along to someone else who has to come next year. They bring something and take something back. They bring a dream and take home a fever. It's not an invasion at all, as previously mentioned it's an infusion.

What is the difference? The difference is the American cowboy spirit. That same entity who stepped off the boat into the sand so long ago and took us from Lexington to Los Angeles by way of the Alamo, and the Number 10 Saloon in Deadwood, has returned to our shoreline and with that same grin, pushes back his hat and extends a welcome handshake to his European cousin who's come here to see my America.

Conclusion

"Where is my John Wayne? Where is my prairie Son?
Where is my happy ending?
Where have all the cowboys gone?
Yippy Yi Kay, Yippi Yi Kay......."
-Paula Cole, 1996

America cries for that "lonely ranger" in the Paula Cole song, Where Have All The Cowboys Gone. Simon and Garfunkle sang, "Where did you go Joe DiMaggio." A generation gone by had heroes to look up to and emulate. Even if they weren't real, the message was, and so was the ideal. What do we have today?

Listen to the words of a Willie Nelson song which says, "My heroes have always been cowboys, and loving the cowboy ways." Well so have mine. Some of the oldest pictures of me are in a Gene Autry suit with my trusty six-guns. If you tell me I smell like a horse I'm not insulted and I still have my first 78 RPM phonograph record. It's on Peter Pan records, and says it is unbreakable, and it surely must be. I have had it since about 1950. The label has a kid in a cowboy outfit like me, holding his 10 gallon hat and twirling a rope, and lists the songs as, Home On The Range, The Old Chisholm Trail, The Big Rock Candy Mountain, and Oh Susanna. The record, like the songs, has stood the test of time, and so has the American cowboy spirit, but now he is on a motorcycle.

His image is occasionally tarnished a bit, but not to the degree of discredit being so awarded by the media. It isn't hard to see bad guys on bad bikes in the movies. In four of Clint Eastwood's films they are the villains. Two have them as buffoons, and in one they are bad cops. Three of Eddie Murphy's do also, and then there are the movies like Cobra, Stone Cold, and Joe Namath's picture C. C. And Company.

How about if we have more of the other side of the coin. Billy Jack was a good guy on a bike and so was Robert Blake in Electra Glide In Blue. Tom Cruise rode motorcycles in Top Gun and Days Of Thunder, as did Sam Elliott in Mask and Road House. All good guys in those movies. Even the hero from the future rode one in Treminator II. There are more, but I think I have made the point. The image ain't necessarily so.

The purpose of this book is to present, that what makes the phenomenon unique and so popular, is that it represents the epitome of the heritage of independence of the the American spirit.

This spirit came over with people, who were less desirables where they were originally, and from the need to burst out and be individuals. Whether they were in pursuit of religious freedom or freedom from pursuit, or even freedom of enterprise, it doesn't matter. They had the spirit in them and passed it on to us.

The idea is that each of us is an independent person in spirit who resents and rebels against being simply told what to do, or how it has to be done. We may be hardheaded but we possess wills too strong to be controlled by the norm.

Many who wear a corporate uniform and fall into the category assigned the name "yuppie" have discovered this freedom even if for short periods. It gives them the opportunity to be rebels and remain within the guidlines of the law. No identity loss.

Stimulation afforded to the masses is more than our sensory systems can handle without downloading a stress overload.

The motorcycle represents power in a world where a person may feel powerless or is otherwise limited. The power in the wind to be part of an alone, even in a crowd, thing. Alone or in a club ride, it's being in a pack, without feeling like just one of the herd. To some a lifestyle, and others an escape, but cowboys all.

When I am much older and mellowed out, and it's *Twilight On The Trail,* and I head ever closer toward *The Last Roundup.* I hope to be able to sit around with my Sons Of The Pioneers albums and as I listen, with the *Empty Saddle* of my beloved brandywine and chrome horse of iron on my mind. I truly hope I will be able to remember the miles and the adventures and the people I knew along the way and imagine I am still out enjoying my love affair with the road, drifting along with the *Tumbling Tumblingweeds.* Forgive me for taking such license with the song titles recorded by these great singers of cowboy songs. I just couldn't resist.

America is a wonderful place. We have to keep it that way so that there is something to leave those who come after us. I have never tired of seeing this land of ours and believe we who live here are truly blessed. Many Native Americans believe that God lives in the top of the Big Horn mountains. Having ridden across the top of the Big Horns at daybreak, I believe it also.

This book was created out of the belief that if we are to continue to have a future, in which individuals may still be allowed to breathe in freedom, we must understand the spirit of that freedom, know of its roots, and the price paid for it, so that understanding where we came from we can have a direction to go into the future prepared to protect it

Marty Rosenblum had this to say in *The Holy Ranger*:
He looked in his rearview mirrors, the sun ahead causing tears, understanding at last that victory comes to the individual who knows the American Past enough to present the future for those who have their gauntlets pulled on, chaps secured and boots on against the bitter years ahead. Out of neutral then into first gear, checking the mirrors to see behind, top gear was reached that morning and held as forward speed was maintained through the first Milwaukee snow shower. The Holy Ranger rode well into that day, returning with sidepipes rumbling in the rhythm of twin cylinders beating as the American pulse is felt by all those who travel this road. (Rosenblum, 83)

To again quote J. C. Rosa in his book, *The Gunfighter*:
The Dust from the last cattle drive has long since settled; the mountain trails and sun-baked streets the gunfighter traveled are no more. But his ghost still rides, and the marks he made on the land are cut deep into the American heritage. (13)

As for the movies and the images that they really portray for us, weren't the characters in Easy Rider just good old modern American cowboys, looking for freedom in the open road? After all, when we take to the roads crossing our land, isn't there really just a little bit of Peter, Dennis, or Jack in each of us?

As long as there are roads to ride, and those of us who's hearts are in the wind and who's spirits are alive in the freedom it provides, the American cowboy will continue to ride into the future.

. The End

Bibliography & Recommended Reading

Allen,O.Tom. HIGH RIDER. Washington,D.C.: Review &
    HeraldPublishing Assocoation, 1983.
Benjamin, Ludy T. Jr., Hopkins, J.Roy, Nation, Jack R.
    Psychology, 2ndEdition,New York: MacMillan Publishing
    Company, 1990
Bloemker, Al. 500 Miles To Go. New York: Coward-McCann,
    Inc., 1961
Bloom, Sol. THE STORY OF THE CONSTITUTION.
    Washington, D.C.: UNITED STATES CONSTITUTION
    SESQUICENTENNIAL COMMISSION, 1935.
Bolfert, Thomas C. The Big Book Of Harley-Davidson.
    Milwaukee: Harley-Davidson, Inc., 1991
Bolfert, Thomas, Buzzelli, Buzz, Chubbuck, M. Bruce,
    Rosenblum, Martin Jack. 1903-1993 Harley-Davidson
Historical Overview. Milwaukee: Harley-Davidson, Inc., 1994
Bolfert, Thomas. The Big Book Of Harley-Davidson. Milwau
    kee: Harley-Davidson, Inc., 1991
Butscher, Stephan A. Customer Clubs and Loyalty Programmes.
    Gower,1998
Carrick, Peter. Encyclopaedia of Motor-Cycle Sport. New York:
    St. Martin's Press,Inc., 1982.
Caunter, C.F., Motor Cycles. LONDON: HER MAJESTY'S
    STATIONERY OFFICE, 1982.
Clymer, Floyd. Floyd Clymer's Historical Motor Scrapbook
    Deluxe Edition. Los Angeles: Clymer Motors, 1950
Clymer, Floyd. Floyd Clymer's Historical Motor Scrapbook.
    Los Angeles: Clymer Motors, 1944
Dary, David. Cowboy Culture. New York: Knopf, 1981.
Davis, Burke. The Civil War: Strange & Fascinating Facts. New
    York:Wings Books, 1960.
Durham, P. and Jones, E. L. The Negro Cowboys. New York:
    Dodd, Mead & Company, 1965.
Eisinger, Larry. THE MOTORCYCLE BOOK. Mecahnix Illus
    trated. Connecticut: Fawcett Publications, Inc., 1951.
Frantz, J.B. and Choate, J.E. Jr. The American Cowboy.

Oklahoma: U of Oklahoma Press, 1955.

Hollern,Susie. <u>Women and Motorcycling The Early Years</u>. New York: Pink Rose Publications and Marketing, 1999.

Howard, Robert West. <u>The Horse In America</u>. Chicago: Follett Publishing Company, 1965.

Lerner, Robert E., Meacham, Standish, Burns, Edward McNall. <u>Western Civilizations</u>. New York: W. W. Norton & Company,1988.

Maclean, Nancy. <u>Behind The Mask of Chivalry</u>. New York: Oxford University Press, 1994

Messick, David M., Tenbrunsel, Ann E. <u>Codes of Conduct</u>. New York: Russell Sage Foundation, 1996

<u>Military Images Magazine</u>. Roach, Harry, Publisher, 1982.
Mill, John Stuart. <u>On Liberty and Other Esays</u>. New York: Oxford University Press, 1991

Mitchel, Doug. <u>HARLEY-DAVIDSON AN AMERICAN CLASSIC</u>. Illinois:
Publications International, Ltd. 1996.

Morganti, Helen F. <u>The Badger Clark Story</u>. Lead, SD No publisher of record, 1960

Rafferty, Tod. <u>The Indian, The History Of A Classic American Motorcycle</u>. New York: Quadrillion Publishing, Inc., 1998

Reid, Peter C.. <u>WELL MADE IN AMERICA</u>. New York: McGraw-Hill Publishing Company, 1990.

Rosa, J. G. <u>The Gunfighter</u>. Oklahoma: U Of Oklahoma Press, 1973.

Sagnier, Thierry. <u>BIKE! MOTORCYCLES AND THE PEOPLE WHO RIDE THEM</u>. New York: Harper & Row, 1974.

Savage, William W. Jr. <u>Cowboy Life</u>. Oklahoma: U of Okla homa Press, 1975.

Savage, William W. Jr. <u>The Cowboy Hero</u>. Oklahoma: U of Oklahoma Press, 1979.

Sprague, W.F. <u>Women and The West</u>. New York: Arno Press, 1972.

Steckmesser, K.L. <u>The Westward Movement</u>. New York: McGraw-Hill, 1969.

Steckmesser, K.L. <u>Western Outlaws</u>. California: Regina, 1983.
Sucher,Harry V.. <u>HARLEY –DAVIDSON The Milwaukee Marvel.</u> California: Haynes Publictions, Inc., 1985.

The American Heritage Dicitonary, Boston: Houghton Mifflin
      Company,1985.
The American Heritage Electronic Dicitonary, Boston: Houghton
      Mifflin Company,1992.
The Oxford English Dictionary. First Edition.
The Weirs Times Special Edition, The History Of Motorcycle
      Week, 75th Anniversary Gypsy Tour. The Weirs, NH:
      Weirs Publishing Company, Inc., 1998
Tindall, George Brown. America. New York: W.W. Norton &
      Company, 1984.
Tocqueville, Alexis De. Democracy in America Vol II. New York:
      Vintage Classics, Div. Of Random House Inc., 1990.
Tocqueville, Alexis De. Democracy in America Vol.I. New York:
      Vintage Classics, Div. Of Random House, Inc., 1990.
Vanderveen, Bart H. Olyslager Auto Library Motorcycles From
      1945. London and New York: Fredrick Warne & Co Ltd,
      1976
Vanderveen, Bart H. Olyslager Auto Library Motorcycles To
      1945.   London and New York: Fredrick Warne & Co
      Ltd, 1975
Wells, H. G. Outline of History. New York: Garden City
      Publishing Company, 1931
Williams, Mark. The Classic HARLEY. New York: SMITHMARK
      Publishers, Inc., 1993.
Wilson, Hugo. THE ENCYCLOPEDIA OF THE MOTORCYCLE.
      New York: Dorling Kindersley Publishing, Inc., 1995.
Wright, David K.. THE HARLEY-DAVIDSON MOTOR COM
      PANY. Wisconson: Motorbooks International Publishrs &
      Wholesalers, 1993.

Jarrett Press & Publications
Book And Product Order Form

Fax Orders: (919) 220-5737

Credit Card Orders Only: Call Toll Free: 1-888-909-7800.
Please have your MasterCard or VISA ready.

Internet Orders: *Orders@jarrettpress.com*   Information: *http://www.jarrettpress.com*

Postal Orders: Jarrett Press & Publications, POB 15277, Durham, NC 27704
All Other Calls Please Telephone: (919) 220-8338

Please send the following books / products:

_____

_____

_____

Book orders should include ISBN: _____

☐   **Please add me to the mailing list for author book signings, public appearances, updates, and upcoming books.**

Company name:_____

Name:_____

Address:_____

City:_____ State:_____ Zip:_____-_____

Telephone: (____)_____ Fax: (____)_____

Email address: _____

Shipping: $2.00 first book $1.00 each additional.   NC addresses add 6% sales tax

Payment:
Cheque ___   VISA ___   MasterCard ___

Card number: _____

Card name:_____

Jarrett Press & Publications
Book Publishers Since 1994

Expiration date: _____
Call toll   *order now*

Jarrett Press & Publications
Book And Product Order Form

Fax Orders: (919) 220-5737

Credit Card Orders Only: Call Toll Free: 1-888-909-7800.
Please have your MasterCard or VISA ready.

Internet Orders: *Orders@jarrettpress.com*   Information: *http://www.jarrettpress.com*

Postal Orders: Jarrett Press & Publications, POB 15277, Durham, NC 27704
All Other Calls Please Telephone: (919) 220-8338

Please send the following books / products:

_____

_____

_____

Book orders should include ISBN: _____

☐   **Please add me to the mailing list for author book signings, public
appearances, updates, and upcoming books.**

Company name:_____

Name:_____

Address:_____

City:_____ State:_____ Zip:_____-_____

Telephone: (____)_____ Fax: (____)_____

Email address: _____

Shipping: $2.00 first book $1.00 each additional.   NC addresses add 6% sales tax

Payment:
Cheque ___   VISA ___   MasterCard ___

Card number: _____

Card name:_____

Jarrett Press & Publications
Book Publishers Since 1994

Expiration date: _____

Call toll   *order now*